A WAR
BRIDE'S STORY

AMAZING STORIES

A WAR BRIDE'S STORY

Risking it all for Love After World War II

ROMANCE/HISTORY
by Cynthia J. Faryon

PUBLISHED BY ALTITUDE PUBLISHING CANADA LTD.
1500 Railway Avenue, Canmore, Alberta T1W 1P6
www.altitudepublishing.com
1-800-957-6888

Extreme care has been taken to ensure that all information presented in
this book is accurate and up to date. Neither the author nor the
publisher can be held responsible for any errors.

Publisher	Stephen Hutchings
Associate Publisher	Kara Turner
Series Editor	Jill Foran
Digital photo colouring	Scott Manktelow

We acknowledge the financial support of the Government
of Canada through the Book Publishing Industry Development
Program (BPIDP) for our publishing activities.

Altitude GreenTree Program
Altitude Publishing will plant twice as many trees as were used
in the manufacturing of this product.

National Library of Canada Cataloguing in Publication Data

Faryon, Cynthia J., 1956-
A war bride's story / Cynthia J. Faryon

(Amazing stories)
Includes bibliographical references.
ISBN 1-55153-959-4

1. Cramer, Gwen. 2. War brides--Canada--Biography. 3. Farm
life--Saskatchewan--Arborfield. 4. Arborfield (Sask.)--Biography.
I. Title. II. Series: Amazing stories (Canmore, Alta.)

FC3549.A72Z49 2004   971.24'203'092   C2003-907173-1

An application for the trademark for Amazing Stories™
has been made and the registered trademark is pending.

Printed and bound in Canada by Friesens
2 4 6 8 9 7 5 3

Cover: Gwen around the time she left England for a new life in Canada
All photographs are from Gwen Cramer's collection.

To my mother, and to all the war brides who
came bravely to this land.

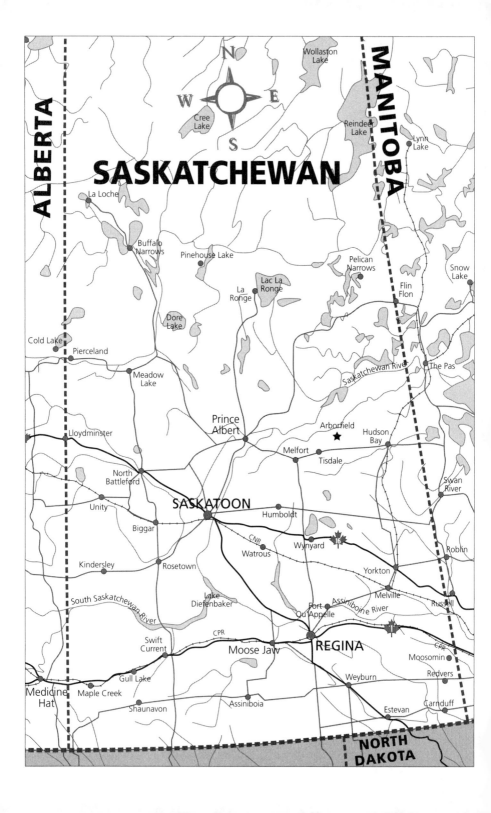

Contents

Prologue

The ship's whistle blows a long blast, followed by two short. Even though it's only four in the morning, and the sky is black over the liquid lead swells of the Atlantic, I get up. Conscious this will be one of the few days left when I'll be permitted to wear the uniform of Air Force blue, I reverently button the large gold orbs, place my officer's cap at the rakish angle of a Canadian flyboy, and shrug into my greatcoat. The coat hangs loosely over the uniform, helping to hide my thin frame; bulk seems to be missing from my ribs, and I smile when I think of what Ma will say when she sees me so skinny. Gwen, my wife, is a great cook, but war rations made mealtime a struggle. And while there was always plenty to eat at the mess hall, 38 missions as a rear gunner robbed me of my healthy appetite. I feel 75, not 25.

Silently, I join other dark figures along the ship's rail. United in war, we are now strangers in peace, and stand soberly hunched together, gazing ahead into the darkness towards the direction of home. None of us knows what to expect. Soon we'll be with family again, we'll return to where we grew up, yet everything will feel different.

"Just like a picture I once saw in a magazine, of POWs standing wordlessly along a stretch of barbed wire fence, shoulders touching, just staring." The sound of my own voice breaks the stillness, and although it is nothing more than a whisper, it echoes loudly around us.

"Funny that," the man next to me says quietly. "I was thinking that very thing."

I turn and smile at him, realizing this man, who has been closer to me than my brother during our time in the service, was becoming a stranger now that the war is over. If I can feel this way about him, how will I feel about Ma and Pa, or worse, how will I react to Gwen when she arrives from England?

I think of my wife, pregnant with my child, patiently waiting to follow me here, and I feel guilt. We were young, scared, and in love. Two complete strangers thrown together by the world at war, with nothing in common but the need to survive. Here I am going home and feeling out of place, but how will she feel when it's her turn to cross the Atlantic? Will we still be in love? We had lived for living's sake, but neither of us had looked beyond surviving the war.

Suddenly, I catch my first glimpse of land and realize that this moment, this instant, is what I had longed

Prologue

for every time I felt the Halifax Bomber leave the earth. This dreamlike homecoming is what I had envisioned with every round of ammunition I fired, every plane I saw explode, and every load of bombs I dropped. I had thought of it a thousand times, dreamed of it at night, and now I am full of emotion and I can't begin to find release. I am more terrified of this — my last journey — than any mission I flew over Germany.

No one is there to meet me when the ship docks in Halifax. And no one greets me at any of the train stations along the way home to Saskatchewan. I stare out the windows of the passenger car and watch the monotonous lines of fences, beginning nowhere and ending nowhere. Nothing has changed. The telephone poles still stand garishly, the land is still flat, and the sky is still huge.

When I reach Arborfield, the whole damn town is there to greet me and the other hometown boys who had gone off to fight. Those of us stepping onto the platform are welcomed with banners, hugs, tears, and music. With tears in my eyes and a lump in my throat, I hug Ma so hard I almost break a rib.

Again I realize that nothing has changed: Arborfield, the farm, the people — everything is as I left it. The only thing that has changed, it seems, is me. A lifetime ago, I left here a boy going off to war to find glory and honour, and to earn the respect of my family and

13

friends. Now I return, a married man with a child on the way.

Soon my wife, my very English wife, who looks like a porcelain doll and wears high-heeled shoes, will leave her home and join me here in Arborfield. I wonder what she'll think of my hometown, with its board sidewalks, mud streets, and piles of horse manure steaming in the snow. I smile as I try to picture her in overalls under the belly of a cow, a bucket between her knees.

"My God, Gwen," I say to no one in particular. "We survived the war, but will you survive Canada?"

Chapter 1
War

On September 1, 1939, Hitler's army crossed into Polish territory, and the German Air Force bombed Warsaw. The German invasion had begun. Months of threats had come to an end; the gauntlet for war had been thrown.

In Golders Green, a community on the outskirts of London, England, people tried to go about their usual routines. The morning of September 3, 1939, began like most September mornings. The suburban gardens smelled of impending autumn, the birds were singing their usual songs, and 17-year-old Gwendoline Haskell was contentedly helping her Aunt Ivy with her sewing in the sitting room of their small bungalow. The two women went about their tasks in quiet comfort, and Gwen, once again, thought about how lucky she was.

Gwen's life hadn't always been happy and serene. In the 1920s, her parents divorced and abandoned her and her sister, Joan, to an orphanage. Not long after the girls arrived there, Joan was adopted, and Gwen never saw her again. After spending a few years in the orphanage, Gwen went to live with her prosperous Uncle Norman and Aunt Ivy, and was given the chance to enjoy all the finer things in life. Growing up, she took dance and elocution lessons, and attended the ballet and the theatre. Her favourite pastimes included visiting the zoo and listening to the bands playing in the park. The only mar on her comfortable life was the heartache that came from missing her sister.

As Gwen and her Aunt Ivy continued to stitch, a piercing wail penetrated the air, sending shivers of dread down Gwen's spine. "An air raid siren," she thought to herself as she stared at Ivy's shocked face. "Planes are coming, with bombs to kill us."

Suddenly, an unfamiliar fear gripped Gwen's body. She thought of her Uncle Norman, who was at work in London, and said a silent prayer for his safety. Then, realizing she and Ivy needed to get to the closest air-raid shelter, Gwen dropped her sewing and rushed to grab her most essential belongings. She ran into her bedroom, but on the verge of panic, couldn't decide what to take with her to the shelter. Finally, she grabbed her journal off the bed and hurried into the hall, where her aunt was waiting for her. Ivy was holding a teapot. The two women looked at one another and Gwen realized that her strong and capable aunt was as afraid as she was.

Ivy and Gwen left the house, joining the rest of their neighbours as they made their way to the nearby air-raid shelter. People were staggering to the shelter in various degrees of shock, carrying blankets, chairs, and other creature comforts they thought to bring with them at the last moment. Like Ivy, some people had simply grabbed what had been within easy reach. They clutched items like pictures, hairbrushes, and books.

The municipal shelter, which was located in the basement of a house, was sectioned into three rooms with two long corridors between them. The inside walls were lined with corrugated steel that was propped into place with beams of timber. Beer bottles filled with fresh drinking water were stacked in every corner of the shelter, and makeshift latrines were located behind a couple piles of sacks.

When Gwen and Ivy entered the main room of the air-raid shelter, they saw that everyone would have to sit very close to one another. Neighbours crowded together, shoulders touching in the dark, drawing comfort in the proximity of others as they faced their own nightmares. The smell of nervous sweat permeated the stuffy room. Sitting in the dim light, Gwen was acutely aware of the other bodies, all damp with perspiration. Ordinarily she would have found the situation repugnant. Now, however, she found it oddly comforting.

There was a hush in the shelter as everyone waited for the first sounds of bombs falling. They waited all day and throughout the night. Finally, in the early morning hours, the all clear sounded; people gathered their items of comfort and made their way back to their homes, wondering what the near future would bring.

Emerging from the shelter after a night of waiting was a surreal experience for Gwen. It took a few moments for her eyes to adjust to the sunlight, and even more time for her mind to catch up with the reality that the country was at war. The landscape of Golders Green hadn't changed; birds were still singing, the sun was warm, and a soft breeze blew the leaves on the trees. To Gwen, however, the world had turned upside down overnight.

Exhausted, Gwen and Ivy walked back to their little bungalow — Gwen still clutching her journal, Ivy her teapot. When they got home, Gwen returned the journal to its hiding place at the foot of her bed, and Ivy washed out the teapot and made tea.

War

As they sipped their tea and ate biscuits, the two women listened to the radio and heard the devastating news they already knew was coming: Britain had declared war on Germany. The biscuits tasted like sawdust after that, and Gwen looked at her Aunt Ivy with tears in her eyes.

India joined with England against Germany and the Third Reich, and Australia and New Zealand quickly followed. On September 6, 1939, South Africa joined the Allied forces, and Canada followed on September 10.

Soon, houses in small villages throughout England, especially those close to the English Channel, were issued bomb shelters. The indoor shelters, called Morrison shelters, were made of thick steel with sprung bottoms and caged sides. The Anderson shelters were similarly made, but were used outdoors, their ends buried in the ground for stability.

Gas masks were handed out to the public, and people were instructed to put sticky paper over their windows to prevent injury in case the glass was blown out in an explosion. Heavy blackout curtains were also hung in every window, and lanterns on all vehicles were disconnected. The grim realities of war had crept into the English way of life.

To Gwen, it seemed the world had truly gone mad. Her family, such as it was, was being split apart. Her male cousins all joined up to fight across the channel, and every available civilian joined a volunteer group to help the troops.

At night, the whirr of German planes, the whistles of dropping explosives, and the distant sound of exploding bombs serenaded the people of England as they tried to sleep. Adding to this symphony was the frequent sound of air raid sirens, which would summon people out of bed and into their shelters.

Emerging from these shelters after a night of bombing was an awful and eerie experience for Gwen. Each morning, smoke and dust from mortar and brick filled the air, dancing discordantly in the daylight's sunbeams. It always took a few moments for Gwen's eyes to adjust to the sunlight and her mind to catch up with the destruction. But perhaps the worst part of these dreamlike mornings was the smell; the acrid sting of burned fuel, TNT, and dust that clung in cloying determination to her olfactory senses.

Most days, Gwen found her way home in a daze, stepping carefully over the countless broken bricks that had been flung into the streets from the blasts, and hurrying to find out if her aunt and uncle's bungalow was still intact. She would stop only if there was a fire burning; when a home in the neighbourhood was in flames, everyone became a firefighter. Bucket brigades were formed, and sacks and shovels of dirt — and whatever else was handy — were hurled into the flames. Battling the fires gave the public something tangible to fight. Though it didn't completely end the feelings of helplessness, it gave most people a focus for their anger and fear.

A year after the fighting began, Gwen was told she would need to find some war work to do. She and Ivy had just returned from North Devon. They had left London to escape the raids, but after only a few weeks of being away, they'd realized they missed Norman and their comfortable house too much, and had gone home. Due to her asthma, Gwen found she wasn't able to work in the Women's Land Army or the Women's Army Corps, so Uncle Norman suggested she volunteer at the Air Ministry in Adastral house in London. He thought the work would help his niece cope. All of England was under siege, and young Gwen had never felt more vulnerable.

After a period of settling in, Gwen found she enjoyed her contribution to the war effort. She especially enjoyed the new friendships she forged with the other girls in her office. Before she knew it, four years had passed, and the war had become a part of her life.

The girls in the office often chatted and exchanged stories of romantic meetings with military men. They pulled the files of the servicemen they were dating, checking the soldiers' backgrounds to ensure they were not being lied to. They giggled over their tea and biscuits, comparing notes and indulging in war gossip.

Although the paperwork at the Air Ministry was easy, the bombing raids continued to make life challenging. After a nine-hour shift at the ministry, and two hours of commuting, by the time Gwen's train pulled into her station at 11 p.m. she was too worn out for anything but tea and bed. Her exhaustion from this gruelling schedule was further aggravated by the strict food rations in place, and by the blackout restrictions, which forced her to travel home at night in the pitch black.

At the end of the working week, if the threat of air raids was minimal, Gwen sometimes accompanied her friends to a local club or show. One of their favourite places was the Review, held in the Windmill Theatre, where talented dancers, singers, and entertainers performed regularly for the troops. They didn't serve liquor there, although it was occasionally smuggled in.

Gwen and her friends also enjoyed the local pub across from the theatre — until a German bomb demolished it. There were many deaths in the bombing, and Gwen knew a number of the people killed. Some of them were dancers from the theatre.

During the last weekend of November 1943, a Canadian girlfriend phoned Gwen up and invited her to the movies. When they arrived at the theatre, the two friends discovered they had already seen the movie, so they went to the club next door for some dancing.

The club was packed, and loud music filled the room. Soon after the girls entered, two Canadian flyboys approached them and asked them to dance. Smiling into the face of Pilot Officer Larry Cramer, Gwen noticed at once how handsome he was, and quickly accepted his invitation. Larry danced liked a dream. He smelled of Canadian cigarettes, and spoke slowly and shyly. As the evening wore on, it became apparent that Larry found Gwen as fascinating as she found him. They danced, laughed, and talked all night.

He told her he was born in a part of Canada called Saskatchewan, where his parents owned and operated a mixed farm just outside a small town called Arborfield. He said it was a very different lifestyle there, slower and more relaxed. He also confessed that he found England strange and foreign. Gwen listened intently to this handsome man, and soon found herself thinking that she would love to visit the place he was from. He seemed genuine and soft spoken, with a wonderful sense of humour.

Larry smiled at Gwen and said he found her very beautiful. She laughed and told him not to string her a line, as she had heard that one before. She also said that she would verify any stories he told her through his records at the Air Ministry office. He chuckled, and then proceeded to tell her tales so tall that she was shocked at his nerve. Gwen knew he was only trying to see if she was interested enough to look him up in the ministry files. She was.

On February 22, 1944, just 11 weeks after they met, Gwen and Larry were married in a London registry office. Though it was wartime and ration vouchers were hard to come by, Gwen's aunt and uncle made sure the wedding was done in style. They hired a Bentley with a chauffeur to drive the bride and groom, and held a small reception to celebrate. Larry's aircrew from Elvington Air Base in Yorkshire all came down in force.

Larry and Gwen spent their honeymoon at the Ritz Hotel in London. Feeling skittish and nervous, Gwen had signed her maiden name, Haskell, at the front desk instead of her married name of Cramer. The desk clerk had immediately noticed the name difference and had frowned disapprovingly. From then on, the staff treated the newlyweds as though they were living in sin. A few days later, tired of the stern looks, Gwen left the large marriage certificate on the hotel dresser for the chambermaid to see. This didn't seem to make too much difference, but Gwen felt better.

On February 28, the last night of their honeymoon,

Larry photographed in 1944

Gwen and Larry were treated to a night of unwelcome fireworks when German bombers swept the London skies. The air raid sirens screamed, bombs whistled as they dropped from their planes, and the sounds of shattering explosions could be heard in the distance. Tired of the war and resenting the intrusion, Larry and Gwen pulled their blankets and pillows into their hotel room closet for the night, deciding not go to the shelter.

Gwen curled up with her new husband, and prayed her family would be kept safe.

Chapter 2
Larry Goes Home

The next year flew by. Larry, now a married man, was given leave to live off the base. He and Gwen found a small house in North York, an area within easy travelling distance to Elvington so that Larry could be called in at a moment's notice. He was finishing his tour of duty, and had been notified that he would be appointed liaison officer to the Free French Forces, and would spend the next year instructing.

The Rudge 500 motorbike Larry bought from the skipper of his bomber crew provided a great deal of freedom and entertainment for the newlyweds during their first year together. At first, Larry had to convince Gwen it was safe for them to ride it. She was hesitant because the regulations for living off base stipulated that Larry needed to be near a telephone while on standby. However, after ripping up the Yorkshire roads and feeling the wind whipping through her hair during their first ride, she was game for more.

During one particular motorbike outing, Larry pulled up to see if his swerving and speed had frightened her. Looking over his shoulder, expecting to see Gwen's face white with fear, he was surprised to see that his beautiful wife was smiling from ear to ear. She looked somewhat comical under her rollers and scarf — she had just done her hair when Larry had convinced her to take a ride.

"Larry, could I have a crack at it?" she asked, eyes sparkling.

"What, you mean — drive it?" He was shocked.

"Yes, you ninny. You aren't afraid of me driving it are you?"

So, off they went. Gwen drove wildly, scarf to the wind, rollers flying, her hair in Larry's eyes. Suddenly, the bike veered to the left, then to the right, and before Larry realized what was happening, they'd bounced over a ditch, bumped along a field, skidded to a stop, and ended up in a heap on the grass.

Gwen, red in the face, a pink roller dangling over

one eye, coughed and giggled. As tears of laughter streamed down her cheeks she sputtered, "I breathed in a bloody fly!" They both laughed harder. Then, with a twinkle in her eye, Gwen said, "Do you suppose the extra protein would be good for the baby?"

Larry looked at his wife in disbelief. Gwen patted her tummy and nodded her head. Her gentle affirmation brought a wide, joyful smile to his face — among all this death and destruction, he was going to be a father.

That night, as Gwen and Larry were lying in bed and drifting off to sleep, they were awakened by the sickening, nasal sound of a German buzz bomb. They heard it at the same time, and both knew there was nowhere to run; the missile was above them, and much too close for them to escape. In the dark, Gwen reached for Larry's hand and clutched his fingers. Larry held hers tightly, then pulled her to him as the tinny, rasping sound got closer. The frightened pair held their breath, waiting for the missile's engine to cut out.

Larry had seen Allied fighters actually tip these missiles over in mid-flight, and then send them back over the channel to meet the Germans. As he listened, he wished one of those fighters would rescue them now, but it seemed more than unlikely; all he could hear was the ominous buzzing of the missile above their home. Hugging Gwen as hard as he could, Larry felt in his gut that their time had come.

"Cuddle up, Gwen," he whispered, hoping she could not hear the terror in his voice. "We can't fight this one. He's too close."

Larry could feel the swell of Gwen's stomach against his own. He closed his eyes and thought of his unborn child. As if she could read his mind, Gwen whispered, "We'll never see our baby." Then she began to cry softly.

Suddenly, the buzzing sound was replaced by a shrieking noise as the bomb descended quickly from above. Gwen and Larry held each other tightly and began to pray.

The explosion that followed shook the house, blowing out windows and cracking walls. But somehow, the bomb had missed them. Their house, perched on the hill above a river valley, was still intact. The missile had dropped right past them and had landed in the valley below, in an area known as Hampstead.

Gwen and Larry left their bed and ran down the hill to see if they could help. Fire was everywhere, and several were homes destroyed. Among the casualties were a number of Jewish people new to the area, children among them. They had recently escaped Germany and found refuge on Britain's soil.

"Oh, Larry," Gwen said quietly as she surveyed the heartbreaking scene. "Oh, Larry…"

Larry Goes Home

* * *

In January of 1945, Larry was granted a few days leave to spend with his wife. These were to be their final days together before he was shipped home. Larry had been grounded months before, and was soon to be repatriated to Canada. Gwen, however, could not go with him. She had to follow at another date, after the baby was born and the proper paperwork had been completed and filed. Gwen and Larry had been married almost a year then, and the baby was due in May.

Larry left for Canada in April of 1945. Mark Lawrence Cramer was born one month later, on May 23, 1945. Larry missed meeting his son by only a few short weeks.

With Larry gone, the months dragged on for Gwen. She was a married woman with a child, yet she was without her husband. Giving up her home in North York, she and Mark moved back into her aunt and uncle's bungalow in Golders Green.

A year later, in March of 1946, a long awaited telegram arrived informing Gwen that she and Mark had been cleared to leave England from Liverpool, and sail to Canada on the RMS *Mauritania*, which would dock in Halifax, Nova Scotia.

The telegram assured Gwen that as a war bride, she

would be looked after from the beginning to the end of her voyage. Transporting the war brides was the responsibility of the Department of National Defence, the Canadian Red Cross, and the immigration branch of the Canadian Department of Energy, Mines, and Resources. The Canadian Wives Bureau arranged for Gwen and Mark's passage, and would deliver them to the ships, distribute information, and assign them to Red Cross officials, who would look after their daily needs.

When it came time to depart for Liverpool, Gwen said her farewells to family and friends. After settling in the transport bus, she watched sadly as her aunt and uncle stood on the street, waving goodbye. She wondered if she would ever see them again.

The transport bus took Gwen and Mark to a local church hall, where many other war brides waited with their own children — over 900 would be travelling on the ship to Halifax. The next morning, after a fitful sleep in a room filled with restless children and emotional women, they boarded a train for Liverpool.

The RMS *Mauritania* stood ominously at the dock in Liverpool. It was a troop ship, but it had been re-equipped with extra bathroom facilities for transporting the women and children.

Gwen and Mark shared a cabin with three other English war brides. One was pregnant, and spent the trip throwing up or sleeping; the other two each had a young child. At the beginning of the journey, many of the women — including Gwen — were simply too seasick to move around or even eat. However, once Gwen's stomach became accustomed to the motion of the boat, she found the food onboard delicious. After years of war rations, the white bread rolls, real eggs, crisp bacon, and fresh oranges were wonderful treats. The first trip to the dining room was a feast for the senses, and Gwen stood there for a moment savouring the smells and sights before her.

Some of the other women had tears in their eyes the first time they saw the food being served. The brides most affected by the delicious spread before them were those from continental Europe, where many had suffered starvation. Looking at these women, Gwen was reminded that as hard as the war had been on England, it had been much more devastating in other countries.

In the evenings, the brides mingled with the rest of the travellers and crew onboard the RMS *Mauritania*. They talked about their new homes, as well as the homes and family they were leaving behind. They watched movies and danced to live music, which was always accompanied by the sound of crying babies, the smell of diapers, and the swaying of the ship beneath their feet. The distractions were welcomed, as they helped alleviate some of the women's anxiety over what to expect in their new county.

The RMS *Mauritania* also had a few troops onboard, and these men helped where they could with the children, and with the brides who were too seasick to be left alone. Gwen had many conversations with the troops about Canada and what to expect. One serviceman laughed when she told him she was going to live in her husband's hometown in northern Saskatchewan. He told her he hoped she liked snow and enjoyed mud.

The Canadian coast finally came into sight on the twelfth day of the journey from England. Gwen stood eagerly at the ship's rail with the other brides, all of them straining to catch a glimpse of their new home.

By the time the RMS *Mauritania* finished docking in Halifax, the icy March wind was blowing ruthlessly. Gwen snuggled Mark close to keep him warm, shocked at how the cold air penetrated every layer of clothing she was wearing. England had never been this cold, and though her coat had always provided more than adequate protection against a blast of ocean air back home, it could now barely keep the chill at bay.

Standing on deck as instructed, Gwen felt forlorn and unsure of herself. Mark, now an active 10-month-old, struggled in her arms, squirming to be set free. Gwen ignored her son's protests and cuddled him closer, realizing yet again that in a few short days, father and son would meet for the first time.

While she held Mark in one arm, Gwen gripped their landing cards tightly in her other hand, fingers white from nerves as much as from the cold. She worried about meeting her new family and felt anxious to get started on the next leg of the journey. Her luggage was piled high on the deck behind her under the letter "C" for her surname, "Cramer." Around her were hundreds of others, all waiting impatiently for help to disembark. Not for the first time, Gwen felt a pang of loss as she thought of her family back in England.

Soon, all the war brides made their way off the ship to the pier below — Pier 21, where so many had landed before. During and immediately following World War II, thousands of war brides entered Canada through this portal. All stood on the decks of various ships feeling the same homesickness, hoping for a happy future in their new country.

As Gwen stood on the pier with the others, she gazed across to the shoreline at the bleak scene that welcomed them. Canada looked stark and felt cold; even the people hugging and yelling greetings couldn't ease her mounting anxiety. She knew she would not relax until she was home, wherever — and whatever — that turned out to be.

All the war brides were appointed two soldiers in uniform, one to help them off the boat with the children, and the other to tend to their luggage. Then each woman was directed to the main dispersal point, which was housed in a large warehouse. There was a band playing on the dock, and people were waving and shouting, welcoming them all to Canada. Some fortunate war brides were greeted warmly by husbands and members of their new families; others stood by forlornly, waiting for more travelling into the vast unknown.

Gwen and Mark waited for someone to tell them where to go next. Still gripping her papers, Gwen watched silently as her luggage was piled close to the dispersal hall for loading onto the train once she had been cleared.

The Red Cross volunteers hustled the groups together. The women and children were ushered into the big main hall, where they were told to check the bulletin board for messages then join the line with their papers, ready to satisfy customs and obtain travel permits.

Gwen hungrily scanned the bulletin board for a familiar name and smiled when she read hers. Larry had sent her a telegram. It read: "I will be waiting for you both in Saskatoon, and we'll spend a couple of days there just the three of us. Ma and Pa are waiting anxiously, and looking forward to welcoming you both home. I miss you. I love you. See you soon."

Seeing the note pinned on the board brought tears to Gwen's eyes. If she was ever unsure of her future in this new country, she now knew her husband was worth the effort of leaving home. Impatient to be reunited with Larry, Gwen asked one of the attendants how many hours it would take to get to Saskatoon.

"Three days ma'am," he answered.

Gwen sighed and fought back fresh tears of exhaustion and disappointment. She had made it to Canada, and now she wanted her husband's arms around her. Three days felt like three years.

Suddenly, one of the war brides standing nearby burst into tears. Her husband had posted a telegram that said he had made a huge mistake in marrying her and told her to return to England, as she was not welcome in his home. As the woman cried uncontrollably, her two-year-old child looking confused, Gwen swallowed a lump in her throat. For the first time, she realized just how big a chance she had taken in travelling to Canada. She loved her husband, but they had been apart for over a year. It had never occurred to her that he might have second thoughts. But for the grace of God, she could have been in that woman's shoes.

Gwen continued to clutch her son in bone-weary

arms, surveying her new country as she stood in line. She could see the landscape through the windows of the hall, or at least what was visible through the sea mist. Tears flowed freely down her wind-bitten cheeks as she thought of England. A few weeks earlier, the English countryside had been in the first blooms of spring. Just days before she had left her home, Gwen had gone for a walk and had gathered purple wood violets. The English forest had thrown a canopy of green above her head as she had wandered; robins had called from tree to tree, and nearby a brook had bubbled and giggled over the rocks, feeding a shallow pond. She'd dangled her feet in the water, and had breathed in the scent of the English country.

When Gwen had arrived home from her walk, her aunt had served tea on fine English bone china. They had munched on biscuits and chatted about nothing in particular. Auntie had reminded her to cross her legs at the ankle and sit up straight, and, even though Gwen was 24, a mother and a wife, she had done as she was told. After tea, Gwen had arranged the violets in a small Waterford vase and had left them on Aunt Ivy's bureau in the front bedroom. The vase had a handmade lace runner to protect the dark well-oiled oak top.

Closing her eyes to the sights around her, and her mind to her place in line, Gwen could almost smell those violets still. The flowers would be in the trash by now, and Gwen wondered if she would ever walk the English countryside again.

England was far away, and as the wild Atlantic waves pounded at the Nova Scotia shore, Gwen tried to stem her renewed feelings of homesickness. She continued to look out at the landscape, noticing grimly that the heavy sea mist had turned everything into a dull grey. Even the trees stood stark and barren against the sky. Their roots clung to round cold rocks, sucking at the salt water and struggling against the wind. This landscape seemed ominous to Gwen in comparison to the lovely wooded neighbourhood back in England. She had known Canada would be different, but she was unprepared for just how different. She wanted to go home, and if not for the words of love on Larry's telegram, she would have broken down and begged to be booked on the next voyage to England.

While Gwen was waiting for her travelling papers, a Red Cross volunteer gave Mark a cup of juice and a cookie, then offered her a cup of tea. The tea was strong, bitter, and laced with milk and sugar. No doubt it had been hot at one time, but now in cold fingers, the drink was lukewarm.

Leaving the pier at last, Gwen and Mark were hustled onto a CN train that was to pass through New

Brunswick, Quebec, and Ontario. Gwen found this part of the trip wonderful; she loved watching the brides getting off at various stops along the way. She laughed quietly at all the nervous men and anxious new in-laws lining up at the stations with flowers, corsages, and uncertain smiles.

Finally, the train stopped at a station in a city called Winnipeg, where she and Mark were to change trains. In his last letter, Larry had referred to Winnipeg as "Winterpeg," and upon her arrival in that town along the river, she had to agree with his assessment. She had never seen so much snow in her life! People were skating on the frozen river at a place referred to as "The Forks." They were bundled up, scarves around their necks and mouths, and though it was a bright day, it looked much too cold to tempt Gwen from the warm confines of the train.

A sergeant from the Canadian army came onboard, greeted Gwen, and offered to take Mark for her. She smiled at him. He smiled back, then guided her off the train and showed her to a waiting room full of people. Gwen assumed they were all there to catch the same CP train that she and Mark were waiting for. She was slightly taken aback when all of these smiling people came up to shake her hand. A moment later, someone laughingly explained that they were all cousins and relatives of

Larry's; they had come to welcome her since he couldn't be there. Gwen, so overcome with gratitude, started to cry yet again.

An hour or so later, the soldier helped Gwen find her place on the next train, giving both her and Mark a hug before he left. Gwen, not sure how to react, did what most English do when bellboys and desk clerks lend a hand: she tried to tip him. The soldier laughed and told her that he was actually Larry's uncle, and that tipping was not a family tradition.

During the final leg of the trip, Mark was a good little traveller. He played, laughed, ate, and slept all the way across Manitoba to Saskatoon, Saskatchewan. While he slept, Gwen spent a good deal of time looking out the window at the winter landscape. Mile after mile of fence posts stuck like brown lumps out of the snow. Every once in a while, a chicken coop, a poorly painted farmhouse, or a pile of hay would appear on the clean, white fields. Cattle chewed their feed and watched silently as the train went by, and now and again, a hawk circled in the huge canopy of blue.

Pretty, Gwen thought to herself as she shivered — pretty flat, pretty cold, pretty deserted.

Chapter 3
Oh Canada!

arry, looking handsome in civilian clothes, was waiting for his wife and son at the Saskatoon station. Gwen cried when she saw him. He kissed her as if he would never stop, until Mark screamed and tried to push him away. Mark wasn't happy to see this tall stranger hugging his mother. He started to yell so loud that everyone within earshot knew how outraged he really was.

Once Mark settled down, the small family walked a short distance to the hotel. On the way, Gwen was surprised at all the food she saw displayed in the stores. Her first dinner with her husband and son was steak, potatoes, and carrots, served at the hotel. Sharing a banana split with Mark for dessert, she began to feel that perhaps Canada was all right after all.

After spending a couple of days in Saskatoon, Larry was anxious to get his wife and child home. He had informed Gwen that they would be staying with his parents on the family homestead, but promised they would only be there for a month — until he could finish fixing up their house in town. Gwen and Larry purchased their tickets to Arborfield and left on the early morning train. As they boarded, Larry warned his wife that life on the farm wouldn't be a picnic. Gwen smiled to herself; she was with her handsome husband and wonderful son, how bad could it really be?

Larry then told her they would be on the train until midnight — and what a train it was. There were no proper seats onboard, just wooden benches. Try as she might, Gwen could not get comfortable on the hard surface, and the clickety clack of the metal wheels on metal tracks made such a racket that she felt she'd go insane. Mark wouldn't sleep, and crawled persistently on the dirty floor. Larry, however, lay stretched out on a bench, snoring contentedly. As he slept, Gwen's anxiety over meeting her in-laws increased with every kilometre travelled. Unable to sit down any longer, she woke Larry up, handed Mark to him, and announced she was off to find the facilities.

Gwen reached the end of the car and passed through to the next. She knew her in-laws would be at the station to meet the train, and she wanted to freshen up. A kind conductor pointed to a door at the end of the car that led to a washroom the size of a very small closet. Once inside the washroom, Gwen shut the door, and was barely able to turn around. She wondered if there was a larger washroom elsewhere, as she couldn't imagine her husband fitting in this one.

Sitting down, she saw a sign directly opposite her. It read: "PLEASE DO NOT FLUSH TOILET WHEN STOPPED AT THE STATION." Odd sign, she thought. Gwen washed her hands and then fixed her hair, using the tiny mirror on the wall. Ready to leave, she pulled the chain above her head to flush the toilet. There was a noisy rush of air, and then the bowl emptied right onto the track. Shocked, Gwen stared through the toilet hole at the ground passing below the train. She couldn't believe her waste had just been flushed out of the train and into plain view!

Gwen stormed back to the car, embarrassed and disgusted. She told Larry what a horrible little contraption the toilet was, proclaiming it utterly uncivilized to flush bodily waste out onto the track where everyone could see it. Larry laughed, which made her more indignant. She vowed she would not go to the washroom again until they arrived somewhere with more dignified facilities.

At midnight, as the train slowed and approached the Arborfield station, Gwen prepared to meet her husband's family for the first time. She smoothed her red silk dress, pinched her cheeks to add colour, and reapplied her red lipstick. Patting her hair into place, she asked Larry if she was presentable. She could see the lights on at the small station in the distance, and noticed several people standing out in the snow. Her stomach began doing flip-flops.

Even though there had been snow on the ground when they had left Saskatoon that morning, Gwen had chosen to wear open-toed high heels for her journey. Now, as the train pulled to a stop, she noticed that all of the people on the platform were dressed for winter. Suddenly, Gwen felt overdressed socially, and underdressed for practical purposes. She looked nervously at her husband. She wanted to make a good impression, but what would these strangers think of her when she slipped and slid through the muck on the platform, then slogged through knee-deep snow to the motorcar in silly shoes?

Larry placed his arm around her and gave her a squeeze and a quick kiss on the cheek. Meanwhile, a man and a woman with smiles on their faces boarded the train and came down the aisle towards them. Gwen's heart began to race as she watched the couple approach — she could not help but stare at the odd-looking pair.

The man, who's crooked grin revealed he was missing a couple of teeth, had a hand-carved wooden pipe sticking out of the side of his mouth. The pipe didn't appear to be lit. He was dressed for the elements, wearing a well-patched pair of work pants, a woollen curler's cap, gumboots that had seen better days, and a Hudson's Bay coat that hung limply on his tall, thin frame. The woman was wearing mittens, a blue print dress under a threadbare wool coat, and a pair of men's boots. On her head was a toque pulled down so low that it almost covered her eyes. Her salt and pepper hair, damp from the weather, stuck out haphazardly from under the hat.

Gwen swallowed and looked to Larry; she was hoping these people weren't his parents. But Larry handed Mark over to the woman, and after a moment had passed, he introduced his wife to his Ma and Pa.

Ma looked at Gwen from head to toe, and judging by the critical expression on her face, Gwen knew Ma's first impression of her wasn't a good one. Ma's frown deepened when her eyes rested on her new daughter-in-law's face. As Gwen stared back, she realized with dismay that nowhere on Ma's face was there even the slightest suggestion of cosmetics. Suddenly Gwen was very aware of her own bright red lipstick, red nail polish, and dyed blonde curls. Her red silk dress felt entirely inappropriate, and the open-toed shoes, ridiculous.

Gwen's heart sunk. First impressions were so important, and by not understanding this way of life, Gwen felt she had struck out. She looked to her husband for rescuing, still hoping there was a mistake and this pair weren't really his parents.

Then, as disillusioned as she was, she gave her new in-laws a warm smile. Larry smiled as well, and took her arm. The journey to Arborfield had been exhausting, and all Gwen wanted was a cup of tea, a hot bath, and a bed. Everything else could wait until morning.

The group left the train and waited on the platform with their luggage while Pa cranked up the 1925 truck he had borrowed from Larry's boss at the grain elevator. For Gwen, climbing into the truck was no easy feat in her tight dress and high heels, but once she was settled, she snuggled up to Larry, who held his sleeping son against his shoulder.

A few minutes later, they arrived at a cute little bungalow that reminded Gwen of her aunt and uncle's home in England. Looking sentimentally at the bunga-low, Gwen smiled to herself and realized that all her fears had come to naught. The house had electricity, a phone, and coal for heat. The stories she had heard from others along her journey about the wilds of Canada, the uncivilized living conditions and strange customs, had been unfounded after all. She only hoped at this point that Ma had bubbles for the bath.

As the group made their way up the walk to the bungalow, Gwen was surprised to see a man and woman standing at the front door. The couple was promptly introduced to Gwen as Larry's boss and his wife. They were very welcoming, and hugged her warmly.

After everyone shed their coats and hats, Gwen and Larry were led to a table laden with all kinds of food. Gwen, now so tired that she felt her head nodding on more than one occasion, could only pick at the food on her plate. The only thing keeping her awake were the countless questions everyone kept asking about her home in England. But to her frustration, whenever she answered their questions, they simply stared blankly at her and asked her to repeat her answer. Gwen wanted to cry. Larry, who had no trouble understanding her despite her accent, had to act as translator. As he spoke, Gwen couldn't help but wonder if the others were simply being obstinate.

Completely exhausted, and not wanting to be rude to her new family and their friends, she leaned over and quietly asked Larry where their bedroom was, as she simply couldn't keep her eyes open a moment longer. Still longing for her bubble bath, she realized she was too tired to make the effort and decided to have one first thing in the morning instead.

Larry smiled and told her they were not at his parents' house; they were at his boss's. His parents' farm was about six kilometres out of town. Then he assured her they wouldn't be staying much longer, as Pa had already gone out to hook the team up to the sleigh.

Gwen looked at him and wondered why he had said sleigh, but decided not to ask. Outside in the cold air, Gwen looked up at the stars above her. She wondered if her aunt and uncle could see what she saw, and then realized it was daytime in England. Biting her lip to stop the tears, she suddenly felt very alone.

The group climbed into the sleigh and then piled blankets on top of themselves. The horses stomped their feet on the frozen turf, impatient for their own barn and bucket of feed. Gwen could smell the animals' sweat, and the acrid odour of fresh manure. Snuggling down in the warmth of the blankets, she decided it wasn't an unpleasant smell after all. In fact, if she wasn't so tired, she suspected the sleigh ride would have been a wonderful experience. But despite her best efforts to stay awake for the ride, her eyelids fluttered closed and she slept all the way out to the farm.

As they approached their destination, Larry nudged Gwen awake. The snow was glowing brightly in the moonlight, and as Gwen struggled to get her bearings, the sleigh pulled to a stop in front of the farmhouse. It was a humble looking building, lonely and forlorn against the white expanse of prairie. The house's siding was unpainted, and bits of tarpaper stuck out randomly here and there. All the stories and warnings Gwen had heard about Canada flooded her tired memory as she untangled her legs from the blankets. Even in the softening light of the moon, the scarred exterior of the farmhouse stared at her apologetically. Gwen sighed.

Entering the only door to the house, the group removed their coats, slipped off their boots, and placed them neatly against the wall. Passing an icebox on the way into the kitchen, Gwen noted the faded and cracked linoleum floor. The kitchen was like no other she had ever seen. It was large and cosy, kept warm by the wood stove that was roaring and crackling in the corner. Wood was stacked neatly against an outside wall, and lying next to the stove on a tattered homemade quilt was a small piglet. The animal was obviously very young and in need of nurturing. A young girl in her mid teens — one of Larry's sisters, Gwen guessed — was at the stove warming milk for the piglet's next feeding. The girl was introduced as Reenie, and she looked shyly over at Gwen and blushed. Gwen smiled uncertainly and then continued to look around.

In the centre of the kitchen was a wooden table with an old-fashioned oilcloth covering the top. The table, surrounded by many wooden chairs, was large enough to seat at least a dozen people. Standing against one wall was a cabinet with a sink for washing vegetables. However, there was no running water. On the floor next to the cabinet was a bucket for slops, and lining three of the walls were shelves stocked with jars of preserves and boxes of Knox Gelatine, Baker's Chocolate, and Magic Baking Powder. Under the shelves were pots, pans, and mugs hanging on hooks. As her eyes scanned the room, Gwen felt as if she had just stepped back in time. Even as tired as she was, her situation hit her hard. Here there would be no luxuries, and lots of hard work.

The group sat down at the large kitchen table, and Ma took Mark with a smile. She told Gwen she'd look after him for the night so that Gwen and Larry could have a good sleep. Gwen wanted to protest, but realized she needed the rest. Besides, Ma had to be capable of babysitting; she'd raised six children.

Larry's youngest sister set out dishes for refreshments. The dishes were plain, old, and functional, and Gwen tried not to compare them to her aunt's fine china. Once again, her eyes welled up with tears as she thought of her family back home. Then, struggling to smile, she told Ma a cup of tea would be lovely.

Ma snorted and said they didn't drink tea, what Gwen needed was a good mug of boiled coffee. A mug was placed in front of her and filled with very strong black coffee. Larry handed her a jug of cream, and told her it was fresh from the cow. Reenie then innocently asked if Gwen had a cow in England.

"Oh yes, there are cows in England," Gwen replied. "But our milk is delivered to our door in glass bottles, by a man in a truck."

Ma and Pa looked at her, and then at each other.

"So's youze never milked a cow?" Ma asked.

"No," she answered.

"Well," Ma said, "we deliver our own milk from the cow's teat to our table. I'll teach youze to milk in a day or two, after you're settled. Nothin' to it, you'll catch on. You can help collect eggs in the mornin's if ya like. I was planning on youze helpin' me cook a roast tomorrow, it's from our steer Willy. Larry said you can make somethin' called york's puddin'?" Then Ma looked over at Larry, her face filled with disbelief at the fact he would marry a girl who had never even milked a cow.

"I'd love to help out where I can, Ma," Gwen said, "but I've never used a wood stove before."

Oh Canada!

Shocked by this piece of information, Ma asked what it was that Gwen *did* do in England.

"All the usual things," Gwen said, looking down at her coffee.

Ma looked hard at this young woman with the red lipstick, dyed hair, and coloured nails, then got up to pour more coffee. But Gwen hadn't even touched hers — she didn't drink coffee.

As she sat at the large kitchen table, Gwen tried to picture herself in the outfit she was wearing under the belly of a cow. She thought of all her dance classes, elocution lessons, and social etiquette. How many times had Auntie made her leave the room and enter it properly with head held high? And how many times had she practised sitting gracefully with her ankles neatly crossed? Should she explain to Ma that she knew how to order just the right cut from the butcher, brew tea perfectly, and make scones that were lighter than a feather?

Gwen felt like crying. Nervously, she looked at everyone staring at her. Out of the need for something to do, she took a big gulp of hot coffee. She then thanked Ma, and asked Larry to show her to their room, explaining to everyone that all she wanted was a bath and to go to bed. Ma snorted and stated that she was not hauling water from the creek at this time of night for a bath. Especially since it wasn't even Saturday.

Larry took Gwen upstairs to one of the bedrooms on the second floor. There were no handrails along the staircase, nor was there carpet on the steps. None of the rooms upstairs had doors; instead, blankets were hung in the doorways. Larry and Gwen's room had a double bed with homemade quilts on it.

In England, and again in Saskatoon, Larry had warned Gwen that things were simpler in his hometown. He had, indeed, told her of milking cows, hunting, fishing, and dirt farming. Gwen had assumed he was exaggerating some of the stories just to pull her leg. But now, standing in the sparse bedroom, she was beginning to realize the stories had been all too accurate.

After undressing and pulling on a nightshirt, Gwen looked out the bedroom window. The stars were bright, and the wind was blowing puffs of loose snow about. Frost was gathering on the outside of the windowpane. Gwen breathed on the glass and then traced her name in the fog.

Sighing, she slid into bed next to her husband and snuggled in under the quilts. Tomorrow she would ask Larry to haul the water so she could take a nice hot bath. It wasn't Saturday, but she needed to feel the comfort of bubbles and hot water. Then, after she was done with her toiletries, she would go to the corner grocer for tea, and show Ma what civilized people drank in England.

Oh Canada!

With a smile on her face, she drifted off to sleep.

Gwen and Larry had been asleep about an hour when an awful racket started up outside their bedroom window. Car and truck horns were honking, pots were clanging, and people were shouting. Gwen wondered what was going on, but it was too cold in the room for her to go to the window and look out. Upon hearing Ma get up and hush up the racket, Gwen rolled over and promptly fell back to sleep.

The next morning, Ma explained that some of the townsfolk had thought the newlyweds needed a shivaree. It was a Canadian custom, where the new wife was dragged out of bed in the middle of the night and forced to cook breakfast for the visitors. This was the woman's chance to show all the neighbours and family what a great wife she was, and how lucky her new husband was to marry her.

Ma, realizing Gwen would be lost in the kitchen with that mob watching, sent them all packing. She didn't want the town to know her Larry had brought home an English girl who couldn't cook or milk a cow, and who wanted to take a bath on a Wednesday in the middle of the night. Ma wondered to herself what other surprises this girl had in store for them.

Chapter 4
Life on the Farm

Her first morning on the farm, Gwen woke to a bright and sunny day. The crispness of the air was apparent in the bedroom she shared with her husband. Rolling over in bed, Gwen suddenly realized that Larry was no longer lying beside her. As she listened to the house creak quietly in the stillness, she vaguely wondered if everyone else was still asleep.

Wrapping herself in a quilt, she got out of bed and looked out the window. She was startled at how flat the landscape was, how huge the sky looked, and how far she could see. Peering off into the distance, she could find no indication that Larry's parents had any neighbours.

Gwen dressed quickly while keeping the quilt as snugly around her as possible. She was focused on one thing: a hot bath. Coming down the stairs, she looked at her surroundings. There hadn't seemed to be a toilet upstairs, so without being too nosey, she poked her head around a couple of corners to locate one on the ground floor. Finally, needing to relieve herself rather urgently, she went into the kitchen to find someone who could point her in the right direction.

Larry and Ma were sitting at the table drinking coffee when she entered. No one else was in sight; the smells of breakfast still lingered in the air, but all evidence of the meal had been removed.

Gwen smiled and said good morning. Ma snorted and asked if she would like coffee since it was almost afternoon. Gwen politely declined. The sun was barely up, yet Ma was treating her like she had overslept. Trying not to feel guilty or indignant, Gwen asked Larry to point her in the direction of the toilet. She explained she wanted to freshen up, use the toilet, and have a nice hot bath to start the day.

As Ma stared at Gwen over her mug, a strange grin crept over the older woman's face. Larry smiled and explained the toilet wasn't in the house, but down the hill in a separate building. Ma chuckled and took a sip of her coffee.

Ignoring the chuckle, Gwen gathered her cosmetics and other toiletries then walked down the snowy hill in the direction Larry had indicated. She thought it odd that the toilet would be so far away. However, many things in Canada were strange to her — perhaps all Canadian farms had bathhouses away from the main house.

Suddenly, Gwen stopped dead in her tracks. Before her, standing pitifully in the snow and well lit by the morning sun, was a small wooden outhouse, not a bathhouse. She was stunned. The structure was so old that the timbers had shrunk, and she could see inside through the cracks in the walls. Despite the brightness of the morning, the wind was blowing bitterly, and Gwen shivered as she listened to the high-pitched sound of the stiff breeze whistling through the knotholes. Walking around the offensive building, her disgust deepened when she saw it didn't have a door — the hole of contemplation was exposed for the whole world to see.

Gwen realized she couldn't wait much longer to relieve herself. Groaning in resignation, she stepped into the outhouse, exposed what was necessary, and whistled loudly so she wouldn't be disturbed if anyone came down the path. Her English posterior was soon covered in goose bumps, and the breeze was so cold it froze moisture on contact. Though Gwen's outer self was chilled to the bone, inside she fumed as she recalled the grin on Larry's face when he had given her directions. Her husband was in for it!

From the outhouse's throne — which was nothing more than a hole in a rough wood plank that had been worn smooth by more bottoms than Gwen wanted to consider — was the pretty view of an overgrown duck pond. The trees in the woods beyond were bare of their leaves, and the snow, still piled high, had started to melt, leaving smudges of muck contrasting with the whiteness. In places, long bunches of grass were sticking up through the drifts.

Gwen had difficulty appreciating the prairie scenery, for as new as it was to behold, the air was just too cold for sitting around and taking in the view. Instead, she did what she needed to do as quickly as possible, all the while whistling nervously and watching for bears.

Finished, and shivering so hard that her teeth rattled, Gwen reached around for the toilet paper. There wasn't any. She looked beside her, behind her, and on the floor. All she could find was a copy of the Timothy Eaton's catalogue, opened to a page that had been half torn out. The realization hit her: not only did she have to suffer the indignity of doing her private business in a facility without a door, she also had to stoop to using printed paper to clean herself up. Her "stiff upper lip" was definitely getting a workout.

In a gesture she felt reflected her thoughts on Canadian farm life so far, Gwen tore out a page from the catalogue's farm equipment section and completed her business. Hopping off the plank, she put herself back together and raced up the path to the house, slapping her backside along the way (it was so cold it had gone numb). Inside the warm house once again, she toasted her rear-end in front of the roaring woodstove while Larry and Ma laughed at her.

Gwen plotted her revenge. That night, she started campaigning for her husband to build a door for the outhouse. He thought she was crazy, but she continued to insist. Eventually, with Ma and Pa laughing at him, he built and installed the door, complete with a crescent moon cutout that let the light in when the toilet was occupied. Gwen thanked him profusely, and felt she had dealt a blow on behalf of the civilized world.

After Gwen had been on the farm for a few days, Ma began to teach her what she needed to know about running a household in northern Saskatchewan. Besides the lack of electricity, the biggest challenge for Gwen was the wood stove. It loomed in the corner of the kitchen, taunting her. Try as she might, she simply could not master cooking with it.

Ma knew exactly when to throw in wood, and how much to add to keep the temperature even for cooking or baking. Gwen, however, would forget to stoke the stove altogether, and it would soon be down to a few coals. Realizing her baking was falling, she'd then pile in the wood, and whatever was in the oven would turn black. Larry would come in from the barn, smell the acrid air, and say it was obvious Gwen had been cooking again.

After a week had passed, Gwen was getting sick of trying to cook with the stove. She was also getting tired of hand-washing dirty laundry in a bowl. Frustrated, she asked Ma when the laundry was due to be picked up and delivered. Well, Ma's face was a picture.

"You're in northern Canada," Ma laughed, "and here we do everything ourselves, youngun', even washing our own soiled clothing."

Gwen, disappointed that she would have to continue to do laundry, asked if she could borrow Ma's washer for her and Larry's clothing and bed linens. Her mother-in-law laughed and said she didn't own a laundry machine.

Ma then ordered Gwen to change her clothes, explaining that she would teach her how to do the laundry. Producing an awful metal tub and a scrubbing board, Ma put the tub on the floor and filled the kettle on the stove with snow. Once the snow was melted and the water was boiling, Ma and Gwen skimmed off the residual black bits from the ground snow, and then poured the water into the tub, on top of the dirty clothing. They used Ma's homemade lye soap and rubbed the laundry by hand on the scrubbing board. Twisting each item of clothing hard, they squeezed out the excess water and threw the laundry into another tub of fresh water for rinsing. After each garment was wrung out once more, it was hung outside on the clothesline.

Gwen's fingers turned red and angry. Her long, polished nails softened in the water and broke off on the scrub board. In England, she and her aunt had always sent the dirty linens out to the laundry, and everything came back cleaned, pressed, folded, and delivered right to the door. Gwen had never even considered the work it took to clean clothes.

Once the clean laundry was dry, it was taken off the clothesline and brought into the kitchen for ironing. Ma heated flat irons on the stove, sprinkled the clothes with water, and then showed Gwen how to slap the irons down, and push and press to remove all the creases. At the end of the day, Gwen found that her perception of dirty clothes had changed quite a bit. In England, she would wear something once and then send it out to be cleaned. But now that she was in Canada, she would wear an item again and again until it warranted the work it took to launder it.

Soon after she arrived at the farm, Gwen wrote a letter home to her aunt and uncle, recounting her Canadian experiences thus far. She wrote about the outhouse without the door, and the clouds of mosquitoes that seemed to hang in the air just waiting for an English meal. She also told them about burning her fingers as she learned to iron, and her mother-in-law's reaction when she called Mark's dirty diapers "napkins." In Canada, napkins were used to wipe the face when eating, not for wrapping around a baby's bottom.

Gwen wrote about her first batch of bread, which was solid enough to build a new chimney, and explained how Ma regulated the temperature to bake by simply adding one stick of wood on the fire in the right place at the right time. Finally, Gwen complained that the townspeople and neighbours — and even Larry's family — thought her aloof and stuck up. It seemed no matter how hard she worked, there was always so much more that needed doing, and her new family looked at her efforts as small and nowhere near good enough.

Chapter 5
Gwen, This is Arborfield

On Gwen's first Saturday at the farm, Ma announced that the two of them would be attending a get-together in town that afternoon. Gwen asked if she could stay home, as she was feeling a bit overwhelmed with her new lifestyle. But Ma firmly said no; the invitation had been extended specifically so that people could meet her new daughter-in-law. Reluctantly, Gwen got all dolled up in London style, and off they went.

When they arrived at the small bungalow belonging to Larry's boss, Gwen's spirits rose. The house looked as quaint in the daylight as it had in the dark of night. At least there, she knew she could fit in.

Gwen, This is Arborfield

As Gwen and Ma entered through the front door, the woman of the house greeted them warmly. She didn't seem to think the picture hat Gwen was wearing was overdone, nor did she seem to notice how dirty Gwen's feet were from walking up the muddy path to the door in open-toed pumps.

Gwen was ushered to the living room, where she stopped abruptly at the entryway and turned bright red. The room was packed with at least 50 women, all of them looking at her expectantly. There were so many women that they could not all be seated on couches or chairs — some were sitting on the floor, and others were standing along the walls. Gwen stared at the strangers in shocked silence. Then, to her further embarrassment, she was led to a decorated armchair and told that she was the guest of honour at a wedding/baby shower.

"A what?" Gwen whispered to Ma.

"You'll see," Ma said with a smile.

A huge basket of brightly wrapped gifts was set down in front of her. She looked at it in confusion.

"Open the gifts," Ma said, "then pass them around for everyone to look at."

Bewildered, Gwen did as she was told. One by one, she opened the parcels, tearing back paper which revealed household items as well as things for Mark. Among the many gifts was an oddly shaped wooden comb. When Gwen, cheeks burning, asked what this device was for, she was curtly told that it was a blueberry picker. As the women exchanged looks, Gwen's discomfort grew. She decided not to ask any more questions, and simply thanked them all for their generosity.

While everyone was enjoying refreshments, Gwen privately asked Ma why the women were giving her things. She wanted to know if they thought she and Larry were too poor to look after their own affairs. Ma, starting to lose patience, told her it was a wedding shower, and that these things were wedding gifts. It was a Canadian tradition, and since she was now a Canadian, she needed to understand the customs.

Gwen had never heard of a wedding shower, and she couldn't help but suspect that these women were giving her gifts out of charity. After all, she and Larry had been married two years. It seemed strange that the community would decide to celebrate the wedding after all this time. However, swallowing her pride, she tried to be thankful and gracious.

As the gathering was beginning to disperse, a woman approached Gwen. This woman had been sitting close by during the gift opening, and her stares had made Gwen very uncomfortable. She was large, at least a few inches taller than Gwen, and almost as wide as she was tall. She also had the biggest bosom Gwen had ever seen.

The woman stood in front of Gwen for a moment, assessing her before speaking. "I guess Larry told you about us?" she finally asked. "How we was engaged when he went off to the war?" She came closer, and Gwen took a step backwards, looking towards her mother-in-law for rescuing. But Ma had her back turned, and was chatting with another woman across the room.

"I waited for him, eh?" the woman continued. "Then heard he married some skirt in England. And I waited four years for him too."

With an angry look on her face, the woman stepped closer again, her double-D pendulums swinging inches away from Gwen's face. "And youze being an uppity outsider an all — no offence."

Gwen looked the woman directly in the ample cleavage and said, "Well, I certainly understand now that he married me on the rebound since it's plain for everyone to see that you are twice the woman I'll ever be." She smiled her sweetest smile. Hesitating only a moment, the woman returned the smile, and the tension eased.

"Well thank you," the woman said. "I suppose you're all right even if ya can't cook and things." Then she walked away. Gwen's smile widened; she had survived her first Canadian social gathering.

The next day, Sunday, it was Larry's turn to drag

Gwen out of the house. He told her to get cleaned up so that he could take her to meet the neighbours down the hill. Larry explained that these neighbours were bachelors, and that they had lived alone since their sister had gotten married and moved away.

Gwen put on her high-heeled shoes, an expensive grey suit, a black fur jacket, white gloves, and a black, wide-brimmed felt hat. Her long, bleached hair was carefully brushed and curled with hot irons from the stove, and it fell nicely a few inches past her shoulders. After pinching her cheeks for colour, she added a touch of red lipstick and felt sure that this time, she would not embarrass her husband.

Larry, waiting patiently by the truck, smiled a wickedly handsome smile when his wife approached the vehicle. He helped her inside, and was still grinning when they left the farmyard. Gwen asked him if everything was all right.

"Of course," he answered, chuckling. "What could possibly be wrong?"

Moments later, they arrived at the neighbours' property. Gwen knew she was overdressed as soon as she saw the tiny tarpaper shack in the overgrown farmyard. Still, she told herself, she was English, and Larry had said these brothers were from the Netherlands originally — surely they would be civilized enough to appreciate a well-dressed woman.

Larry knocked on the door to the shack, and a gruff voice yelled for them to enter. As the door swung open, Gwen stood on the front stoop and gawked at the three men lounging around a roughly built wooden table. To her surprise and embarrassment, each of them was in various stages of undress. The men were obviously surprised to see Gwen, and they stared openly at the well turned-out woman at their door.

Finally, one of the brothers, the one wearing long-johns and trousers held up by suspenders, pushed a chicken off one of the wooden chairs and offered the seat to Gwen. The second brother, clad only in long-john bottoms with the "trapdoor" slightly askew, ran down to the well to draw water in order to boil fresh coffee. The third brother never moved from the table. He was wearing nothing on his top half, and though she could not see his bottom half, Gwen was almost certain he was naked from the waist down, too. He looked at her and blushed, and she looked at him and blushed.

Gwen kept her eyes averted after that. She drank her coffee, grateful for something to keep her occupied, while Larry chuckled and talked farm talk with the two brothers who were wearing clothes. At the end of the visit, the two brothers walked her and Larry out to the truck, while the third, still blushing profusely, sat firmly in his chair.

The next day, Gwen was once again faced with the task of mastering the kitchen. Ma could bake 16 loaves of bread at a time. Each loaf was fluffy and perfect, and after having lived through years of war rationing, the smell of the baking bread nearly drove Gwen mad. She felt like she was in heaven's kitchen, even though the stove came from Hades.

Indeed, the wood stove was not Gwen's friend. She would forget to stoke it, and dinner would be half raw, or she stoked it too much and everything would be burned. All the cooking skills she had learned back in England were suddenly useless. Humbled, Gwen wondered what Ma must have thought of her, a grown woman who didn't know how to do laundry or iron, and who couldn't even cook.

To make matters worse, Gwen was fairly certain that Ma didn't believe any of her stories about England. Whenever Gwen spoke of her aunt's bone china that was as thin as eggshells, the central heating in the little bungalow at Golders Green, or the milk that was delivered in glass bottles, Ma just looked at her in amazement. Ma also laughed at Gwen's accent, and said that she hoped Mark would learn to talk properly.

Of course, Ma and the wood stove weren't the only challenges for Gwen. It seemed that in Canada, almost everything had a different name: ladders in her stockings were called "runs," and the green grocer was called a "mercantile." Often, Gwen was afraid to open her mouth when she was in the presence of townspeople. If she called the truck a motor car, she was uppity. If she referred to sausages and mashed potatoes as bangers and mash, she was being silly.

Luckily Mark, being so young, fared better. As the first Cramer grandson, his grandparents spoiled him to distraction. Ma and Pa tried to treat Gwen as a daughter, but her strange ways continually made her an outsider. Mark, however, was their son's child, and therefore he had an immediate place of honour in the family.

Not only did Gwen have to do her best to win the hearts of her in-laws, she also had to conquer her fear of wild animals. She didn't like berry picking because of the threat of bears. Even the gophers, as cute as they were, made her nervous with their scurrying about. There was one animal, however, that managed to intrigue her — at least momentarily.

Larry first told her about this mysterious creature when they went for a walk in the woods one afternoon. As they strolled along, Gwen worried about the bears, but Larry told her that he knew for sure there were no bears in the area. Gwen looked at him in disbelief and asked how could he know that. Smiling, Larry said it was because treesqueaks didn't like bears, and if there was a bear in the area, the treesqueaks would hide.

"Treesqueaks?" Gwen questioned.

"Gwen," he said, "didn't I ever tell you about treesqueaks? They're my favourite animals. They're soft like rabbits, with big brown eyes like a deer, and they sit in the trees high above the ground calling to each other. Listen." He stopped talking and waited.

Sure enough, up high and slightly to the left, Gwen heard a creaking sound coming from one of the trees.

"There," said Larry, "did you hear the treesqueak?"

"Yes," smiled Gwen, looking up into the trees to catch a glimpse of the creature. "I want to see one Larry."

When the story of the treesqueaks was relayed to the family at the dinner table that night, Pa laughed so hard that tears fell from his eyes. Ma looked at Gwen in bewilderment, and then chuckled. Larry roared. Gwen, red in the face and recognizing how gullible she had been, tried to take the teasing in good faith, but she silently swore to pay her husband back.

Realizing how embarrassed Gwen was, Ma asked her to tell them how she and Larry met, as they had never heard the story.

"Well," said Gwen, relaxing after the teasing, "we met at a club, and since I worked at the air ministry I knew he pulled a good screw so I told him he could knock me up at eight."

Suddenly, the only sound in the kitchen was Larry choking on his coffee. Ma and Pa stared at Gwen with open mouths. Confused, she could do nothing but stare back at them. After a moment had passed, Pa got up from the table.

"No need for that kind of talk," he said, leaving the house.

Ma followed suit, leaving her son and daughter-in-law alone in the kitchen. Gwen then looked imploringly at Larry, trying to understand what she had done wrong.

Later that evening, Larry tried to explain to his parents that in England, the terms "screw" and "knocking up" had very different meanings than they had in Canada. But even though Ma smiled and nodded politely after the explanation, Gwen knew that her mother-in-law didn't buy a word of it.

Chapter 6
Town Life

fter spending a month on the Cramers' farm, Larry, Gwen, and Mark were finally moving into a home of their own in town.

Town! Gwen could hardly contain her excitement. Even if Arborfield was made up of nothing more than a group of houses, one rickety wooden sidewalk, a beer parlour that only permitted men, and a couple of stores, at least it *sounded* civilized. Besides, they were moving into their own house. No more wood stove, no more coal oil lamps, and no more outhouse.

Or so she thought. On first inspection, Gwen discovered that the house did not have an indoor toilet, but instead boasted the inevitable outhouse in the big back-yard. This wasn't the only disappointment. The sink in the kitchen had plumbing, but only a cold-water pump. When the family needed hot water, Gwen had to use the stove — the wood stove — that stood in the corner of the kitchen. Of course, she often forgot to stoke up the fire; there were plenty of cold washes in the first weeks on their own, to say nothing of half-cooked meals and bread that came out like buckshot.

Larry and Gwen, with all of these challenges, were still very happy to be off the farm. Shortly after they moved, Gwen found out she was pregnant with their second child. Cheerfully, she busied herself with fixing up the house for the new arrival. The nursery required wallpaper, and one day, when Larry was at work, Gwen took Mark down to the hardware store to pick up what she needed. While she was there, she also bought some paint and a few other things to make the redecorating easier.

After paying for her purchases, she realized she would not be able to carry everything home with a toddler in tow. Fortunately, there was a man near the counter who seemed to be an employee. He looked a little old to be an errand boy, but Gwen thought it was wonderful that the shop owner would give this small, elderly man a job. The man kindly offered to carry the items home for Gwen. She gratefully accepted, happy that there was at least one shop in town that did business the same way the English did.

By the time they reached the house, Gwen was feeling quite sorry for the older man. The items were heavy, and he was skinny. In fact, it looked like he could have really used a good meal. She opened the front door of the house for him, and he thoughtfully put the items in the room where they would be used. Gwen reached in her purse for a tip, and felt terrible when she discovered she only had a quarter. Apologetically, she handed over the coin and thanked him "ever so much." The little man chuckled and thanked her, putting the quarter in his shirt pocket. As he made his way down the front walk, he looked back at the house and chuckled again.

When Larry arrived home from work, Gwen told him the story, and asked if he would give the man something extra the next time they were in the hardware store. Larry laughed and said like heck he would, the little man was the town's millionaire. Not only did he own a couple of sections of land outside Arborfield, he also owned the hardware store, several houses, and a garage.

Gwen figured it would be a long time before she would live that one down — and she was right. Soon the story of the crazy English girl tipping the town millionaire a quarter was being spread around the community.

After having settled into the new home, Gwen decided it was time to invite Larry's boss and the boss's wife over for dinner. Gwen vowed to herself that she'd show them all what a great cook she was by serving them a traditional English meal. She rose early to begin work on the meal, preparing the roast beef by searing it on the outside in hot butter and spicing it the way her aunt had taught her. She peeled carrots and blanched potatoes, and placed them around the roast, along with onions and celery. Then, humming happily to herself, she put the roast in the oven and turned her attention to dessert.

It was a hot day in August, and Gwen decided that fresh peaches served with English-style clotted cream would be a refreshing dessert. She washed, sliced, and pitted the peaches, putting the clotted cream on them before placing them in the icebox to keep cool until dinner. Then she cracked several eggs, whipped them by hand until they were frothy, and put them in the icebox until they were needed for the Yorkshire pudding.

Setting the table, Gwen was careful to put the butter in a dish of ice so that it wouldn't melt in the heat. She also made aspic jelly, and placed it on the table alongside the butter.

Pleased with everything, she washed, changed, and waited for her company. They arrived right on schedule, and Larry served them pre-dinner drinks in the front room.

After a polite period of time had passed, Gwen excused herself to take the roast out of the oven and start on the Yorkshire pudding and gravy. As she opened the wood stove, her heart hit her feet. She had forgotten to stoke the stove and it was completely out. The roast was red and barely cooked, the carrots were still crunchy, and the oven was nowhere near hot enough for cooking the Yorkshire pudding. Gwen told Larry to stall the company with another drink while she handled the emergency.

Unfortunately, while she was struggling in the kitchen, the ice around the butter melted, overflowed the dish, and soaked the tablecloth. The aspic jelly was also beginning to melt, and it leaned precariously to one side, threatening to land on the table.

Gwen carved the roast as best she could, slicing off the parts that looked cooked. She called everyone to the table, and her company sat down just as the aspic jelly got tired of leaning. The roast was so rare it almost jumped off the serving dish, and Gwen was so distraught that she was ready to cry.

Larry made some jokes, poured her a large glass of sherry, and soon she was feeling better. She figured at least the dessert would be fine; the peaches didn't need to be cooked, and they certainly wouldn't melt in the heat.

But as it turned out, the peaches weren't at all ripe; they were hard and sour. Gwen almost cried again when she brought them out to the table. To make matters worse, the cream had curdled, and even sugar couldn't sweeten the fruit up enough to make it edible.

Despite all of this, the company was very gracious, and as far as Gwen knew, they never told a soul about the dinner — if they had, it would have been all over town in no time flat. But what Gwen didn't realize was that the couple had no idea the dinner was a failure; they simply thought the English had peculiar taste in food.

Not long after the disappointing dinner party, Ma asked Gwen to accompany her on a visit to a farm deep in the bush. The family that lived on the farm was poor, and the woman had several children. Ma warned Gwen that the woman was not careful about her appearance, so not to expect too much. Gwen simply laughed in response.

When they arrived at the farm, Gwen was stunned. Surrounding a very dilapidated house was the most beautiful garden she had ever seen. It seemed the woman was able to grow anything.

However, upon entering the farmhouse, Gwen

quickly realized the woman's talents didn't extend much beyond gardening. Her house — if you could call it that — was nothing more than an old, unpainted shack with a homemade board table and some benches inside.

The woman had been baking that day, and there was bread rising on the counter. But because there were no screens on the door or windows, the bread was covered with flies. As the women had tea and chatted, ducks waddled in and out of the house at will. Then, in the middle of the conversation, the woman plopped her two-year-old on her lap, lifted her top and, while farm hands and her husband came in and out of the kitchen, let the child suck noisily. Gwen, coming from a country where bottles were the normal method of feeding children, was most embarrassed, and tried to look everywhere but at the woman. Ma just smiled widely, and chuckled.

During the course of the visit, the woman's husband, who seemed clean and nice enough, brought in the family goat. Gwen's mouth dropped as he stood the goat on the table where they were sitting, and milked it. She was speechless. Ma, deciding that her daughter-in-law had had enough of a culture shock for one day, said it was time for them to be on their way home.

After visiting the farm and seeing the woman's wonderful garden, Gwen was inspired to try her own hand at growing things. She went to the hardware store and read the seed packages for sale, picking out a package she felt she could handle without too much difficulty.

Bringing home the seeds and following the directions closely, she set out the area and asked Larry to help her get it ready for planting. Larry broke the sod and hoed the area free of weeds and rocks, then Gwen shooed him away. She truly felt she had something to prove: English or not, she could grow a garden just like anyone else.

When Larry was at work, she reread the planting directions carefully. She was to put the seeds in hills and cover them with dirt. It didn't say anywhere how high to make the hills, so she formed a couple of rows about a foot apart with hills about a foot high. On the top of each hill, she carefully placed one seed and covered it over with a bit of dirt, then watered it. Daily, she went out to look at each hill for the first sign of new growth. Within a few days there was a small sprout of green and Gwen was thrilled. She began to tell the neighbours about her garden.

One neighbour came over to look, and smiled widely as she praised the garden. Apparently, the woman commented to Ma about it in town one day, and asked Ma if she knew what the funny English girl thought she was growing. So Ma, curious, decided to pay her daughter-in-law a visit. When Gwen showed her the backyard, Ma burst out laughing. Only one hill sprouted a single vine. On that vine was a single pickling cucumber. Gwen was very hurt, she was quite proud of that cucumber.

When summer arrived, Gwen and Mark picked all kinds of berries that grew fairly close to town. Gwen refused to take Mark too far away, sure that they would stumble upon a bear. With Ma's help, she canned much of the fruit they picked, and made pies and cobblers out of the rest. By the end of the summer, she had canned 90 litres of saskatoons and several litres of blueberries. Larry was very impressed with how quickly Gwen was adapting to prairie life.

One day, Larry brought home a case of crab apples and told Gwen not to tackle them until he returned from work the following day, as she had never canned crab apples before. Gwen, however, ignored his request. She decided to can the crab apples while Larry was away at work so that she could surprise him with a dish of them for dessert after dinner that night.

Gwen hunted through her recipe book and found directions for canning crab apples. Cleaning them all, she stoked up the woodstove, and by the end of the day she had the whole case put up.

Larry was very impressed when he got home from

work and saw 26 jars of fruit sitting on the kitchen counter. After dinner, he waited eagerly for Gwen to dish up dessert, as crab apples were his favourite. Pouring a liberal amount of cream over the plump fruit, he thought it a bit odd when the cream appeared to be curdling, but he dug in with gusto anyway. Almost immediately, he choked and sputtered. Gwen hadn't canned the crab apples in syrup; she had pickled them in vinegar.

Chapter 7
Trapping

Pa was quite a trapper, and ran lines all winter. Every week, weather permitting, he made the long trek into the wilderness to check his lines. He was mostly after ermine, beaver, and rabbit furs. Larry often accompanied his Pa, taking his rifle along so that he could supplement the larder with whatever game he could shoot. Gwen enjoyed rabbit, as long as she didn't know what it was ahead of time. Venison was also okay, but it had to be cooked right. Ma's venison was wonderful, but Gwen's had a long way to go.

One November afternoon, Larry told Gwen that he thought she needed a change of pace. He offered to look after Mark so that she could go with Pa to check the traplines. She was thrilled, wanting to learn as much about her new country as she could. She also felt that since she wore fur, she should see first-hand how it was acquired.

After loading the sleigh, Larry bundled up Mark and drove his small family over to the parents' farm. He planned to visit with Ma while Gwen and Pa were off trekking. The lines Pa was checking that day were close to home, they were mostly along the creek and the duck pond, and a few were set along a rabbit trail in the woods.

It was a crisp, clear day, and as Gwen and Pa breathed, clouds of white puffed out of their mouths. Though the temperature was cold, Gwen loved bright, winter days on the prairie. It seemed as though she could see forever; the land was so flat, the sky so huge, and the white of the snow made everything look clean. Gwen swore that it was so flat in northern Saskatchewan that if a person's dog ran away from home, three days later that person could stand on his or her porch and still see it running.

Gwen had to struggle to keep up with Pa, and she watched the woods constantly for bears. Pa laughed at his daughter-in-law; everyone knew bears hibernated in the winter, but Gwen was fixated on the creatures. Every picnic, walk in the woods, or trip to the outhouse was an ordeal for her. Every time she saw a dark shape in the distance, spotted tracks in the snow, or heard a noise outside at night, she was sure a bear was lurking nearby. It made no difference that Larry and his parents assured her that bears hadn't been sighted in the area for years. She simply didn't believe it.

The first trapline in the woods proved productive. Three snow-white rabbits had been caught in the snare. They looked twisted in death, as if they had fought valiantly near the end. Though Gwen felt a twinge of sympathy for the rabbits, she realized that the snare would have killed them quickly, and was satisfied the animals had barely suffered at all.

Pa kept Gwen at a distance and off the rabbit trail so that her scent wouldn't come close to the line. Careful to touch only what was necessary, he freed the frozen carcasses from the snare. He explained he had to replace the snare's old wire with a new one that didn't smell of death, so other animals would continue using the path. Then he carefully took a rabbit skin out of his pack and laid it on some fresh snow. Unwrapping it, Pa revealed a pair of mitts. Without touching the outside of the mitts, he slipped his hands in them and reset the lines.

Pa explained that the mitts had been left outside on the line for a week so that the smell of human would be faint or erased altogether by the wind and cold temperatures. Then they were carefully wrapped in a fresh rabbit skin and put in his pack so that the rabbits and other animals wouldn't find the odour offensive. Gwen was fascinated, and realized that this man — who was lacking many social graces and would undoubtedly appal her Aunt Ivy with his demeanour and manners — was educated and intelligent in ways she could only imagine. She suddenly recognized that out there in the woods, how you sipped your tea really wasn't important.

As Pa worked, he talked. He was usually so quiet on the farm, and Gwen enjoyed discovering this new side of her father-in-law. He told her of the early Native tribes that once roamed over this land, and of all the Native artifacts that he'd found on the homestead when he first broke sod in 1914. He had discovered ancient hunting camps, as well as arrowheads, stone blades, and hammers of smoothed rock.

Pa told Gwen that he admired the Native way of life. Early Native peoples were so in tune with the world around them that when they made a kill, they prayed over the dead animal and asked its spirit to forgive them. Believing waste was against the gods of the earth, sky, and sun, they used every part of the animal. Ma and Pa both hated waste. They spent much of their time using and reusing items.

The next trapline Pa decided to check was the one at the beaver pond. He had placed traps over the bank where the beavers came ashore to harvest their birch trees and drag them into the water.

As Pa hauled the first trap out of the water and onto the bank, Gwen saw that it had a fresh catch. A young beaver, crying like a baby, was caught by one front leg. The animal's little moans and whimpers sounded human, and when Pa hit it over the back of the head with the blunt end of his hatchet, it raised its one good paw as if to ward off the blow. The sound was like that of an egg breaking.

Gwen felt ill as she watched Pa clean the still-warm animal. He explained that the frozen carcasses could be taken home and thawed before skinning, but that he preferred skinning the warm ones on the trail, especially beaver, since the family didn't eat beaver meat.

While Pa skinned the animal, Gwen turned her back and closed her eyes. Her mind kept replaying the sound of the beaver's cries and the skull cracking that put the poor creature out of its misery. She decided she couldn't stomach seeing any more, and asked Pa if she could go back to the farm. Surprised, but trying to be understanding, he pointed her in the direction of the path home. She wasn't far, and Pa promised that when he finished at the pond he would follow to make sure she arrived safely.

That evening, when Gwen got home, she threw away all the fur she had brought from England, all the hats and ornamental collars. After seeing the beaver's suffering, the items no longer seemed fashionable. All she could see when she looked at them was death. From then on, she swore that she would only wear fur for warmth. If animals had to die for her, then she would make sure that her clothing reflected their sacrifice and not her selfish vanity.

The day's outing had also increased her respect for her father-in-law and all he did. He worked hard for his family, and did so without complaint. When Pa heard about Gwen's reaction to her excursion, he chuckled and shook his head. "The English have strange ways," he said.

Just weeks after Gwen went with Pa to check his traplines, she gave birth to her second child. Larry and Gwen's daughter, Wendy, was born in the local nursing home. She was a pretty little thing, with big eyes, and lots of dark hair.

Chapter 8
Back to the Farm

Gwen and Larry had been living in town for two years when Larry and his brother Murray decided to go into a farming partnership. Purchasing an old farm outside of Arborfield, the brothers began making their plans to grow grain.

The winter before the family was to leave their home in Arborfield to move out to the farm, Gwen decided she would put her dance training to good use. To earn some extra cash for Christmas, she started a dance school. Soon, she had about 15 pupils, and another English war bride assisted her.

The two planned a Christmas concert. Gwen wanted

some money to buy Mark a tricycle and Wendy a big doll. She and Larry were also trying to save for the move, and the extra cash from the ticket sales would certainly help them.

The night of the concert was cold but bright. Larry was the master of ceremonies for the evening. He had taken on extra work to earn money for some badly needed farm equipment. In addition to his grain elevator job, he was working part-time helping the local electricians fill and deliver all the Christmas orders. He was very tired, and fortified himself with a bottle of coke that had a shot of rum in it.

Someone also laced the children's punch with moonshine, and as the evening wore on, Larry's jokes became funnier and the crowd became noisier. Gwen was mortified when she discovered that everyone at the concert was getting drunk on the punch. She enlisted some help, made fresh, alcohol-free drinks, and the concert went on. All in all, the show was a hit; the kids were adorable, the parents were proud, and Gwen was pleased with the turnout.

After the concert, there was a dance to top off the evening. By the end of the event, Gwen had made enough money to pay for the refreshments, the hall rental, and the band. She also had a tidy sum left over to put towards the upcoming move and buy a few Christmas presents.

A photograph of Gwen and Larry
taken around the time they left Arborfield.

The children had a good Christmas. Mark loved his bike and wouldn't go to sleep at night without parking it at the end of his bed. Wendy loved her doll, but she liked her brother's bike better.

When spring came after another long winter, Gwen and Larry packed up their house, said goodbye to their neighbours of two years, and moved to the farm. The property was only a few kilometres from Ma and Pa's homestead.

The farmhouse was a draughty old wreck of a place, but Gwen worked hard to make it as cosy as possible. The heater was more than 20 centimetres off the ground, and the loose windows and cracks under the doorways kept the floors cold. Gwen worried that her family would all freeze when winter arrived. But Ma, ever practical, gave her some rags and showed her how to make braided rugs for the floor.

After that, nothing in the house was safe. Any article of clothing Gwen could get her hands on was ripped into strips and braided. She also sewed tubes of cloth, stuffed them with scrap material, and laid them along window ledges and doors to try to keep out some of the cold air.

Ma and Pa owned an old Durant car. Since Larry and Gwen now had two children, their truck wasn't appropriate for transporting the whole family for long distances. So, for the occasional outing, they borrowed the Durant, which ran fine except for the fact it continually ran out of water.

One sunny summer day, after the family had settled into the farmhouse, Larry and Gwen decided to take the children out for a ride in the country. They packed a picnic, and some extra water for the Durant, and went to find a place where the children could play and explore.

It had been a particularly hot summer, and most of the watering holes and creeks had long since dried up. Except for a few muddy spots in the bottoms of the creek beds, there wasn't any ground water to be found.

On the way home, the car overheated and needed more water. All the water they packed had been used, and the ditches were dry. Since they were still too far to attempt walking home, Gwen suggested that Larry try to find a farm somewhere nearby. Larry nodded in agreement and promised to be back soon. A few minutes later, he emerged from the bush holding a rusty can filled with water. Smiling, he poured it into the car's radiator, and off then went.

As they drove, Gwen marvelled at how fortunate it was that Larry had found a farm so close by. Larry chuckled and said he didn't get the water from a farm.

"A creek then?" she asked.

"No." he answered, "it was left over from the juice I drank at lunch."

Gwen was disgusted, and Larry laughed all the way to the nearest riverbank, where they filled up with fresh water for the trip home.

Back to the Farm

That fall, right after the harvest, the farmers in the area held their annual jamboree at the curling rink in town. Every year, the party included games, raffles, and a dance with refreshments. The band was made up of local musicians, and occasionally Pa played the fiddle or called the square dances.This year, however, Ma and Pa decided not to attend. Instead, they offered to look after Mark and Wendy so that Gwen could go to her first prairie jamboree.

Excited, Larry took Gwen into Tisdale, about 60 kilometres away, to buy new clothes for the occasion. On the night of the dance, they dolled themselves up. Larry had even purchased a new pair of shoes.

The children were dropped off at their grandparents' house, and Gwen and Larry made their way to the dance. When they arrived at the curling rink, Larry parked the truck in front of the building and told his wife he needed to run over to the store to buy some cigarettes. Gwen nodded, got out of the truck, and waited for Larry in the entrance to the hall, listening to the music.

She waited a long time. Every now and again, she'd go outside to see if she could see him coming, but no such luck. He was gone so long she thought something must were happened to him and she began to worry. Pacing between the rink and the truck, she looked up and down the street, growing more and more anxious as time went on.

When Larry had left Gwen at the truck, he'd decided to take a shortcut to the store by cutting across someone's backyard. Little did he know that the people who owned the property had just recently dug a new hole for their outhouse. Earlier that day, they had dragged their outhouse off the old hole, and planned to fill it in the following morning.

In the dark, Larry had missed seeing the old sewage-filled hole, and he fell in all the way up to his chest. It took him at least half an hour to pull himself out, gagging and vomiting the whole time. He arrived at the curling rink plastered with sewage, and weak and sick from the smell. Gwen stared at her husband in shock. The stench was unbelievable, and while she was concerned about his well-being, she couldn't get near him for the smell.

Larry climbed into the truck and opened the window; Gwen got into the passenger's side and opened her window as well. They drove home with Larry hanging his head out one side for air, and Gwen hanging her head out the other. Of course, between gasps, Larry was cursing and gagging, and Gwen was laughing and gagging.

There was a bright harvest moon shining that night, and Gwen made Larry stand outside in the farmyard and strip off his clothes. She brought him the metal tub and some of Ma's homemade lye soap. The stove was out, so Larry, standing naked in the moonlight, had to scrub himself with cold water from the pump. He shivered, gagged, and shivered some more. Finally, he was clean enough, and he came inside covered in a blanket. He looked so pathetic that Gwen burst out laughing all over again.

The next day, Larry buried his new suit and shoes, and he and Gwen went to pick the kids up from their grandparents' house. Ma and Pa chuckled hard when they heard the story of the night's escapades. Gwen told them Larry looked like a Rodin statue, all white in the moonlight. Larry glared at her, and they all laughed. Gwen was pleased — it was the first time since she'd arrived from England that they were laughing at something someone else had done. She began to feel like part of the family.

It was a week before Larry could stomach eating.

On New Years Eve, Ma offered to mind the children so that Gwen and Larry could try to attend another local dance. This time, Larry avoided taking any shortcuts, and the couple had a good time at the party. However, as soon as the New Year came in, they decided to hurry home, as a bad snowstorm was on its way. Larry, trying to get to there as quickly as possible, swerved too sharply around a bend and hit a snowdrift about a kilometre from the farm. The couple had to walk the rest of the way, and Gwen, wearing dancing shoes, was chilled to the bone by the time they reached the house. The next day, Larry retrieved the truck and collected the children from his parents. That New Year's dance was Gwen's last venture away from the farm for the next three months, as storm after storm hit.

One of the first things Larry had done when they had moved to the farm was run a clothesline from the house to the barn. This line acted as his guide in the blizzards so he could find his way to the barn and back without getting lost. When he told Gwen how a whiteout could get you lost feet away from your house, Gwen thought that he was pulling her leg. However, after the first blizzard hit, she realized his story was not so far-fetched after all — in fact, it was frighteningly accurate.

The first winter on the farm was a hard one. Gwen found herself housebound with two small children for weeks at a time. Her slight frame was no match for the wind that howled and almost toppled her whenever she ventured outside. She was always bundled so thoroughly against the cold that she was afraid if she ever did fall down, she wouldn't be able to bend enough to get back up again.

Larry didn't seem to slow down much that winter.

He went to town once a week for the mail and supplies, same as Pa. He did the chores, looked after the animals in the barn, and helped haul tubs of snow into the house for melting, and wood for the stove in the kitchen. Throughout the winter, Gwen suffered long bouts of homesickness, cried sometimes for days, and barely spoke to others. The brutal weather was a shock to her. She had known there was snow in Canada, but she wasn't prepared for this. The cold was like nothing she had ever experienced, and with every passing day, the house seemed to grow smaller, closing in on her.

Gwen spent many hours pouring over letters from her family back in England. Occasionally, she slammed cupboard doors in frustration, and threw books or dishes. No one, not her in-laws, her new acquaintances in town, or even Larry, could understand her frustrations.

Chapter 9
"Bear! Bear!"

The following spring, Larry and his brother decided to work the farm in two shifts, daytime and nighttime, rotating every two weeks. The first night shift was to be Larry's. The plan was that every evening at dusk, he would head to the fields to plough and prepare for planting, and then come home every morning at dawn.

Gwen quaked at the idea and said, "You can't leave me here all night on my own. I'm too scared. We're miles from anywhere."

Larry laughed and told her to leave the coal oil lamp on and she'd be perfectly safe. To ease her mind a bit, he filled the lamp for her and lit it before he left; she

was frightened of the thing. He took the other lamp
|with him.

The first night passed smoothly, and Gwen and the
children slept well. When Larry came home that morning, his wife seemed content and rested, and he thought
things would be easy from that point on. Gwen, however, couldn't help but feel a little disappointed that her
husband hadn't even acknowledged her achievement.
After all, she had managed to spend a whole night on
the prairie alone. She knew farm wives were supposed
to spend many nights on their own, looking after livestock and children while their husbands were away. But
she was from England, and for that reason alone, she felt
some recognition of her accomplishment should be
noted. Larry, of course, simply laughed when she
brought it up later that day. Then he filled and lit the
lamp for her and went off to work, just as he had the
night before.

Darkness fell, and Gwen trimmed the lamp low.
The children drifted off to sleep and Gwen, weary from
a hard day's work, went upstairs to turn in as well. But
the second she started to drift off, there was a loud
bump outside the window, and she heard the children's
wagon being knocked around the yard.

Not surprisingly, a bear was the first thought that
came to her mind. She was sure the animal had smelled

the children and was trying to break into the house. Again she heard a thump, and her heart started to race. Terrified, she spotted the lamp burning on the other side of the room. Thinking she could set the bush outside on fire as a signal for help, and possibly even scare the bear away with the flames, she tossed the lamp out the window with all her might.

Unfortunately, the lamp blew out as it fell from the window, and everything went dark. Gwen heard the sound of metal hitting the ground off somewhere in the distance. There was no fire, and without the lamp, the whole house was shrouded in blackness. Gwen was near hysterics.

Worried about the children's safety, she ventured into the dark hallway and felt along the wall until she reached their room. Waking Mark, she scooped Wendy into her arms and the group felt their way back along the hall to Gwen and Larry's room. Then, venturing out into the hallway again, Gwen pushed all the furniture she could move down the stairs and lodged it against the front door. Dressers, beds, night tables, bedding — everything she could shift or toss, bumped and crashed down the staircase until there was nothing left to throw.

Meanwhile, the thumping and shuffling outside continued. Gwen, fearing the worst, stuck her head out her bedroom window and yelled and screamed as loudly as she could, over and over, hoping that Larry would hear her and come running.

But no one came, and hour after hour ticked by as the animal noises continued in the yard. Gwen lost her voice with all the screaming, and the children lay frightened in the bed, in the dark.

At about 4 a.m. it started to rain, and the rain turned into a downpour. Larry, who had been trying to plough, realized it was too wet to continue, and he packed up to go home early. Arriving home just as the grey was beginning to show on the horizon, he was surprised to find that he couldn't open the front door. There was no light showing from the upstairs window, and no signs of life anywhere in the house. Larry banged on the door and called for his wife to let him in.

Finally, a voiceless Gwen stuck her head out of the upstairs window. She wanted to warn him to watch out for the bear, but her voice came out as a dry whisper and, out of frustration and fear, she started to cry. There was so much furniture on the stairs that she couldn't even get down them to let him in.

Mark came to the window and told his dad that the door was stuck and they couldn't get down the stairs. So Larry wiggled a window open and crawled through. After clearing the furniture from the stairs, he came into the bedroom with a lamp. Gwen was still crying, and

Mark had to explain that there was a bear outside.

Curious, Larry went outside in the new morning light to investigate. He found the lamp about a metre away from the bush. It was empty of oil and a little bent from hitting the ground, but still serviceable. Soon after he found the lamp, Larry found the family cow, chewing her cud after making a meal of the kitchen vegetable patch. Gwen, overtired the night before, had forgotten to lock her in the barn. Daisy, the family Jersey, was the bear.

All the same, Gwen flatly refused to be left alone with the children the following night. After packing up some bedding and other essentials, she informed Larry that if he insisted on working at night, then they would all have to go out to the field together. Larry agreed and told her he would tow the bunkhouse out to the field he was working on. That way, she and the children could sleep nearby, and he could keep on working.

The bunkhouse was used for threshing crews and labourers during the busiest part of the season. Built on skids, it was often towed into the fields for night crews. Larry hooked the bunkhouse to the tractor and towed it, bumping and banging, out to the field. After checking to make sure there were no mice in the stove and pipes, he lit the lamp for Gwen and told her that if she needed anything — or was frightened by another cow — she

"Bear! Bear!"

was to wave the lamp in the window as a signal, and he would come running.

When he left, Gwen warily took in her surroundings. The bunkhouse was a dreary affair, with an old iron bedstead, one tiny, dusty window, and a lone cupboard fastened to the wall. Beneath the cupboard, enamel cups and other appliances dangled precariously on rusting hooks. A large potbellied stove stood in the middle of the room, flanked by two wooden chairs. Gwen sighed. For tonight, this was home, and the kids went right to sleep.

Everything was fine for a while; the bunkhouse was in the centre of the field, and Larry was working in circles around it. However, as the night wore on, his circles were getting bigger and he gradually moved farther and farther away from Gwen and the children. The farther away he was, the more nervous Gwen became.

Dozing fitfully, Gwen jerked awake upon hearing an unfamiliar noise outside. As she listened, she realized that Larry's tractor sounded a long way off. Soon, she was sure she could hear animal noises, and imagined all sorts of predators out for a night's hunting. Limp with fright, she grabbed the lamp and started swinging it frantically in the window, praying Larry would notice it.

He did, and a few minutes later, he buzzed his way over on the tractor and asked what was wrong.

"I saw eyes looking in at us through the window," Gwen explained, stammering.

Larry took his lamp and walked around the outside of the bunkhouse to inspect the soft earth. He laughed. It was only a deer, he told her, and since the deer in Canada preferred grain and grass to skinny English women, she had nothing to fear. Then he shook his head and told her to go to sleep so he could get some work done.

Gwen was furious, and still frightened beyond reason. As the sound of the tractor faded into the night, her panic rose and she waved the lamp in the window again, determined that he would not leave her alone in an old bunkhouse in the middle of a field.

Once again, Larry drove over on the tractor, but this time, he didn't bother to step foot in the bunkhouse. Instead, he hooked the bunkhouse up to the tractor and dragged it around the field while he carried on with his work. Inside, the stove jiggled, the cups banged, the walls creaked, and Gwen fumed. Only the children slept while they were dragged in circles around the field for the rest of the night.

In the morning, Larry's brother came out to the field to take over. When he saw Larry on the tractor, towing the bunkhouse, he started to laugh. Soon, the whole town was talking about the bear, the deer, and Gwen being towed around behind Larry's tractor all night.

The spring was a difficult one for Gwen and Larry. Mark came down with pneumonia and was admitted to the hospital in Tisdale for a week. Wendy was crawling everywhere, and soon was pulling herself up to standing position. With all the canning and preserving Gwen had to do on top of running to and from the hospital, looking after an active baby, and trying to harvest, she had her hands full.

One Saturday, Larry's sister came to help Gwen with the children and the canning. Mark had only been home a couple of days, and Wendy was determined to follow her brother everywhere. As the two children raced around the house, Gwen and her sister-in-law set to work on the canning. Gwen had picked all the beans and chopped them so that they were ready for the jars. On the stove was a tub of boiling water to blanch the vegetables, and another of boiling brine to pour over them in the jars before sealing. Larry's sister had laid the highchair and some kitchen chairs in the doorway to the kitchen to keep the children away from the hot stove.

Struggling with a hot pot of beans, Gwen turned and drained the boiling water into a bucket on the floor, then went over to the sink full of cold water, where she plunged the vegetables before putting them in jars. As she turned from the sink, she saw Wendy. The baby had crawled through the hole in the highchair, pulled herself to a standing position, and was taking a couple of shaky steps across the kitchen floor with her hands extended. Gwen yelled and rushed forward to grab the child, but she was too late. Wendy fell as she reached the bucket of boiling water, knocking it over and dousing herself from head to toe.

Wendy screamed, Gwen screamed, and Larry's sister ran to fetch Larry from the field. Angry blisters were quickly forming on the side of the baby's face, as well as on her arms, stomach, and legs. Gwen placed butter and ice on Wendy's delicate skin, and then wrapped her in a clean, wet sheet to reduce the burning.

Larry charged into the kitchen and scooped up the screaming toddler. Gwen raced on ahead and got into the truck so that Larry could place Wendy on her lap. They drove six kilometres into town, and when they pulled up in front of the doctor's office, their hearts hit the floor. On the door was a note stating the doctor was away fishing. So, all they could do was drive another 60 kilometres to the nearest hospital in Tisdale.

The burns were bad, but fortunately for Wendy, the doctor tried a new drug to see if that would help the healing process. Wendy was given one of the first doses of penicillin to be administered in the area, and was soon well on the road to recovery.

Nevertheless, the episode was the last straw for Larry and Gwen; they decided to pack up and move to Edmonton. Larry would find work in the city, Gwen would have electricity, and the children would have doctors close by.

It wasn't a difficult choice to make, to give up the farm. The crops were poor, and farming was a lot of work with no returns and quite a bit of expense. In the two years they had been on their farm, one crop had rained out, and a clover crop had been blown away by the wind right before the harvest. The family was tired of struggling with farm life, and Gwen finally admitted that try as she might, she would never be a farmer's wife.

With bittersweet goodbyes, the Cramer family packed their things and made for the city of Edmonton. Gwen knew she would miss many things about their life in northern Saskatchewan: Ma, Pa, the community dances. Of course, there were things she wouldn't miss, but would never forget: the outhouse without the door, the treesqueaks, and Ma's majestic wood stove.

Epilogue

The day shone clear and bright. Somewhere in the distance a firecracker exploded. It was October 30, 1988, and people were getting ready for Halloween.

Next to a small Pentecostal church in Chemainus, British Columbia, there was silence in the graveyard. A wind stirred the trees and a maple leaf, brown with touches of gold, drifted slowly to the earth in a spiral of autumn colour. Gwen Cramer stood holding the arm of her eldest son, Mark, as the minister began the last burying rights of her husband, Larry Cramer.

Around Larry's gravesite stood men and women clad in legion uniforms, and around Gwen were her five children, their spouses, and 14 grandchildren. Each child marked the path of the family's travels since Gwen had immigrated to Canada in 1946. Mark, the eldest, was born in England; Wendy in Arborfield, Saskatchewan; Bryan in Edmonton; Cynthia in Calgary; and the youngest child, Della, was born in Red Deer, Alberta. All the grandchildren were born on Vancouver Island, British Columbia, where Larry and Gwen had finally settled in 1966.

They say you can take the boy away from the farm

but you can't take the farm out of the boy. In Larry's case, the saying proved true. In Chemainus the couple had retired on an acre of land, where they cared for a dairy cow, chickens, a fishpond with koi and turtles, and an enormous vegetable garden.

As happy as Larry had been in Chemainus, Gwen had been equally content; not only had she been living close to the ocean, she also had indoor plumbing. At the time of his death, Larry and Gwen Cramer had been married 48 years.

Today, Gwen lives in a highrise in Victoria, British Columbia. Everywhere in her home are pictures of Larry, as well as her family here in Canada and in England. Gwen speaks with an English accent, her hair is coloured, and she never leaves her apartment without looking her best. The receptionist at her doctor's office refers to her as Mrs. Hollywood because she is so well turned-out.

When asked what she would change in her life if she had the chance, Gwen said she wouldn't have agreed to go out to the farm after the war in 1946. She said she was never a farm girl, and while the people were wonderful and the town was cute, she was a lime in an apple barrel.

Between the years 1942 and 1947, the Canadian government transported nearly 48,000 war brides and their 22,000 children to this country. Some war brides couldn't make the transition, and left their husbands to return to their families back home. Gwen said the thought had crossed her mind once in the middle of a blizzard, with crying children and the wind howling through the cracks under the doors. However, even after all these years, she's glad she came, glad she stayed, and is very proud to be a Canadian.

Acknowledgments

This story was the true story of Gwendoline (Haskell) Cramer. The situations depicted in this book were taken with her permission from her journal and memories, and augmented by historical facts.

Photo Credits

All photographs are from Gwendoline Cramer's own collections.

AMAZING STORIES™

UNSUNG HEROES OF THE ROYAL CANADIAN AIR FORCE

Incredible Tales of Courage and
Daring During World War II

HISTORY
by Cynthia J. Faryon

ISBN 1-55153-977-2

About the Author

A mother of three, Cynthia J. Faryon is an internationally published author and freelance writer residing in Richer, Manitoba. Canadian born, she focuses her writing on Canadian content, covering topics such as travel, family issues, biography, and history. This is Cynthia's second book in the Amazing Stories series.

AMAZING STORIES™

MARIE-ANNE LAGIMODIÈRE

The Incredible Story of
Louis Riel's Grandmother

HISTORY/BIOGRAPHY
by Irene Ternier Gordon

ISBN 1-55153-967-5

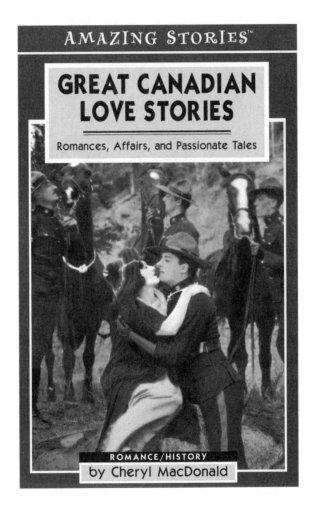

AMAZING STORIES™

GREAT CANADIAN LOVE STORIES

Romances, Affairs, and Passionate Tales

ROMANCE/HISTORY
by Cheryl MacDonald

ISBN 1-55153-973-X

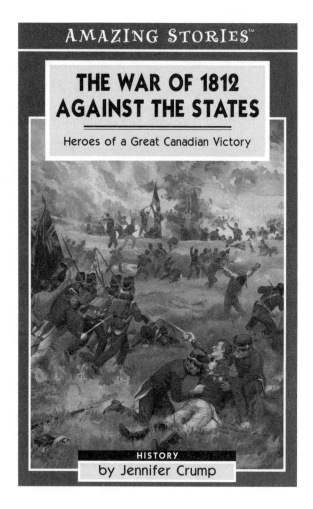

AMAZING STORIES™

THE WAR OF 1812 AGAINST THE STATES

Heroes of a Great Canadian Victory

HISTORY

by Jennifer Crump

ISBN 1-55153-948-9

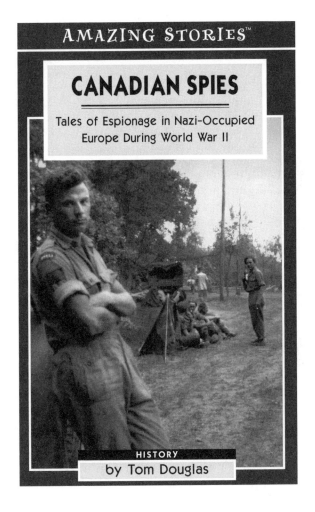

AMAZING STORIES™

CANADIAN SPIES

Tales of Espionage in Nazi-Occupied
Europe During World War II

HISTORY

by Tom Douglas

ISBN 1-55153-966-7

OTHER AMAZING STORIES

These titles are available wherever you buy books. If you have trouble finding the book you want, call the Altitude order desk at 1-800-957-6888, e-mail your request to: orderdesk@altitudepublishing.com or visit our Web site at www.amazingstories.ca

New AMAZING STORIES titles are published every month. If you would like more information, e-mail your name and mailing address to: amazingstories@altitudepublishing.com.

Comments on other *Amazing Stories* from readers & reviewers

"*Tightly written volumes filled with lots of wit and humour about famous and infamous Canadians.*"
Eric Shackleton, *The Globe and Mail*

"*The heightened sense of drama and intrigue, combined with a good dose of human interest is what sets* Amazing Stories *apart.*"
Pamela Klaffke, *Calgary Herald*

"*This is popular history as it should be... For this price, buy two and give one to a friend.*"
Terry Cook, a reader from Ottawa, on **Rebel Women**

"*Glasner creates the moment of the explosion itself in graphic detail...she builds detail upon gruesome detail to create a convincingly authentic picture.*"
Peggy McKinnon, *The Sunday Herald*, on **The Halifax Explosion**

"*It was wonderful...I found I could not put it down. I was sorry when it was completed.*"
Dorothy F. from Manitoba on **Marie-Anne Lagimodière**

"*Stories are rich in description, and bristle with a clever, stylish realness.*"
Mark Weber, *Central Alberta Advisor*, on **Ghost Town Stories II**

"*A compelling read. Bertin...has selected only the most intriguing tales, which she narrates with a wealth of detail.*"
Joyce Glasner, *New Brunswick Reader*, on **Strange Events**

"*The resulting book is one readers will want to share with all the women in their lives.*"
Lynn Martel, *Rocky Mountain Outlook*, on **Women Explorers**

UNSUNG HEROES OF THE ROYAL CANADIAN AIR FORCE

AMAZING STORIES®

UNSUNG HEROES OF THE ROYAL CANADIAN AIR FORCE

Incredible Tales of Courage and
Daring During World War II

HISTORY

by Cynthia J. Faryon

PUBLISHED BY ALTITUDE PUBLISHING CANADA LTD.
1500 Railway Avenue, Canmore, Alberta T1W 1P6
www.altitudepublishing.com
1-800-957-6888

Publisher	Stephen Hutchings
Associate Publisher	Kara Turner
Editor	Jill Foran
Digital photo colouring	Scott Manktelow

We acknowledge the financial support of the Government
of Canada through the Book Publishing Industry Development
Program (BPIDP) for our publishing activities.

Altitude GreenTree Program
Altitude Publishing will plant twice as many trees as were used
in the manufacturing of this product.

National Library of Canada Cataloguing in Publication Data

Faryon, Cynthia J., 1956-
Unsung heroes of the Royal Canadian Air Force / Cynthia J. Faryon

(Amazing stories)
Includes bibliographical references.
ISBN 1-55153-977-2

1. Canada. Royal Canadian Air Force--Biography. 2. World War, 1939-
1945--Aerial operations, Canadian. 3. World War, 1939--1945--Personal
narratives, Canadian. 4. Airmen--Canada--Biography. I. Title. II. Series:
Amazing stories (Canmore, Alta.)
D792.C2F37 2003   940.54'4971'0922   C2003-911126-1

Amazing Stories® is a registered trademark of Altitude Publishing Canada Ltd.

Printed and bound in Canada by Friesens
4 6 8 9 7 5

To all the heroes of World War II,
and their amazing stories.

A map of western Europe as it looks today.

Contents

Prologue

The drizzle in Victoria, British Columbia, fogs the windows and makes the road slick. My Chevy van lunges forward, carrying me to adventure, to a dip into the past that will stand sharply in my memory.

The driveway to the West Coast home is steep, and a grey haired gentleman in his 80s meets me at the door with a smile. I've been told he is a hero, but to me he simply looks like someone's father, or grandfather.

"Hi, Cynthia," he says, shaking my hand, "I'm Ken Moore."

His house is warm and welcoming, filled with rich fabric and wood. There is a magnificent window in the living room that reveals a breathtaking valley view.

Ken sits on a couch across from me, and next to him is a plastic bag filled with photos, newspaper clippings, and letters — the standard sort of material that is saved, cherished, and placed into scrapbooks that will serve to depict a life lived.

Usually collections like these are given to me by family members anxious to recapture a life after a loved one has passed. But in this case, the man whose life we are here to talk about is sitting right in front of me. Showing the scars of battle in his expressive eyes, he's ready to share his story.

Leafing through his collection of memorabilia, I discover a citation signed by King George VI. "Not many of those in existence," Ken says proudly, "and here, look, a photo of my crew." He rattles off their names, drawing attention to the mascot sitting front and centre. "Dinty" is the mascot's name; he is a stuffed panda in full air force battle dress.

Ken's voice cracks with emotion. "We were never apart you know. Commissioned and non-commissioned officers alike, we ate, drank, played, flew, and even bunked together. It was against regulations, but they listened when I told the higher-ups it had to be that way. I swear it was the only reason we survived.

"The RAF thought the Canadians were young, high-spirited, and too un-disciplined, yet they still extended to us an undefined kind of respect. We were farm boys, many of us, and we were given opportunities that would never have happened if not for the war. Prairie boys, some of us poorly educated, and there we were rubbing shoulders with the likes of royalty, as well as military and political giants."

He sighs and fights the tears that are gathering in his eyes. Then his voice gives out and he looks away to regain control. He has a strength and dignity that eludes description as he gazes out the window, and back 60 years.

"The emotion catches me unawares," he whispers. "It floods, and suddenly I'm back there. No one prepared us for

that kind of memory. And I know I'm not the only one who experiences the flood. I went to England for the 50th anniversary of D-Day. Liverpool accommodated almost three million visitors during that time, and we all experienced that powerful flood. It seemed to catch us all by surprise. I guess it permitted us a time of mourning together.

"We were just kids, you know. We didn't know we were doing anything special. We were simply putting one foot in front of the other and hoping we survived."

The interview lasts an hour, and covers a period in Canadian history that changed the shape of the world.

Chapter 1
First Mission of a Rear Gunner

A s he stands outside the air force hut, Larry Cramer looks southeast in the direction of Holland and Germany. It is evening and the trees are boldly silhouetted against the darkening sky. The world seems to be losing clarity with the coming of twilight.

"Peaceful," Larry thinks to himself, "and it's almost flight time."

Larry is at the Elvington Air Force base in York, England. He and the rest of his aircrew are about to embark on their freshman sortie, and while excited to be officially part of the war effort, Larry feels his stomach doing cartwheels. He takes a deep pull on his cigarette and blows the smoke into the air pensively. The time has come at last to set off somewhere into the unknown, to seek out targets, and to help the Allies win this war. The date is May 23, 1943, and the targets are the munitions factories in Dortmund, Germany.

The aircrew's Halifax bomber (often called a kite or a heavy) is fit for action. The bomber's call letter is "E," for *Edward,* and it stands waiting on the field in a parking bay close to dispersal. *Edward* has had some maintenance done, and Larry's skipper, Pilot Officer Ron Pritchard, has already taken the kite up for a test flight.

Larry takes one more pull on his cigarette and stomps it out on the English soil. For a moment he thinks of his folks back in Arborfield, northern Saskatchewan. Right about now, Pa would be milking the cows and Ma would be getting the darning out. If he were at home, he'd be cleaning stalls and brushing the horses. But he's a long way from home.

After briefing, there is a short reprieve and then preparation begins in earnest. Pilots and navigators consult together, studying the flimsies provided by intelligence. The flimsies list the night's colours for aircraft resins and Very recognition lights, which are placed on the wings of the Allied aircraft to help with identification. The lights are changed for every operation, as is the code word for aborting the mission.

After his pre-flight meal, Larry makes his way back to the barracks to get his personal things in order. He takes a moment to write a letter home, puts his effects together with a list of future ownership, and adds what's left of his pay in the envelope with the letter. Going through this, Larry feels like he's already died, and knows that once he takes off into the night, the world will carry on as if he never existed. He feels lonely, and he tries to ignore the macabre thoughts running through his mind as he prepares to kill and to be killed.

Transport finally arrives to take the crews to the hangars. The men silently pile into the vehicles and bump their way out to the airfields, where they collect their flight maps and receive last minute instructions. When the crews get to the hangars, Larry sees navigators working around a large table with topographical maps and plotting charts. His nervousness has left an emptiness in the pit of his stomach, and he walks through the hangar feeling haunted.

Moments later, Larry slips on his Mae West and adjusts it for comfort, checking that it's reasonably intact and liable to inflate properly if his luck runs out and his "ass gets a dunking," as the skipper likes to say. Grabbing his helmet, Gee board, maps, and flashlight, Larry tucks a bulky parachute under one arm and heads outside to wait for the transportation out to the kites. He feels a slight chill in the air and thinks of how cold it will be at 18,000 feet.

As Larry waits with the rest of the men, the padre hands out the flying rations, as well as the emergency rations and escape kits. The doctor then offers caffeine pills to anyone who wants them. Larry puts a couple in his pocket, and turns his collar up against the stiff breeze. He can't imagine needing the pills, but figures it's better to have them on hand just in case.

Five minutes before take off. Jimmy Coles is on the far left of the picture, Pilot Ron Pritchard is wearing the cap, and Larry Cramer is second from the right.

Soon the men are scrambling into the transport vans, relieved to be moving again instead of waiting and wondering. The navigators hug their bags of equipment while Larry clutches his parachute and the 60-pound panniers of ammunition for his guns. As the vans progress, each crewmember is dropped off at his dispersal point with shouts of "keep your bottoms down and heads up chaps," and then, "we'll see you for tea."

Finally, Larry and his fellow crewmembers are dropped off at their aircraft. They stand beside the kite with mounting unease, smoking their last cigarettes and doing their best to look nonchalant. Every member of the aircrew is conscious that this is his freshman operation. They're anxious to go, but none of them want the ground-crew boys to see their excitement and nervousness.

Suddenly, flares signalling the Stand by Stations command are shot from the tower. Larry climbs into the Halifax, manoeuvres around the bomb load, and squeezes through the fuselage to his position in the rear turret, almost directly above the tail. He hangs his parachute on the hook outside the entrance to the compartment and takes his seat inside. The height restriction for a rear gunner's compartment is six feet. Larry is six feet and half an inch, leaving no extra space.

As he settles into his compartment, Larry double-checks his ammunition and oxygen supply, tests the swivels, and cranks up the intercom. His flight suit is heated, but Larry knows he will be battling to stay warm once they are airborne.

One by one, the seven crewmembers confirm their readiness over the intercom. Then there's a pregnant pause as they feel the kite hesitate. Thunk. The chore-horse connector sockets into position, supplying the force to turn the four 1480-horsepower Rolls-Royce Merlin 22 engines. The ground crew hooks up the booster battery assembly to each engine in turn. A muffled high-pitched whine begins as the port propeller on engine one begins to turn. Hesitantly, almost reluctantly, the engine coughs and hiccups as wisps of smoke rise from the exhaust. After a few turns, the Merlin fires to a rumbling thunder. Then engine two fires, followed by three and four, all leaping to life without hesitation. The Halifax bomber shudders and trembles beneath Larry like a dragon on the verge of flight. The giant is awake, and the four propellers are spinning so quickly that they're nothing more than a smudge against the skyline.

Larry's excitement is building. Once more, before it's too late, he runs a gun check and then bends forward to latch and secure the turret hatch. The kite is throbbing with the unleashed power of the piston engines, and he can feel the vibrations from the rest of the squadron kites, all vying for their piece of the asphalt. Above the crew, the bomber stream from the other air bases across England is forming with a deafening roar.

It's dark in the rear turret compartment. Larry pulls on his leather helmet, which has goggles and chin straps. The helmet covers his ears, muting the sounds of the strange world around him. The relative quiet is a welcome relief, but it adds to his feeling of isolation in the turret. For the next five and a half hours Larry will be alone with four .303 Browning machine guns as his only companions.

Through the intercom, Larry hears the skipper report to the tower that they are ready for takeoff. Bracing himself, he takes a deep breath. When the okay comes down, the skipper,

Pilot Officer Pritchard, signals to the ground crew, who pull the wheel chocks away from the tires and move clear. Pritchard studies the control column, swings the rudder pedals left then right, re-checks the brakes, and runs the engines to the upper limits. Satisfied that everything is in working order, he pulls the two throttle levers all the way back and works the rudders with his feet. The Merlins shift from a skull-splitting whine to a low rumble as the Halifax lumbers forward. Members of the ground crew look at Larry and give him the thumbs up. He returns the signal on behalf of the rest of the crew. Then, the engine noise increases sharply once again as the kite turns to port, picks up speed, and pulls out of the parking bay. The colossal metal bird lumbers along the tarmac to the downwind end of the airfield, lining up at the starting hut.

The skipper's voice crackles over the intercom, "All set? Have we said our piece, then?" One by one, the crewmembers acknowledge their readiness by raising their right thumbs and proclaiming, "Aye, Skipper."

It's completely dark now, and Larry prepares himself for take off. He is seated in a backward position. He doesn't mind travelling backwards once he's up in the air, but the initial sensation of lift off always makes him feel uneasy.

As the kite arrives at the takeoff point, it stops at a right angle to the runway for the final engine run-up. Pritchard engages 30 degrees of flap just as the flashing green light on the windscreen at the hut beside the port wing switches to steady. This light tells the crew the previous plane has cleared the strip and their kite is next to go. Larry's heart catches in his throat. This isn't training. This is the real thing.

The sound of the engines builds into a battle cry of power and the port throttles are pushed ahead to counteract the torque. The Halifax shudders to escape its locked brakes, and the wind from the propellers rushes into the aircraft.

The roaring of the engines subsides as the brakes are released. Pritchard keeps the aircraft stationary until he has enough power to obtain rudder control. He then advances the throttles to fully open and hands them over to the engineer, who holds them steady, leaving the pilot's hands free for the control column. The plane speeds up, and then swings sideways when the torque of the propellers catches a slight crosswind. The cockpit crew barely feels the slide, but to Larry, who sits almost directly over the tail wheel, the sensation of whiplash is intense.

Adding to Larry's discomfort is the shaking and rattling of metal on metal as the kite strains and pitches from side to side. He is helpless to do anything but hang on to what he can — including his pre-flight meal. The live ammunition jostles and clinks ominously in the fuselage, the turret sways and vibrates, and the kite barrels forward, straining for the sky. Finally, an almost imperceptible change in altitude registers in the pit of Larry's stomach. As the tail lifts up, the shift is more palpable. Pritchard pulls back on the control column and the kite is off the ground, pushing upwards and forwards between the white streaks of light lining the airstrip, one on either side. There is a final thump as the wheels bounce once after finding air, and Larry watches the last of the lights slide beneath him and away. Rising against the headwind, the bomber labours steadily into the blackness above.

Out of habit, Larry searches for other planes. Looking above, below, starboard, and port, he sees Halifaxes, Lancasters, and Whitleys. Together, these planes make up a massive force of bombers in the stream. In all, 826 aircraft are assembling into formations for this raid on the city of Dortmund. Moving together like a flock of starlings in a ballet of death, the planes head for the English Channel and the waiting continent.

The first faint wisps of low cloud fly past Larry's bubble, and all at once the plane is enveloped in a thick, grey mist. He feels a double thump somewhere beneath and behind him as the landing gear locks into place. The aircraft wobbles slightly as it continues to climb, heavy with full fuel tanks and over 13,000 pounds (nearly 6000 kilograms) of bombs in its belly. A thin sheen of ice forms on the upper surface of the wings, glistening in reflected red and green. The intercom is silent as all who have a window are gazing intently out into the night, watching for enemy or friendly planes that may get too close. Now and again, Larry catches sight of the exhaust flames from the other bombers, and his stomach settles down. It's comforting to know that he and the rest of the crew are not alone.

The skipper levels the heavy aircraft at 18,000 feet and cruises at 330 km/h.

It's very cold in the turret — Larry's heated suit and mittens are barely keeping him warm. Every few minutes he wiggles in his seat and flexes his toes to make sure they're still awake. As the bomber nears enemy territory, its external lights are extinguished.

At the unseen Heligoland turning point, the plane heads south, crossing the enemy coast that is somewhere beneath them but totally obscured by cloud cover. So far, there has been no challenge to their intrusion, but each crew member has a gut feeling that it won't be quiet for much longer. Somewhere up ahead, the pathfinders are marking the way, and the fighter escort is preparing to engage anyone who stands in the path of the Allied force. Finally, after an hour and three quarters of flying time, they are closing in on the target area.

In the complete blackness, Larry can barely make out the shapes of the nearby bombers; they are mere shadows, revealing only the slightest glimmer of grey metal in the moonlight. Larry's hands are icy, but they are sweating. He feels his fingers cramping, but he can't take his gloves off to rub them; the equipment in the turret is too cold and his bare skin would stick to it. His eyes hurt from combing the skies for the first glimpse of trouble.

Suddenly, Larry hears the crew's mid-upper gunner, Jimmy Coles, whisper into the intercom. Jimmy sees the flash of tracer bullets, indicating fighter activity, not too far up ahead. Larry swivels around in his turret and notes the blue searchlights quartering the sky. Some of these searchlights are flitting about randomly in small groups, but others are concentrated in cones consisting of 20 or more lights. One of these cones has a Lancaster bomber pinned to the sky while red bursts of heavy flak from German anti-aircraft guns explode all around. The Lancaster dives immediately and directly at the blue light, feigning a move in one direction then quickly turning in the other. The pilot is swift, and very lucky. The searchlights scatter and then move on to other targets, ones that are not as fast.

Everywhere Larry looks is the bump and flash of flak, and the *Edward* is flying right into the thick of it. Below the heavy, the ground is lit with lines of reconnaissance flares. As the bombers up ahead drop their load and climb roaring into the sky, the target is criss-crossed with streaks of white and flashes of red, where fires have started. Larry tears his eyes away from the action below to keep a lookout for enemy fighters coming in from behind. With all the lights, flashes, and explosions, he's glad the Very lights on Allied planes are obvious, because his trigger finger twitches whenever a fighter advances. Every nerve and muscle in his body is alert and ready.

As the Halifax nears the drop site, flares, gun flashes, streams of flak, and the ever-present searchlights all vie for Larry's attention. Feeling confused and overwhelmed, he fights his panic and gives the pilot directions that will help the crew to avoid the dangers surrounding them. Larry's hands are at the ready, his eyes are constantly scanning, and his mind is travelling faster than the kite. Everywhere he looks there are explosions; planes carrying friends and allies are shot to pieces and plunging helplessly towards the ground.

It's not the fear of dying that plays tricks on Larry's eyes and has his nerves jumping. Instead, it's the responsibility that comes with his job. His guns — his four .303s — won't be used to gain ground or to shoot men in defence of his life alone. Larry is responsible for protecting the lives of his crewmates while the kite forges ahead to the target and drops 13,000 pounds of high explosive and incendiary bombs on the enemy below.

Larry dares not let his eyes fail him during the mission, for he knows that if he were to make just one mistake, he would not be the only one to suffer. If he blinks and misses a Junkers, if he says "corkscrew port, Skipper" when he should have said starboard, or if he gives a direction a fraction too soon or a split second too late, the aircrew could all die and he would be to blame.

Larry's thoughts are broken by the sound of the intercom. He hears the bomb aimer tell the navigator to flip the master switch, and the pilot to open the bomb doors, while he sets his selector switch to release all the bombs together. They commence the attack of the target with a steep dive from 9800 feet, break cloud at 1200 feet, and let go of the bombs.

Instantly, alarms begin to sound in Larry's ears. There's a hang-up and the bombs can't clear the doors. Larry tries to ignore the mayhem over the intercom and focuses his eyes on the sky around him. Flak is exploding all around them, the searchlights are raking the air in search of sitting ducks, and his kite is fully loaded — a ticking time bomb.

Larry's knuckles turn white from tension as he grips his guns hard and sits forward, straining to see. The hair on the back of his neck stands up, and suddenly he can smell the enemy coming at him — but from where? Yes, there it is, a Junkers 88 is heading straight for him, cannons ready. Larry quiets his breathing, waits until he's sure it's too late for the enemy pilot to pull up and out, then yells into the intercom, "Hun, Skipper, 10 o'clock, corkscrew port!" Pritchard manoeuvres the plane and the Halifax disappears from range just as the Jerry fires.

The Jerry's mind is focused on the kill and he isn't prepared for the heavy's dodge. Larry's timing is perfect. The Junkers' guns fly a stream of wasted ammunition right where Larry had been. Then the enemy plane corrects its course and attempts to follow the heavy bomber's gyrations.

"Starboard, Skipper, and dive!" Larry hangs on as he feels the fully loaded bomber groan and whine with the violent evasive manoeuvres. A rivet pops out of the metal plating above his head and pings across the rear turret. The whole crew prays that their kite holds together.

"For God's sake, Larry," the mid-upper gunner swears at

him from his perch, "I can't get him in my sights. Shoot already!" Larry takes a deep breath and calms himself. Continuing to shout manoeuvres, he calculates where the Junkers 88 will appear next and prays that his instructions are timed for when the enemy is inside the attacking curve. This will force the Junkers into a steeper turn, and if Larry shoots right into the space that the Halifax has just vacated, the enemy aircraft will fly right into Larry's bullets.

Larry squeezes the triggers — "Raaataataaaaaatat" — and the bullets race away like a deadly string of beads. The Junkers 88 is hit, and shrapnel flies in all directions as the tip of one of its wings explodes. What's left of the enemy aircraft plummets towards the ground, trailing flames and smoke as the cloud cover obscures its descent. None of the aircrew can see a parachute, and because of the thick smoke and flak, they cannot confirm the plane is actually downed. Nevertheless, Larry knows he got the Jerry.

But his elation is short-lived. Out of the corner of his eye he sees a Lancaster, tail section gone, twirling down to the ground below like an autumn leaf. Crewmembers are falling out of the Lancaster's wounded belly — some with parachutes opening, and others without. Then a Halifax is hit, and yet another.

Larry's bomber comes around to attack the target again. The bomb aimer calls directions to the skipper. This is their first mission, and they know they could just fly home and jettison their load, but none of the crew wants that. They all want their freshman mission to be recorded as a success. The men pray that the hang-up has been reversed so they can dive in, drop their load, and get out of there.

"Right, right-steady-left-steady-steady-steady... bombs gone!" The bombs pepper the air behind them, seeming to hover in a deathly quiet above the target area lit by flares, flak, and flames. Larry watches as the bombs hit their mark, sending clouds of smoke and debris high into the sky. This explosive action automatically opens the shutter on the plane's fixed camera and releases the flash bomb. Pritchard flies the kite straight and level until the camera is finished taking photos of the target sight, all the while keeping close watch on the flak and anti-aircraft guns. Photos are secondary to the safety of his kite, but without the pictures, the crew may not be credited with the trip.

Once the photos are taken, the skipper sticks the kite's nose down in a shallow dive, builds up speed in the four Merlins, corkscrews and climbs aggressively away from the target, and banks left for home.

The Halifax has successfully dropped its load of bombs on the target, and the photos can confirm it. The *Edward* is one of 12 bombers that left Elvington with Flight A to join with the 825 other planes from all over Britain. Of the 12, only 6 returned, and it wasn't the flak, the searchlights, or the enemy aircraft that kept the returning crews on their toes during the long and lonely flight home. It was the visions of exploding planes, blown out cockpits, and smoking black holes where the gunner usually sits. It was the memory of bombers and fellow fighters falling aimlessly from the air like the dead leaves of autumn. And it was the knowledge that yet again, they had friends who were no more.

There is nothing Larry and his crewmembers can do for the men who were shot down but put Xs on the squadron photos under the young faces of the fallen; fresh, youthful faces of men who ate, drank, laughed, and joked with Larry and the others before their mission, but who will now remain forever young.

* * *

Flying Officer Lawrence George Cramer was awarded the Distinguished Flying Cross for this mission. He successfully completed 38 missions as a rear gunner with the Royal Canadian Air Force. He died in 1988 in Duncan, British Columbia.

Chapter 2
Taken Prisoner

Lloyd Kidd takes off his uniform and pulls on a dark blue turtleneck. He then dons his battle dress shirt and trousers, and slips wool socks over his feet for added warmth. The air-force issue overalls, which zipper from the right ankle to the left shoulder, are set aside. He'll put those on after he visits the latrine. Lloyd makes sure he uses the toilet before each operation. Undoing the zippers and buttons of his overalls to relieve himself at 18,000 feet in the frigid cold is a nasty experience that is rarely repeated.

After visiting the toilet, Lloyd steps into his overalls, then pulls a pair of leather gauntlets over his silk gloves. The gauntlets extend past his wrists and will help to keep his hands warm during the flight. Lloyd reminds himself once again that while he's in the air he must not remove his gloves to use the flight instruments. If he does, his fingers will stick to the frozen metal. The cold in the aircraft rivals the winters back home in Saskatchewan.

Lloyd chuckles to himself, remembering that one winter, when he was just seven years old, he'd tried to open the latch on the gate at home with his mouth because he had thought it was too cold outside to take his mittens off. Of course, his lips had quickly stuck to the cold metal, and his mother had had to pour a pitcher of warm water over the latch so that he could free his lips without pulling off the skin. She'd been laughing while she did it. Lloyd's own smile widens at the memory. After a moment, he shakes himself out of his reverie and continues with his preparations. Usually he tries not to think of home.

Almost done dressing, Lloyd steps into his pair of black flying boots. These are nothing more than stout walking shoes with suede and lamb's wool uppers extending up over the calves for warmth. In a small pocket inside the upper boot, Lloyd stores the compass and knife that the Royal Air Force provides to each of the aircrew in case of a bail out behind enemy lines. The knife is for slashing away the knee extensions off the boots, providing more mobility for cross-country hiking.

Searching his pockets, Lloyd throws away any evidence that might assist an enemy interrogator in the event that he is shot down and taken prisoner. He then makes sure that he has his special pencil, also RAF issue. The pencil twists apart below the pink eraser, revealing a small map of occupied Europe with escape routes marked. Lloyd slips a picture of his family into the New Testament he received when he first joined the air force and tucks the Bible into his overalls pocket. If one of these items doesn't help him stay alive, perhaps another one will.

Lloyd Kidd is a wireless operator/air gunner (W/AG) posted with No. 78 Squadron at Middleton St. George, England. It's the night of October 2, 1942, and there is a bomber raid scheduled for Krefeld, Germany.

This is Lloyd's 21st sortie, but for some reason it doesn't feel like a routine run. Taking extra time, Lloyd puts his things in order, tidies his sleeping area, and throws out what he doesn't want prying eyes to see. He writes a letter home and leaves the envelope on his bed, sealed and ready for delivery in case he doesn't make it back.

As he walks out of the barracks, the door to the building closes behind him with a hollow thud. Though the sound shakes him, Lloyd continues walking. He heads for the parachute room, where his chute is checked for safety. As it turns out, the chute is too wet to be useable, and he is issued a dry one. Stamped on the outside of the loaner parachute are the instructions "Return in 48 hours." Lloyd takes these orders as a good omen.

Unfortunately, his optimism doesn't last long. Right

before takeoff, the Gee (aircraft radar) malfunctions and has to be removed. Already 20 minutes behind schedule, the crew realizes there is no time to replace the unit, even though flying without it will make the kite a blind target for night fighters. Resigned to the problem, the crew sits tight as their plane climbs into the darkened sky. On this particular night, Lloyd is flying as air gunner.

The journey to the target is tense, and the crew is still half an hour off the bombsite when a Junkers 88 swoops down out of nowhere and nails the kite with both guns before anyone sees him coming. A stream of incendiary bombs flies through the air and hits both the starboard engines. The kite catches fire, and all power to the craft's interior is cut off, as are the hydraulics for Lloyd's turret. The intercom is dead, leaving no means for communicating evasive action to the pilot. As Lloyd watches the smoke billow from the two burning engines, the pilot orders the crew to abandon the aircraft. Lloyd obeys and bails backwards from the turret at 15,000 feet.

His descent is uneventful until he hits a tree and falls the last 10 feet to the hard ground below. He buries his chute quickly, managing to smile once again at the 48-hour warning written on its side. Cutting away his uppers, he extracts the escape kit from his pencil and leaves the landing site at a run.

Hours later, right after the sun comes up, Lloyd finds shelter in a bluff and falls into a restless sleep. He's woken up by the sound of two children playing nearby, and spends an uneasy couple of hours hoping they don't discover his hiding place. Once they leave, he dozes fitfully again, waiting for darkness to fall before daring to travel further. After a few more hours have passed, Lloyd cannot stand to wait any longer; he crawls out of his hiding place at dusk.

Cautiously making his way along a country road, he suddenly comes face to face with a German soldier. The soldier greets him with "Heil Hitler." Lloyd returns the greeting and salute, and the Jerry is on him in an instant. Lloyd is marched at gunpoint to the nearby village and locked up for the night in the local jail. All of his possessions are confiscated except the Bible and the picture of his family.

Early the next morning, Lloyd wakes up to find two Luftwaffe officers of the mighty German air force standing before him. They have come to transport him to a fighter station, and offer him a German cigarette and a black bread and sausage sandwich. Knowing his stomach couldn't possibly handle the smoke or the food, Lloyd refuses the offer. He is then taken to the train station and sent to Frankfurt am Main, home of the infamous interrogation centre. Bracing himself for questioning, Lloyd's anxiety mounts as he recalls the stories he's heard about the horrible treatment endured by prisoners of war in Germany.

The interrogation process is as awful as Lloyd feared. After refusing to answer any questions, he is stripped of his clothing and left overnight in a dank cell without food, water, or the comfort of a blanket. In the morning, cold and desperately hungry, he is questioned once again. And once again, he refuses to repeat anything but his name, rank, and service number. Days pass, and after enduring an exhausting series of interrogations and severe restrictions on food and water, Lloyd learns that the enemy is finished with him. He is put on a train headed for Stalag VIIIB, a German prisoner of war camp near Lamsdorf, Poland.

There are several compounds at the POW camp, and many of the prisoners there are Canadians who were captured in France. Their hands are tied with twine from Red Cross parcels, and from the look of the angry red abrasions on their wrists, the twine has been there a long time. Soon after his arrival, Lloyd is given the same treatment. The Germans explain that they are exacting their revenge for what the English are doing to German soldiers in British POW camps. After a few weeks, the twine is cut off and replaced with handcuffs, leaving sores that are slow to heal. A few months later, these also are removed.

Life at the camp is anything but pleasant. To ease the prisoners' confinement somewhat, the Red Cross sends parcels that contain tins of Spam, cigarettes, chocolate, clothing, and other items. These parcels are the only luxury keeping many of the men alive, as their daily rations are comprised of a chunk of black bread and a bowl of cabbage soup. Lloyd dreams often of the black bread and sausage sandwich he declined when he was first captured.

In January of 1945, the POWs hear the booming of guns

as the Russian army closes in on the Polish border. To prevent the Russians from getting their hands on the prisoners, the Germans decide to evacuate Stalag VIIIB and transport the men to another camp. Each prisoner is given a Red Cross parcel and, wearing only the flimsiest of clothing, they are marched out through the snow. The POWs refer to this as a death march, as many of them won't survive the ordeal.

The prisoners march until darkness falls and the Germans order them to stop. Lloyd spends the first night of the journey sleeping on a coal pile. His feet are blistered, and he takes his boots off before going to sleep. When he wakes up in the morning, his feet are swollen and his boots are frozen stiff. Not having much choice in the matter, he jams his sore feet into the boots and marches another full day. The next few nights are better, as the guards find haylofts for the men to sleep in.

En route, Lloyd develops a severe case of dysentery and the medical officer deems him too ill to continue the march. The German soldiers leave him at a train station with another group of POWs being transported to a different camp. At the station, the prisoners are packed 40 plus into livestock cars that are meant to hold eight horses. The railway cars have no windows or ventilation, and the sliding doors are locked from the outside. Each car has a small can in the corner for human waste. Though most of the prisoners are exhausted, no one can lie down because there isn't the room. Lloyd is still very ill, but there is nothing he can do but endure.

Overheated and suffering from dehydration, the prisoners are finally let out of the boxcars during one of the scheduled stops for water. The men pour out of the cars like drunken sailors, eager to quench their thirsts. Lloyd stretches, enjoying the freedom of the open air, and then earnestly gulps his ration of water.

As he drinks, Lloyd suddenly hears the unmistakable sound of a North American P-51 Mustang airplane in the distance. His heart skips a beat and he begins to search the sky. When a number of Mustang fighters come into view, Lloyd and the other prisoners wave fervently at their allies, smiling and hopeful. But before the men can hope for too long, the allied fighters dive at the train with guns blazing. Germans and POWs alike are mowed down where they stand.

Lloyd leaps for the safety of a nearby ditch and lies as flat as possible as a Mustang passes overhead. Around him, the dirt puffs as 0.5 calibre shell casings pummel the ground. For a moment, he despairs at the thought of being killed by friendly fire after having survived the horrors of the POW camp.

While Lloyd takes refuge in the ditch, the Germans begin to fire back at the Mustangs. Soon the planes leave the area, no doubt believing that their mission was a success. Lloyd emerges slowly from his hiding place, and though he is relieved to have survived this latest ordeal, he is immediately saddened by the carnage that surrounds him. Leaving the dead bodies where they fell by the train tracks, the remaining

German soldiers gather the surviving prisoners and continue the journey to Stalag IXC, near Kassel, Poland.

The living conditions for Lloyd at Stalag IXC are not much different than those at the previous camp. Watery cabbage soup and hard black bread are served once a day. Three times a day, the prisoners are tortured by the smells of the meals being prepared for the guards. For some of the men, the food situation is so dire that they hunt rats and devour them with relish. They also eat worms, beetles, ants, and anything else that can be chewed and swallowed.

Even with the constraints of captivity, the camp has a band, an orchestra, a theatre group, and a football team. The prisoners are also required to take part in work detail, leaving the camp under heavy guard to toil on road construction or community improvement projects. Though no one enjoys the work, it gives them all a break from the camp, and takes their mind off the lack of female company and the constant craving for food.

Occasionally, a prisoner attempts an escape. Stalag IXC is a simple compound, enclosed by wire fences. When a prisoner dares to step outside the wires, however, the German guards are swift. For the lucky ones who are caught trying to escape, death comes as a quick blast of bullets. For the not so lucky, punishment is slow and brutal. Would-be escapees are beaten almost to death and then returned to their beds, battered and bruised. Lloyd sees these men suffer and knows that the best chance for his own survival is to simply wait and endure.

Taken Prisoner

Lloyd Kidd became a POW in October of 1942. He is finally released when the camp is liberated and closed by General Montgomery and his Desert Rats in April of 1945. Within a month of being freed, Lloyd is on his way home to Saskatchewan, still carrying the picture of his family. The picture is worn, faded, and bent, but it is intact.

Chapter 3
We All Wish to be Pilots

he heavy Lancaster bomber rattles its way off the tarmac and the aircrew brace themselves for the inevitable lift of their stomachs at takeoff. As the crew leaves England behind, the farewell committee salutes them, and another bomber powers up to follow.

It's dusk, and the tops of the clouds are on fire with the setting sun. Below, the island of Britain is already shrouded in darkness. Blackout curtains are tightly drawn in every room of every house, and what vehicles are on the roads are driving blind without lanterns or streetlights. The land looks like nothing more than a black rock surrounded by the shifting shades of the ocean.

The date is February 2, 1945, and the heavily defended target of tonight's raid is Wiesbaden, Germany. The bomber stream is facing intense anti-aircraft fire, powerful searchlights, and countless enemy fighters. Strain shows on the faces of the crew and stress tightens their every nerve as the Lancaster thunders to the drop zone, swept along in the midst of the stream like a fish in a strong current.

One of the crew is Flying Officer William "Billy" Eugene McLean. Born in Toronto on January 10, 1920, Billy grew up during the roaring twenties, and suffered the restraints of the hungry thirties. His pre-war job was in an aircraft assembly plant, and it was there that Billy began to dream of becoming a pilot. In 1941, he enlisted in the RCAF in the hopes of fulfilling his dream.

The competition was fierce. It seemed that everyone who enlisted in the air force wanted to be a pilot. Billy could understand the attraction. To him, there was nothing more appealing than being in control of an airplane, conquering the skies, and leaving the confines of the earth behind. Of course, there was also the glory to consider. Billy loved to listen to the stories of the dogfights from World War I, and the tales of the heroes already emerging from World War II. He knew that Canadian pilots were making a mark in the European skies, and he longed to be among them.

And now here he is, 25 years old and flying his fifth sortie as skipper and captain of a four-engine Lancaster. His crew is still considered green without the 15 missions necessary to increase their odds of survival. By the time their kite approaches the bombing site, the target is already a hive of activity. Smoke is filling the air from previous bomb loads finding their mark. Pathfinders are still in the area, marking and remarking the drop zone for the incoming wave of bombers. Flak is booming and bursting with flashes of red and puffs of smoke. German searchlights are combing the darkness, their brightness so intense that they momentarily blind the pilots of the Allied planes.

When a searchlight finds a bomber, it stays with it. Other searchlights then hone in, illuminating the plane so that the anti-aircraft artillery can shoot it out of the sky. This procedure is called coning, and once a plane is subjected to it, a bomber pilot has mere seconds to try to throw the lights off its track. If the bomber is in the wrong position for faking turns or making drastic manoeuvres, it becomes a sitting duck. Even with a quick response, only rarely do bombers manage to escape the anti-aircraft fire completely once the lights have marked them.

As the searchlights in Wiesbaden continue to rake the sky, Billy takes his bomber in for the final dive. Once the bomb load is released, he keeps the kite level long enough to allow for the obligatory photographs, and then pulls up and away. Suddenly, the searchlights find the Lancaster, and the giant kite is caught in the air like a deer caught in the glare of headlights. Temporarily blinded by the bright blue light, Billy is unable to make the manoeuvres and corkscrews that are

A Lancaster bomber

necessary to break the light's contact. The crew holds their breath as the interior of the metal mammoth glows in the surreal illumination from below. There seems to be a short pause, and then a violent explosion rocks the kite. Flak has found its mark, exploding a wing and sending fuel, flames, and debris in every direction. As if in slow motion, the Lancaster hangs there for a moment, then slips backwards and sideways as it begins its descent to the hard earth below.

The bomb aimer climbs up from his position below to give assistance to anyone still alive. The wounded Lancaster is pitching and spinning out of control towards the ground, throwing around everything and everyone not strapped down.

Flak is still booming and banging, and shrapnel from the bomber's wing is flying everywhere. A large piece of red-hot metal shoots into the cockpit, embedding itself in the floor between Billy's feet and the rudder bar. Billy ignores the burning metal and continues to fight with all his strength to right the wounded aircraft. Putting his extensive knowledge of the workings of the heavy into play, he manages to slow the spiral, but only long enough to give the crew a few extra minutes.

While Billy struggles with the controls, the bomb aimer grabs a flight jacket and wrestles with the glowing chunk of metal, trying to extract it from the body of the kite. All of a sudden, the flight jacket catches fire, burning the bomb aimer's hands. He continues to beat back the flames in the cockpit, but it is obvious that his efforts are useless.

The end result is inevitable. The kite is toast, but Billy knows that if he can fight the downward spiral for long enough, he can buy time for his crew to bail out. The fire in the cockpit is hindering him but by allowing the bomb aimer to continue fighting the fire he is forfeiting the man's chance for survival. Realizing he can't permit a member of his crew to sacrifice his life for a lost cause, Billy orders the bomb aimer to leave the fire and save himself. The bomb aimer reluctantly follows orders.

Billy doesn't want to die, but he cannot live at the expense of his crew. He remains at his controls and as the flames lick his boots and orders the rest of his men to abandon the aircraft. The crewmembers who are still able to move scramble to the escape hatches. The ground is rapidly approaching, and no one knows if their window of escape has already passed them by.

Before the mid-upper gunner leaves through the front hatch, he notes that Billy's boots and jumpsuit are completely in flames. Yet despite this, the skipper remains focussed, still fighting to keep the kite steady by pulling the nose up as high as he can so that as many crewmembers as possible have a chance to bail out. As he jumps to safety, the mid-upper gunner knows that the pilot's opportunity to save himself has already come and gone. Billy is quickly being engulfed in flames. Mercifully, the rumbling of the wounded bomber drowns out his anguished cries.

Ready to bail out next, the bomb aimer wrestles with the unresponsive form of the flight engineer. He fastens the flight engineer's parachute with hands so burned they are hardly functional, and turns to drag the man through the escape hatch with him. The cockpit is now fully engulfed, but the skipper, who is a ball of flames, is still at the stick, maintaining whatever control possible as the aircraft plunges to its demise.

Suddenly there is another blast, and the bomb aimer is hit in the stomach by a flying object. The force of the blow throws him through the hatch and out of the aircraft. Moments later, suspended by his parachute, he watches what is left of the Lancaster plummet to the earth and explode on impact. A mercifully quick ending to what must have been an agonizing experience for Billy McLean.

The bomb aimer, who is one of only two crewmembers to make it out of the Lancaster alive, knows that he has Billy to thank for his life.

Many ordinary Canadians fought to be pilots, to soar above the clouds, and to be free of the earth. Some wanted the glory, others the thrill of adventure, and most, when faced with extraordinary circumstances, chose to be heroes.

Chapter 4
Adrift on the North Sea

F lying low over the lead-silver ocean in a heavy bomber is an awesome experience. Flying low over the lead-silver ocean in a heavy bomber without enough fuel to reach the airbase is something else again. Croft is the most northern airbase in Bomber Command, making for longer trips, and increasing the danger of running out of fuel on the way home. Those who are on their way to Croft but must make their landing at another airstrip are inconvenienced, but live to tell of it. Those who are on their way Croft and are forced to land in the sea would be lucky to survive the experience, as only 13 percent of all aircrew live through a ditching in the ocean. Survivors of a ditching become instant members of the

Goldfish Club, and receive a goldfish patch to be worn on their battle dress. This is sent compliments of the Lindholme Dinghy Company, suppliers of the safety rafts in the bombers.

Many men flying in bombers from No. 434 Squadron at Croft have felt the knot in the pit of their stomachs when the pilot announces there isn't enough fuel to reach home. All it takes for such a shortage is a headwind to slow the path of the heavy.

On August 16, 1944, Flying Officer John Wagman, pilot with No. 434 Squadron, is detailed to attack Kiel, Germany. Hailing from Saskatchewan, he is part of a bomber crew that includes five other Canadians: Sergeant Wilf Odegaard from Saskatchewan, navigator; Sergeant Hugh McMillan from Alberta, bomb aimer; Sergeant Hank Kaufman from Ontario, wireless operator and air gunner; Sergeant Des Burke from Ontario, mid-upper gunner; and Sergeant Jack Archibald from Quebec, rear gunner. Sergeant Jock Cameron, a flight engineer from Scotland, rounds out the seven-man crew.

The Kiel attack is rough with severe anti-aircraft fire and night fighter activity. On approach to the target, John Wagman's kite is hit by flak, severely damaging the bomber and gouging the gas tanks, causing serious fuel loss. At take-off, a kite is fully loaded with 8000 litres of fuel. After the bomb drop, John's Halifax has only 1700 litres remaining. At this realization, his stomach hits his boots. He announces the situation over the intercom, and he can hear his crew groan.

Not only is there not enough fuel to make it back to Croft, it's unlikely they'll even make it back to England. The best the crew can hope for is to make it to the English coast and ditch the plane as close to home as possible.

In order to stretch their fuel supply, John pulls back on the air speed and flies as low over the North Sea as possible to minimize the effects of the headwind. When it becomes apparent that they won't make it to the English coast, the wireless operator, Hank Kaufman, breaks radio silence and starts sending out the estimated position for ditching, approximately 64 kilometres off the coast. Even after the order is given for the crew to take up ditching posts, Hank chooses to remain at the wireless, sending location signals for as long as possible to increase the likelihood of a quick rescue.

Moments before impact, Hugh McMillan and Hank scramble to the fore and aft fuselage sections of the kite and lie stretched out full length with their feet braced against the front spar, facing upward. Meanwhile, Des Burke, Jack Archibald, and Jock Cameron brace themselves, clasping their hands behind their heads and pressing their backs up against the rear spar, facing backwards. Everyone remains still. They expect the aircraft to skip along the water and come to a stop, as this is what they were told would happen back in training.

However, the Halifax bomber and the North Sea have other ideas. Due to the damage caused by the flak, the kite hits the water without levelling out and splits on impact. As the kite breaks in half at the rear spar, Jack, Des, and Jock are thrown into the dark sea. The Halifax bounces back into the air, swivels slightly, and crashes down once more. Everything that is not buckled down is sucked out of the aircraft, including the pilot. The remaining men, Wilf, Hank, and Hugh, are shaken, but glad to be in one piece. Bleeding only slightly, all three seem to have escaped serious injury.

To order to avoid being sucked under water when the kite sinks, the three men climb out of what remains of the Halifax through a hole in the fuselage. Inflating their Mae Wests with their bottles of carbon-dioxide, they jump into the ocean and swim away from the doomed plane. The back end of the kite is nowhere to be seen; neither are the four other crewmembers. An overwhelming hopelessness envelopes the men. The sky is black, the waves are relentless, and the ocean is frigid. Even in the warm summer months, the North Sea is too cold for a man to survive longer than two hours. Wilf, Hank, and Hugh cling to each other for added warmth, knowing that hypothermia isn't far away. Praying that a plane will be sent out for them soon, the men try not to dwell on the fact that no one will be able to see them until daylight. They had hit the water at 2:45 a.m.

With their heads barely bobbing above the swell, the three fight to keep hope alive by talking, about anything and everything. The subject doesn't matter; all that matters is the human contact and the sound of their own voices. Then faintly, off to the right, they hear something besides the endless waves and their weakening speech. It's the voices of the rest of the crew! They have all survived the crash, and suddenly there is a renewed hope to hang on together until help comes.

Just as the sky begins to lighten, the men see a half-inflated dinghy sticking out from the wing section of the aircraft. Though it is missing the emergency kit that holds rations of food, water, and the billows to finish inflating it, the dinghy will still help the crew get farther away from the sinking craft, and farther out of the water.

Hank, Wilf, and Hugh swim back to the wreckage and pull the dinghy free. The three climb on board and paddle to the rest of the crew. Then, with a combined effort, the men manage to manoeuvre the raft a safe distance from the remains of the Halifax. All seven crewmembers are riding so low in the waves that the bottom half of their legs are submerged. Wet and cold, they huddle for warmth in the dirty grey of pre-dawn. Each one prays that daylight will bring an Air Sea Rescue plane.

Daylight breaks at 5 a.m. The warmth of the sun revives the crew and the light bolsters their hope. They have made it through the night! Surely help is on its way. At 7 a.m., there is a loud sucking sound, and the largest part of the kite rolls over until all that is visible is one wing sticking 50 feet straight up in the air. The crew stares in silence at their disappearing plane. It's a sad moment, and it hits them hard.

Suddenly, discouragement replaces hope. Fearing the worst, everyone but Hank recites the Lord's Prayer.

Hours later, the only sounds on the water are the hovering sea birds and the ever-present lapping of waves against the inadequate dinghy. Then they hear it, a throaty throb of engines coming closer. Four Halifaxes are making their way across the water, and one of them spots the wreckage and the pitiful dinghy below. The planes signal to each other, and all four wag their wings at the survivors. The kites stooge and circle around the dinghy so as not to lose site of it in the swells. One aircrew shoots off a Very cartridge. Another crew drops a smoke float, but their aim is too accurate and the downed men have to push the float away to prevent it from setting fire to the dinghy.

Finally, at 2 p.m., almost 12 hours after the initial ditching, an Air Rescue Hudson drops a fully inflated dinghy, along with an emergency kit containing milk, food, cigarettes, waterproof matches, and four dry flying suits. The men figure that either the rescuers can't count, or that no one believed all of the aircrew could have survived. It's decided that those who are wettest and most injured will don the dry suits.

Taking another turn above the raft, the rescue plane drops a message in a waterproof container. John Wagman decides that since he is the skipper, it's his job to swim out for the message. He sheds his warm, dry suit and stands on the edge of the dinghy, naked and shivering. But after sticking one toe into the frigid water he yells, "To hell with it!" and crawls back into his warm flight suit. The men aren't going anywhere. They decide that the message can't be that important, and if it is, someone will tell them about it when they come and pick them up.

The Air Sea Rescue launch finally arrives from Grimsby at 4 p.m. Climbing aboard the boat, the survivors gratefully dress in the warm civilian clothing they are given. Then, suspecting that the men might be in need of something hot to eat, a crewmember of the launch takes out a can of mock turtle soup. The can has a wick running through its centre that, when lit, will heat the soup from the inside. After lighting the wick, the launch crewmember sets the can on a nearby table. As the soup heats, the survivors laugh and joke, happy to be alive.

All of a sudden, the men go quiet and turn their attention to the hissing can on the table. With mounting horror, they realize that the launch crewmember forgot to puncture the can before lighting the wick. For a brief moment, they simply stare at the container as it continues to build pressure. Finally, one of the men snatches the can and heaves it out to sea with all of his might. It explodes before hitting the water, sending soup and pieces of tin in all directions. The aircrew lets out a collective sigh of relief and chuckle at the thought that, after surviving the flak, the fighters, the ditching, and the cold North Sea, they are almost killed by shrapnel from a can of mock turtle soup.

Chapter 5
Friendly Fire

I t is January 7, 1945, and the aircrews of Nos.12 and 626 Squadrons are preparing for a night raid on Munich. Doug Crowe is used to the pre-flight routine. This is to be his 24th sortie, and he manages to function on automatic even though the apprehension and nerves he always feels are still present. His aircraft is a Lancaster Mk1 called *Old Sugar 2*. Fully loaded, she waits patiently out on the tarmac.

Old Sugar 2's crew includes five Canadians: Flight Officer R. Marshall Smith, pilot; Flight Officer J. Ken Yeamans, navigator; Flight Officer Dave Rymer, bomb aimer; Flight Sergeant Doug Crowe, mid-upper gunner; and Sergeant Cyril Lane, flight engineer. Rounding out the aircrew are two non-Canadians: Flight Sergeant Geoff Magee from Australia, wireless operator; and Sergeant William "Bill" McLean from England, rear gunner. Bill McLean is new, introduced to the others at briefing. He is replacing the crew's original rear gunner, who was killed on the way home from laying mines.

The men in the aircrew are uncomfortable with taking on a member that has never flown with them before. Rear gunners are paramount to the safety of the kite. Without a reliable man in the rear turret, the bomber has a blind spot that leaves the crew vulnerable to attack from behind and below. The enemy fighters know this, which is one of the reasons why the life expectancy of a rear gunner is only five weeks — night fighters rely on the element of surprise and aim to hit the rear gunners first.

Old Sugar 2 takes to the air at 6:44 p.m. As the bomber stream approaches Soissons, France, they run into heavy cloud, and Pilot Marshall Smith adjusts their course slightly to 090 degrees. While they climb to clear sky, Dave Rymer reports seeing the starboard navigation lights of an aircraft too close to the port side of the heavy. Kites in the main bomber stream don't normally display navigation lights this close to the target, so the crew is immediately on their guard. Suddenly, there is a bright orange flash, and the kite jumps, sending the crewmembers flying. Doug feels nauseous as air rushes around him. *Sugar* is hit — severely. Swivelling around in his mid-upper turret, Doug's worst fears are realized when he sees that the rear gunner's turret has been completely blown out. There is only a gaping hole where Bill once sat.

Now flying at 15,000 feet, the Lancaster is about 19 kilometres northeast of the main track. The wounded kite starts into a slow, diving turn that Marshall is unable to pull up from. He struggles for a few seconds, and then orders everyone to abandon the bomber. Doug climbs down from his turret and reports that the rear gunner is nowhere to be found.

Everyone left on the plane is scrambling to evacuate. Everyone, that is, except Marshall. He sees that the kite is too close to some U.S. troops doing manoeuvres on the ground, and also spots a small village and a U.S. Army field hospital nearby. Marshall decides that in order to avoid further catastrophe, he must continue to fight for control of the bomber. He wants to give the crew enough time to safely bail out, and perhaps more importantly, he wants to prevent the kite from crashing too close to the hospital or the village.

The rattling and banging in the aircraft is enough to break teeth, and the stench of smoke is getting stronger. As the rest of the crew leave by either the front hatch or the rear door, Marshall remains at the controls, trying his best to hold back the crash. *Old Sugar 2* is headed straight for the town of Laon, France.

Just before losing total control, Marshall gives all the power the kite has to all four engines. This forward thrust carries the aircraft forward, allowing it to clear the town, the hospital, and the troops before crashing into a railway cutting beyond. *Sugar* bursts into flames on impact and finally blows up at 9:00 p.m. The body of Pilot Marshall Smith is thrown 15 metres from the wreck.

The five remaining crew, after bailing out at 15,000 feet, hit updrafts from the heavy cloud cover. At times they are pushed higher into the air instead of drifting down. Most of them take about 30 minutes to make the descent, but Ken Yeamans, the navigator, takes 45 minutes. Independent of one another, the crewmembers bury their chutes in the snow and, following standard procedure, head away from the crash site.

Doug Crowe lands in an open field surrounded by trees. He knows he is close to the front lines, but isn't sure where exactly he has landed. Looking around the field for a way out, he finds and follows a fence line. After walking some distance, he comes to a gate that opens onto a lane. This lane leads him to a small village.

Thinking that he might need to find shelter for the night, Doug carefully scans the village to determine the location of the church. He then approaches some French farmers, who invite him into their home. The Frenchmen call the village priest, and a short time later, a U.S. Army vehicle arrives to transport Doug to a U.S. military traffic control point. There, Doug is reunited with crewmembers Ken Yeamans, Geoff Magee, and Cyril Lane. Their names are forwarded to the Supreme Headquarters, Allied Expeditionary Forces (SHAEF), who notify the squadron that they are alive. Dave Rymer is also located some distance away, and taken to

SHAEF headquarters in Rheims. Bill MacLean and his rear-gun turret, however, are never found.

Flight Officer R. Marshall Smith was never officially recognized for his selfless act. Still, the fact remains that had the pilot abandoned his post to save himself, his crew and countless strangers would not have survived the *Sugar*'s crash. In facing his own death to save people he had never met, Marshall Smith committed an act of extreme bravery and heroism.

* * *

There is a difference of opinion as to what actually happened to *Old Sugar 2*. The above account has been comprised from the official record. However, there is another version of the story. On the evening of January 7, 1945, U.S. troops near Laon had been firing anti-aircraft guns at some bombers, thinking they were Jerries. *Sugar* had been flying so closely to the bomber displaying navigation lights that there is some speculation she was hit by friendly fire.

Chapter 6
Shot Down Behind Enemy Lines

Many who dream of being pilots want to fly Spitfires. These planes are flown solo, simply the pilot versus the enemy. The glory, the stories, and the action associated with these fighters draw countless hopeful recruits to the RCAF. Of course, the harsh realities of fire, bullets, ditchings, and death are rarely considered until a Spitfire pilot is on a mission and staring them in the face.

Manitoban Jack Hughes is a fighter pilot in the RCAF, stationed with No. 402 Squadron out of Redhill, England. On July 15, 1942, he is one of many pilots who will be flying rhubarbs (offensive fighter sweeps on targets of opportunity) into France. The Redhill airfield is shared between a Polish squadron and Nos. 402 and 602. The plan for the upcoming mission is for the Poles and 602 to fly into France and, like hounds at a foxhunt, sniff out the enemy at railway yards, canals, and roadways. Jack and No. 402 Squadron are instructed to stand at the ready in case they are needed for defence.

The first wave of Spitfires takes off at 11 a.m., leaving Jack and the others at 15-minute readiness. Jack is out at his aircraft talking with the ground crew when two red scramble flares — the signal ordering immediate takeoff — are triggered.

Leaping into action, the pilots of No. 402 are strapped in and have their engines running in minutes. Jack's Spitfire is second off the line, flying number two to the commanding officer (CO). As soon as he reports that he's airborne, the air controller replies, "Buster 180 deck," giving Jack the go-ahead to fly maximum speed due south below the clouds.

The Spitfires drop down to the English Channel, where there are several flyers submerged just off the French coast, and where Allied rescue boats are being attacked by German Messerschmitts 109s (Me109s). The Me109s are hitting the vessels in pairs, and several of the boats are in flames.

The CO quickly manages to break up the attack in progress, and the rest of the Allied planes fly a defensive circle around the rescue boats. Suddenly, the Jerries forget the boats altogether and turn their attention to the Spitfires, who are now at a disadvantage, as they're in a defensive position.

Shortly after the attack reprieve, an enemy squadron of Focke-Wulf fighters (Fw 190s) shows up to relieve the Me109s, who are short on fuel and ammunition. On their way out, a pair of Fw 109s dives in for one last hit on the boats. Jack doesn't think twice about going after the two enemy fighters; he is bent on saving the men in the water from an ugly death.

Diving after the Me 190s with guns rattling, Jack makes a couple of hits and then breaks off. When he looks back over his shoulder with the idea of going around again to finish the job, he sees an Fw 190 on his tail, less than 300 feet away. Jack guns the Spitfire's engine, but it's too late. The rounds come out of the Jerry's cannons like red-hot baseballs. They smash holes through the port side of the Spitfire's fuselage and then exit out the starboard side, igniting the fuel.

In an instant, the flames from the gas tank are sucked into the cockpit, covering Jack from helmet to boots. A message comes over the radio: his buddies see he's in trouble and have his tail covered. Though he is wounded and still wearing his burning flight suit, Jack manages to remember his training. Almost automatically, he puts his ejection plan into action. This is a plan he has often gone over in his head, but until now, it is one he has never had to use.

Moving quickly, Jack reduces his speed by pulling up into a loop. He is not only strapped into his aircraft, he is also attached to it by oxygen and radio connections. Jack pulls the oxygen fitting and radio plug out from the dash of the Spitfire,

A Spitfire pilot with all his equipment. The pilot is wearing his Mae West but would also have his parachute strapped on when flying.

then drops the seat, pulls the pin on the seat harness, and stands up. He kicks the control stick forward to create a burst of momentum that he hopes will help spring him up and out of the burning aircraft as the kite throttles forward.

Unfortunately, Jack can't jump as easily as he had planned. The radio cord is tangled on the seat lever. Jack is on fire, his plane's engine is stalling, and he can't reach down to get the cord loose. Crouching down on the seat with his hands on the edge of the cockpit, he leaps out of the aircraft with all his strength, ripping off the oxygen mask and earphones in the process.

As he flies through the air, Jack looks over at his Spitfire, which is entering its death spiral. He then pulls his ripcord and feels the chute pulling away from him underneath his body. When executing his escape plan, Jack hadn't taken into consideration that he would still be catapulting upwards from the momentum of the aircraft, causing the chute to open beneath him and upside down. As he starts to fall, Jack realizes he's in danger of landing on his own parachute, rendering it useless. Without wasting another second, he does a backflip in the air and makes a dive towards the chute. He races past it head first, and the chute flips around and opens properly, yanking Jack into an upright position.

The flames plaguing Jack's gear are almost out, but his hand is bleeding profusely from a shrapnel wound. As he descends from the sky, he wraps his ripcord around his wrist to stem the flow of blood. Losing track of time, he doesn't realize how close he is to the water, and he hits the English Channel without getting the chance to release his harness.

After a few seconds of struggling, Jack manages to release the parachute harness buckle, and three of the four straps fall away as they are supposed to. The fourth, however, catches on something, and the chute starts to drag Jack with the current. Lungs bursting, he kicks off his flight boots and pulls the lever on his CO_2 bottle to inflate his Mae West. Soon, his head breaks the surface of the water, and he gratefully breathes in the misty ocean air.

Pulling out his emergency dinghy pack, Jack inflates the

raft and climbs aboard. The channel had doused the remainder of the flames on his uniform, but he is badly burned, and the saltwater is causing him excruciating pain. His flight suit is charred and tattered, and he has a head wound, an injured hand, and countless small abrasions. Reaching into the side compartment of the dinghy for the first aid packet, Jack discovers that both it and the escape kit are missing. This means he has nothing with which to dress his wounds, and worse still, he has no flares to send off to help with his rescue.

Jack pulls his chute from the water and tucks it into the raft for easy access. He figures that if he hears a Merlin engine thunder by, he will throw the chute out and use it as a signal. However, if rescue doesn't come with daylight, he'll tie the raft to the chute and use it to sail across the channel and home.

With his last act of survival completed for the night, Jack tosses the drag anchor into the water to keep his dinghy from drifting too far with the current, and then passes out from exhaustion and loss of blood.

Sometime around dusk, the noise of wooden trawlers in the surf wakes him. Jack opens his eyes and sees one boat in front of his dinghy and another one coming up alongside it. He tries to stand up and wave his arms, but he can't keep his balance. Within moments, a net is thrown over the side of the trawler and two seamen scramble part way down. Reaching over, they grab Jack by his shoulders and hoist him up over the side of the boat, then place him facedown on the deck.

They pin him there and frisk him; they are looking for weapons and trying to verify that he is RCAF.

Jack soon realizes that he is not on a fishing boat, but a disguised English minesweeper. He asks one of the crew how they found him in the overcast weather, and the crewmember explains that they had seen a fireball and had followed its path downwards, taking a bearing between the two boats. The boats then had to continue their sweep of the area before investigating further, but they later located him only a little ways off from where they had figured he would be.

Jack is taken below deck, where a medical officer cuts away his clothing and swabs, cleans, and bandages his wounds. Once he is dressed in warm overalls, he sits on the edge of a bunk and wishes he had something for the pain. A thoughtful sailor brings him a good shot of rum. Later, another sailor brings him a shot of brandy. Jack falls asleep warmed to the bone.

Sometime in the night, he awakens with a start. Things seem too quiet. The boat's engine has stopped, and the vessel feels empty. The light of the ship's compass casts a blue light over everything, and tentatively, Jack makes his way on deck. Sticking his head up far enough to see, he finds the boat is docked, and there are English servicemen milling around the beach area. The boat has landed in Dover on the south coast of England. Jack is home.

As soon as he is able, Jack returns to his squadron to commence active duty. He is one of only a few to have survived the air battle on July 15, 1942, and his act of heroism includes not only his brave defence of the survivors in the water, but the actions that saved his own life against daunting odds.

Chapter 7
Death Before Dishonour

I t is almost midnight, and the ground begins to shake as kites take off from the Gransden Lodge airbase in England. The aircrew members not taking part in the night's operations lie in their bunks, counting the planes as they take off by listening to the rumble and roar of the Merlins. These men silently wish their comrades and friends a safe journey, steeling themselves for the possibility of loss. Sleep will be light and fitful at the base, and tensions will ease only when the planes return in the morning, revealing how many men have vanished. One lost heavy bomber means seven friends and brothers are gone or missing.

It is April 27, 1944, and there is a bomber stream of

120 Halifaxes and 16 Lancasters flying in the night's operations. The target for these bombers is the marshalling yard at Montzen, Belgium. The intent of the operation is to disrupt the movement of military equipment to the German forces along the coast of France in preparation for the D-Day invasion. The mission is expected to encounter only light resistance: a few small anti-aircraft guns, but no searchlights.

The commanding officer and master bomber for the pathfinding mission is Flight Lieutenant Reginald John Lane, born in Victoria, British Columbia. Edward "Teddy" Weyman Blenkinsop, also from Victoria, is the squadron leader, deputy master bomber, and next in line for CO. Both men are flying with No. 405 Squadron based at Gransden Lodge. This is to be Teddy's 38th operation.

Lane and Teddy are both approaching the target area in Lancaster bombers. Closing in on the drop zone, the two pilots see the markers left by the other pathfinders. The raid is just beginning, and as the first bombers drop their loads, the flares and markers are obliterated. As planned, Lane's kite flies in and releases more target markers from 4500 feet, redefining the drop site for the next wave of bombers. The raid is on in earnest soon after, and Teddy's plane dives in to drop additional flares, keeping the target well marked for the main force.

About 20 minutes later, their jobs are done. Teddy's aircraft heads home as ordered, while Lane's crew stays a little longer to take care of late arriving bombers. That's when things start going wrong.

The enemy fighters arrive on the scene earlier than anticipated and manage to penetrate the bomber stream, shooting from below and within. In the smoke and flak, the Allied fighters protecting the bombers have a tough time warding off the enemy; the falling bombs and the close proximity to their own Allied aircraft limit them. The air battle follows the bombers away from the target and along their route home. The Germans are merciless in their attack, and the bombers continue to battle for their airspace and safe passage. Ammunition slices through the air, and the bombers are in almost as much danger from stray friendly fire as they are from the enemy guns.

Twenty-four minutes after the raid begins, Lane watches as bomber after bomber is attacked and shot down by night fighters who are working from inside the stream with great success. Seeing the struggle in the air, Lane drops his kite as low to the ground as possible in order to confuse the intercept radar of the enemy aircraft and hopefully save some Allied planes. The anxiety among his aircrew is thick as each pair of eyes combs the skies. The men are sickened by the losses, but helpless to do anything more. Then, straight ahead, Lane watches as the ninth kite in the stream is hit dead on, blindsided by a Me109. All stare, horrified and helpless, as the plane blows up and target markers explode from the pathfinder bomber like fireworks at a picnic. Then the realization hits Lane: that was Teddy's plane.

Lane swallows hard at the bile rising from his gut and

tries to concentrate on what he has to do. No one could have survived that explosion. The aircrew struggles to shelve their grief and attend to their own survival, but Lane is having difficulty remaining detached. He finds Teddy's loss harder to deal with than others because the two had bonded over their mutual hometown roots.

It's a quiet and sombre group that lands back on English soil. The grounded airmen awaiting their friends' return count the landings at 3 a.m. and wait in vain when the number is short. Fifteen bombers are unaccounted for; a heavy price for what was supposed to be a very straightforward mission. Fifteen bombers equal 105 men killed or missing in action.

The next day, surviving aircrews do their best to ignore the empty chairs in the mess hall. Bunk detail cleans out the personal lockers of the missing servicemen, and the dreaded letters are composed and sent off by war-weary officers. All know the empty spaces will soon be filled with new recruits. While saddened, grief is a luxury that can't be indulged at this time. The preparation for D-Day must take priority.

* * *

Teddy Blenkinsop leaves the target area as soon as he receives the order from Commander Lane. There is confusion everywhere: smoke, bombers, and the thumping and bumping of flak. The absence of searchlights is a blessing, but it soon becomes clear that there is another, more immediate threat. Bombers are being shot down from inside the main stream. The Allied escort is having difficulty defending the bombers due to the enemy fighters' proximity to friendly aircraft.

Teddy hesitates for a moment and tries to come up with a plan to help with the defence of the bomber stream. Like Lane, he decides to drop altitude to confuse the radar of the fighters, giving the enemy a false reading on the middle of the stream. He hopes his move will also draw some of the Jerries lower so that the Allied escort can get clear shots at them.

Almost immediately after he drops altitude, his rear gunner begins to yell manoeuvring instructions into the intercom. As Teddy starts to respond, he hears a loud thump and a terrible roar. A force rips him out of the cockpit and throws him clear of his kite, which is now 10,000 feet in the air. Still conscious, Teddy manages to pull the ripcord to his parachute, and while fighter activity continues all around him, he drifts unnoticed to the ground and lands behind enemy lines. He is the soul survivor of his crew, and except for a few minor cuts and bruises, he is uninjured.

Upon landing, Teddy takes his air force issue knife, pencil, and compass from the pouch of his overalls before stripping them off. He swallows his caffeine pills to ward off exhaustion, and then uses the knife to cut away the uppers from his flight boots. Burying his chute and any unneeded flight equipment, he pulls off the rubber end of the pencil and extracts a map of the target area with likely escape routes marked.

As he travels away from the drop site, he works out his location by remembering the last reports of his navigator, and by taking direction from his compass and the stars. Teddy runs to put as much distance between himself and the crash site as possible, hoping in his haste that his location estimates are close enough.

Over the next two days, Teddy manages to meet people who have connections with the Belgian Resistance. The underground plans to smuggle him back to England, arranging for a guide to take him overland through France and then into Spain. But at the last moment, Teddy refuses to go. He sees the effort the Resistance is making on behalf of the Allied forces and feels that with D-Day coming, he'd be more valuable in Europe.

The Resistance welcomes Teddy and issues him false Belgian national papers. Over the next few months, he helps fight the Germans from behind the lines, attacking rail yards, blowing up bridges, and aiding other escaping airmen. During one of his secret missions, Teddy is picked up by the German Gestapo and taken to St. Gilles prison, in Brussels.

The Germans do not know that Teddy is RCAF, and they hold him as a Belgian national who is part of the Resistance. While at the interrogation centre, Teddy taps a Morse code signal on the steam pipes in his cell, relaying his identity to other prisoners at the facility. Eventually, the information he relays is passed on to England, and then to his family in Canada.

After being interrogated at St. Gilles, Teddy is transferred to Hamburg, where he is held as a Belgian national and forced to work in the shipyards. While labouring at the shipyards, he manages to escape his captors and makes his way back to Belgium to rejoin the underground. However, on August 11, 1944, the Gestapo catches Teddy again. This time around, the Germans discover that he is a member of the RCAF, and while he should be sent to a POW camp like most prisoners belonging to the Allied forces, he is sent instead to Neuengamme Concentration Camp, near Hamburg.

Life in the concentration camp is beyond difficult. Teddy and his fellow inmates suffer through starvation, hard labour, physical abuse, unsanitary conditions, and insufficient medical care. In November of 1944, Teddy becomes very ill. The lack of food, water, and medical attention accelerate the decline of his health. Between Christmas and New Years, it is discovered that Teddy has developed tuberculosis. He dies shortly after the diagnosis.

There is an unofficial story that Teddy Blenkinsop succumbed to heart failure after receiving a fatal injection at Neuengamme, but this story has never been substantiated. It is assumed that his body was cremated at the concentration camp on January 5, 1945, with a number of other bodies. But again, this assumption cannot be confirmed with certainty. What is known for sure, however, is that Squadron Leader Edward Weyman Blenkinsop, Canadian with the RCAF, died a hero.

Chapter 8
She's Going Down

D-Day. The very whisper of it brings a tremble of excitement and a measure of fear. Everyone has heard the rumour, and everyone knows it's coming. It's also common knowledge that on the day of assault, No. 224 Squadron will be an active element in keeping the threat of German U-boats, now skulking in the Bay of Biscay, away from the masses of invading forces.

On June 2, 1944, the aircrews of St. Eval airfield cram into the aerodrome, not far from the Cornish coast. About 4000 servicemen and servicewomen are gathered together to hear the specifics on the invasion of the European continent. Air Vice-Marshal Sir Brian Baker steps up to the microphone and begins to brief the anxious crowd. "As everybody in the south of England must now be aware, a most daring and highly organized movement of troops and equipment, which has taken months to prepare and perfect, is very shortly to take place in the shape of an invasion of the Continent of Europe. This enterprise must not fail — whatever the cost …Many lives and vast quantities of equipment will depend upon your efforts, not only during the passage of the ships in the initial assault, but during the period of build-up of the bridgehead afterwards." The Air Vice-Marshal ends his speech with "Good luck and good hunting."

Of course, for many of the Allied aircrews, the efforts and assaults have already begun. Earlier in the morning of June 2, an aircraft from No. 407 Squadron sank a U-boat as it turned the corner at Ushant. Now, every crew at the airbase will be closely watching the orders being posted in anticipation for their turn to fly.

Among those who wait is Flying Officer Kenneth Owen Moore, a Canadian with No. 224 Squadron. He is 22 years old, and the pilot of a Liberator bomber set to fly defence operations in preparation for D-Day. As the Allied fleet moves in to invade the European continent, Ken, his crew, and many other Liberators will comb the waters, attacking enemy vessels in an effort to keep them away from the invading fleet.

Ken's crew is made up of ten men, seven of whom are Canadian. In the time they have worked together, the crewmembers have become very close. Ignoring rank and protocol, they eat together, bunk together, and drink together.

Ken insists on it, and for whatever reason, the powers that be let him have his way. The crew is a tight unit, and Ken considers his men to be the finest there are.

On June 7, 1944, Ken's Liberator crew are flying "G" for *George* on their first English Channel patrol. Their mission is to guard the channel all night to ensure no U-boats make it into the strait.

As their Liberator climbs into the air, the crew looks back over England, which is eerily silhouetted against the night sky. The moon is high, bathing the Atlantic in leaden light. While the bomber continues on its path, the men keep their eyes to the ocean, searching for signs of enemy patrols. Ken doesn't even think to check on his crew or to verify who is at which station. He knows that everyone is where they are supposed to be. The men operate like a well-oiled machine — so much so that when Ken gets an itch on his arm, he half expects his second pilot to reach over and scratch it.

Everything is quiet at the beginning of the patrol. As the Liberator approaches France, the crew spots a few fishing vessels lying off the enemy-held coast, but overall, things seem peaceful. Ken does a fly-by, banks, and begins a second pass. During the second pass, at approximately 2:15 a.m. on June 8, the aircrew makes visual contact with a U-boat, later identified as U 629.

The German submarine is clearly visible in the moonlight. Fully surfaced, it is travelling through the English Channel like a racehorse out of the gate. From the Liberator,

The crew of the Liberator. Ken Moore is kneeling second from right, holding the crew's mascot, Dinty. Al Gibb is kneeling, far left.

Ken's crew can see the unmistakable black outline of the submarine's conning tower. Inside the tower, seven Nazi sailors are manning the guns and waiting for the kite to get into range. The crew jumps into action.

The radar operator, reading the blip on the screen, starts relaying information within seconds of the sighting. Ken does the calculations quickly in his head, as there is no time for more accurate measurements. The second pilot looks after the engines and sets up the automatic camera to record the attack. The navigator sets up his bombing panel, checks the six depth charges, and sees that the bombing doors are opened. The wireless operator flashes signals and coordinates back to the base so that they know a target has been sighted. The engineer is in position in the open bomb bay to watch the effects of the depth charges, and the gunners start firing on the U-boat from a couple kilometres off starboard. The crew works quickly, as they know they only have about 30 seconds if the U-boat suddenly decides to submerge.

The Liberator flies in and attacks. Crewmember Al Gibb opens up with the nose guns, scoring numerous hits on the conning tower and deck. Gibb also shoots two of the Nazis gunners and they fall into the sea. The U-boat returns fire immediately, and intense flak is coming at the kite. Ken flies as evasively as he can without compromising their own chance of a hit.

The Liberator's crew then spots a few of the U-boat crew running along the deck of the submarine. As one of the kite's guns open up, Ken sees a German sailor grab his stomach and fall into the water. The Liberator swoops in closer to the U-boat, and as it flies over the conning tower, all four engines vibrating, the bomb aimer drops six depth charges down the stick. It's a perfect straddle — three on either side of the German vessel. The U-boat is blown out of the water with such great force that one of Ken's gunners reports seeing the submarine's bottom rise right out of the sea. Astonished by the sight, the gunner cries, "Oh, God, we've blown her clean out of the water!"

Ken flies closer to make another run in, and sees the heaving waters, the huge amounts of debris, and distinct patches of black oil forming on the green of the ocean. In the oil patches are darker spots, which he presumes are bodies. Before the crew continues on their way, the wireless operator sends a "Definite Kill" message back to the base, giving details and locations.

"Lets get another one," Ken says half joking.

Just east of the Liberator's first conquest, another U-boat has opened fire on a French fishing fleet. The fleet, consisting of about 20 vessels, cuts their nets and quickly leaves the area. Soon after, the Liberator's bomb aimer spots the second U-boat, number U 373, travelling across the English Channel ahead of them. He shouts out a warning over the intercom, and Ken makes a weave to port, putting the U-boat on their starboard side. The crew prepares for yet another attack.

The second battle is training-perfect, and almost a duplicate of the first. Lit by the moon, the U-boat is fully surfaced and boldly slicing its way through the channel. The Liberator crew opens fire from the nose turret about two kilometres out, and Ken flies in for the kill. Unlike the previous U-boat, however, this one is already gunning for the heavy. The Germans are shooting a perfect fan of tracer from the conning tower, and Ken has no choice but to fly through it and hope for the best.

As Ken does the fly-in, the depth charges straddle a line about 10 feet behind the tower, four on one side, and two on the other. The hit is perfect, and it slices the vessel from starboard to port. The Liberator banks to starboard for a fly-by, and the aircrew sees that heavy oil is trailing the U-boat, and its stern is dipping down into the sea.

For a moment, the aircrew is disappointed, as it looks like their attack didn't result in a kill, merely a disabling. Ken is about to tell the wireless operator to make the call for someone else in the area to come in to finish the job, as they have used the last of their charges. But just as he opens his mouth to give the order, the mid-upper gunner starts yelling.

"She's going down! It's just like a Hollywood picture!"

Sure enough, when Ken looks out again, he sees that the U-boat is sliding slowly — nose first — into the sea. Someone in the crew remembers to turn on the Liberator's Leigh Light, and the sudden illumination reveals three yellow dinghies filled with Germans floating among the debris and oil slick. And while the Germans don't look too happy, the men on the Liberator are quite pleased. Ken Moore and his crew have had a successful night — the two U-boat sinkings were completed in 22 minutes.

Between June 7 and June 29 of 1944, at least 12 U-boats were destroyed in the same spot that the U 373 met her fate at the hands of Ken Moore and his Liberator crew. By the end of World War II, approximately 781 German U-boats had been destroyed, and more than 30,000 enemy seamen were killed on those vessels.

Chapter 9
Prisoner of War

O n July 16, 1944, the prisoners in compound K Lager of POW camp Stalagluft VI are informed that they will be moving. The camp, which is located near the Lithuanian border, is a potential target for the advancing Russians, and as a precaution, the inmates are to be transferred further inland to Stalagluft IV, at Grosstychowo, in Pomerania (a region that now straddles northeast Germany and western Poland). The prisoners are told to leave all their personal belongings behind and to pack only their kits. They will be leaving at 6 p.m. sharp.

Robert "Bob" L. Masters is one of the 650 prisoners who will be making the journey to the new camp. Born in Nelson,

British Columbia, in 1922, Bob has been a POW for two long years. He was serving as an air gunner with No. 51 Squadron when he was shot down over Germany in 1942, captured, and brought to Stalagluft VI. And though life has been interminably hard since then, he has been able to find comfort in simple luxuries.

Over the last two years Bob has accumulated a small but important store of possessions from the Red Cross parcels issued to the prisoners. Among these luxuries are a hairbrush, a toothbrush, and a Bible. Like many of his fellow prisoners, Bob is upset when he is ordered to leave his treasured possessions behind. As he and many of his inmates try to think of ways to smuggle their belongings to the new camp, they quickly realize there is another object they must somehow bring with them: the camp radio. The radio is carefully disassembled and the parts are hidden in pockets, shoes, and even body cavities.

A few hours before the prisoners are to set out, the POW camp is in chaos. Only months before, there had been an escape at the camp, and the Germans now have no idea how many men are actually interned there. Wanting an accurate count before moving the POWs, assemblies are called.

Bob is among the many prisoners who organize to confuse and frustrate their captors. They play the shell game with the guards; every time a section of men is tallied, a few sneak to the back of the compound to be counted again. By the time the count is finished, there are more men officially at the camp than were ever brought through the gates. A small victory, perhaps, but if the Germans don't know how many prisoners there are, they may not notice if a few escape during the trip.

Bob Masters is in the first column moving out. The initial leg of the journey is relatively short, and the prisoners soon arrive at a train station, where old livestock boxcars are waiting for them. Bob is nudged into a car with about 40 other prisoners, and the doors are slid shut, bolted, and locked from the outside. There are no windows in the boxcars, no ventilation of any kind, and the men barely have enough room to sit down.

The train arrives in Memel, Lithuania, at 10 p.m. Bob marches with the rest of the men to a nearby wharf, where the SS *Insterburg*, a 1500-tonne coastal freighter, stands ready. The boat's tween-decks have been removed, and the 650 POWs are instructed to leave their meagre belongings on deck and crawl below through the manholes. The floor of the freighter becomes a sea of bodies; each man is allotted just enough room to sit with his knees under his chin. For three days, the prisoners are kept below like this. Only one man at a time is permitted on deck to relieve himself, but the majority of the men do not bother to leave the hold.

Once a day, a black kettle of lukewarm cabbage soup is lowered through the hatches, but no one has cups, spoons, or bowls, and only a few prisoners can actually get to the soup. The only comfort the prisoners are afforded is the ventilation through the hatches above, which are mercifully left open for most of the voyage.

On the third day, the ship docks at Swinemünde naval base, located on the Oder River estuary. None of the POWs are given the time to find their own kits on deck, but are instructed instead to take the first one they come to and move along. This sparks rumours that the Nazis are planning to execute all the prisoners. Foremost on everyone's mind are the 50 men murdered by the Gestapo after the Great Escape a few months earlier.

The prisoners are organized and marched off the ship, then ushered back into boxcars. The sun is unbearably hot, and the unventilated cars stifling. Bob, like many of the prisoners, hasn't received water since he first left the camp. The heat in the boxcars is unbearable, and Bob soon feels faint.

Shortly after everyone is packed in and locked down, the air sirens sound as a port cruiser starts firing off rounds. A smoke screen is laid over the port, and the train stays in the smoke and oppressive heat until the all clear is given. Some of the prisoners pass out. Fortunately, they arrive in Kiefueide, Pomerania, a few hours after the train pulls out.

At the rail yards, the men are paired and handcuffed together for the march to their new camp. The column is led by teenaged Kriegsmarine sailors, who are enthusiastic Nazis, and impatient. The other guards on the journey are Volksturm World War I veterans, who are much more tolerant than their younger counterparts.

Prisoner of War

The column is ordered to march out in double time. The men at the back of the column take time before they can comply. Once underway, there are occasional pile-ups as the prisoners at the front of the line tire and those at the back catch up.

Bob is one of the few prisoners to be marching without handcuffs. One of the older men is in bad shape after the train ride, and Bob and another prisoner are allowed to keep their hands free in order to help support this man during the march. As the prisoners struggle on in double time, starving, parched, and exhausted, they suffer the added challenge of marching on a road made of uneven cobblestones.

The guards have dogs with them, as well as hand-held bayonets and rifles. The younger sailors brandish the weapons with obvious enjoyment. The dogs attack unchecked, and rifle butts are used to hit prisoners across the head if the guards feel the men aren't travelling fast enough. The bayonets are wielded with relish, wounding many prisoners. The Germans are merciless, but the column must keep moving.

After about a kilometre of marching, the prisoners turn on to a dirt road that seems to be going deeper into the bush, leading nowhere. The murmuring among the men in the column increases, and Bob tries to calm the fear that is mounting inside him. Whispers of execution and a mass grave are circulating. Prisoners begin looking to the left and right of the road, straining to see if they can spot any open trenches dug out in the fields beyond. Bob continues to support his fellow prisoner as they march, but he wonders if he is helping the older man to survive only to lead him to his grave.

When Stalagluft IV finally comes into sight and the prisoners see the barbed wire fence, the postern boxes, and the bleak compound buildings, the faces of even the weariest of the men break out into smiles of relief. The journey is over, and there will be no executions.

Water is finally issued in a limited quantity, and every POW lies down where they are, succumbing to their exhaustion. The trip lasted for three brutal days, and ended in a three-kilometre run. The 650 POWs are now interned in a safer camp, where their kits can be returned to their rightful owners, and their illegal radio can be secretly reassembled. Bob Masters is happy to have done his part to help his fellow inmates. He and most of the others will remain in this camp until it is liberated in 1945.

Chapter 10
Capture and Escape

There is a hot wind blowing as Flying Officer Raymond John Frederick Sherk climbs into his Spitfire and prepares for takeoff. Hailing from Hamilton, Ontario, Ray enlisted with the RCAF on September 16, 1940 and once overseas, joined the air offensive on the African continent. He is stationed with No. 601 Squadron, and on this night, he and two other fighters have orders to conduct a seek out and destroy mission on an ammunition train in the vicinity of Charing Cross, near Mersa Matruh, Egypt.

The three Mk IX Spitfires go through their engine checks, running up the Merlin 70 engines and testing the pressure and drops, the flaps, and the rudders. Of all the fighters to date, this Spitfire is the quickest and most responsive, judged to be at least on a par with its German counterpart, the Fw 190. With a well-trained pilot at the stick, the Spitfire Mk IX is a formidable foe.

Taking to the skies, the buzzing of the three fighters sounds more like a chorus of oversized mosquitoes than a group of deadly aircraft. They head for their target in formation; the squadron leader is in the lead, with one Spitfire off the right wing and the other off the left. Each pilot is keenly aware of the airspace around him.

Flying relatively close to the ground to avoid radar detection, the men comb the railway tracks looking for their target. Keeping an eye on their steadily declining gas gauges, the three are forced to turn back before sighting the ammunition train. Out of the blue, two Junkers 52 dive in towards the Spitfires from above, guns blazing. The three planes split up, outflank, and shoot down one Junkers while the other banks and runs.

Heading for home, Ray switches his fuel supply from the long-range petrol tank to the main one. Suddenly there is an air lock, and the engine sputters. Flying only 200 feet above the ground, Ray doesn't have enough time to recover the engine, and is forced to land on enemy soil. Keeping his nose up, he glides as best he can and uses the rudders to control the landing. The Spitfire comes to a stop, but only after sustaining damage to the fuel line. Ray realizes his only way home will be as a guest on another aircraft, or on his own two feet. He is over 60 kilometres from Allied lines.

Capture and Escape

After reporting his location and situation to his flight leader on the wireless, Ray is ordered to leave the Spitfire and make his way to the Allied lines on foot.

Stripping off his excess gear, Ray takes only what he needs: his escape kit (with compass, knife, and maps) and his emergency rations. He starts walking due east. About two hours into the hike, two Spitfires fly overhead but don't see him. He walks through the night, stopping at a secluded spot just before sunrise to eat, drink, and sleep until darkness falls again.

When evening approaches, Ray leaves his refuge and starts off again. As he draws close to the Allied lines, he is caught unawares by an Italian patrol and captured. He is searched at gunpoint, and everything except his clothing is confiscated. He is then taken by jeep to a nearby camp, and escorted to the officer in charge.

Ray remains calm and stares blankly at the Italian officer. The officer smokes a cigarette and stares blankly back. He is holding Ray's personal belongings, and he decides to return the prisoner's pack of cigarettes before the interrogation begins. Ray smiles, knowing his compass is still hidden in the cigarette package, then gives the officer his name, rank, and service number — nothing more. The two men smoke and laugh, and the next day Ray is moved out by field ambulance to the Italian Army's headquarters.

Ray has walked over 64 kilometres in 24 hours and is exhausted by the time he reaches enemy headquarters.

Despite his exhaustion, he watches closely for any means of escape. He is certain that if he escapes, he could find his way back to Allied lines with the use of his compass. All he needs is the right opportunity to make his getaway.

Ray quickly discovers that the intelligence officer at the Italian headquarters speaks fluent English and is not as easy-going as the previous interrogator. This one doesn't laugh and smoke, and he won't put up with Ray's refusal to divulge any further information. He barks questions at Ray and grows impatient when they are not answered. The officer then tries a number of approaches, asking the same questions in different ways in order to trick the answers out of his prisoner. Alert to these tactics, Ray still manages to stand his ground.

Unhappy with the results of the meeting, the officer orders that Ray be issued a German flying suit instead of an English one, and sends him to sleep on the sand with the guards. That night, Ray slips away while the guards slumber. He manages to cover about 90 metres before the guards discover he's missing. Ray briefly considers making a run for it, but realizing that he may be shot down if he tries, he chooses instead to pretend he was merely relieving himself, and returns to the camp.

The next morning, Ray is taken by truck to El Daba. Arriving at 5:30 p.m., he and a guard are given instructions to hitchhike further on. But when they have no success flagging down a ride, Ray is jailed in El Daba and turned over to the Germans. He is then brought to a tent for more interrogation.

Capture and Escape

At first, Ray is relieved when he sees a Red Cross official enter the interrogation room. The official is a pleasant man by the name of Corporal Barnes. He explains to Ray that the German authorities require him to fill out many forms, and asks for Ray's patience and cooperation. The fighter pilot simply smiles. The official then presents Ray with a pen and a bogus form on which there are approximately 30 questions. Ray fills out his name, rank, and number, and then hands the form back to the German. The official stares at the near empty form and suddenly flies into a rage. Yelling and cursing, he produces examples of forms that have allegedly been completed and signed by other prisoners of war.

Ray looks at these forms calmly, but none of the signatures seem familiar to him. Of course, even if he had recognized a name or two, it wouldn't have changed his mind. He knows that he cannot fill in the forms. No matter what they do, he will resist helping the enemy. Ray asks if he can smoke, extracts a cigarette from the package with the compass in it, and smiles to himself.

Annoyed at Ray's refusal to cooperate, the German interrogator orders him stripped and searched, but again, the compass in his package of cigarettes is overlooked. When the strip search is complete, Ray is escorted to another tent, where all of his clothes are taken. He spends a cold and lonely few days in the tent, naked and waiting.

It is October 3, 1942, when the German official realizes the flying suit Ray had been wearing earlier is a German one.

Ray is then accused of being a spy, and is interrogated further. Once again, he refuses to give any answers beyond his name, rank, and service number. And once again, the interrogator flies into a rage. As the German fumes, Ray calculates the level of threat and decides that in order to avoid being harmed, he needs to volunteer some answers. He lies to the interrogator, stating that he belonged to No. 74 Squadron, and that his Spitfire had been shot down on September 26. Somewhat mollified by the misinformation, the interrogator orders that Ray be dressed and moved to share a tent with another prisoner.

The other prisoner in Ray's new tent is a South African who claims to be a lieutenant and air observer from a Halifax bomber. It doesn't take long for Ray to realize the man was assigned to the tent to pump him for information. Ray and the South African are moved to Mersa Matruh the next day. The informant tells Ray that he is going to be flown to Italy in a Ju52 for cooperating with interrogators, and then he advises Ray to cooperate as well. When Ray ignores this advice, the South African gets annoyed and tells him he is a fool for keeping his mouth shut, as the remainder of his captivity will not be pleasant. Shortly after this, Ray is handed back to the Italians.

Ray is assigned to a tent that is already occupied by another prisoner of war. This prisoner identifies himself as a pilot from Southend-on-Sea, England. He is rough around the edges, and his knee is bandaged from an apparent wound. As the men chat, the prisoner tells Ray that he'd been shot down in a Wellington, and had walked for nine days before being captured. Ray relaxes when the stranger is able to give him the name of his wing commander. Convinced this pilot is both English and a prisoner, Ray reveals to him that he is from No. 601 Squadron and had been picked up the day after he ditched his plane. Ray also shows the English prisoner the compass in the package of cigarettes.

Later that day, he is turned over to a German guard and the two hitchhike to Fuka, en route to El Daba. On the way there, the guard demands Ray's cigarette package and removes the compass. The German then cocks his revolver, and Ray knows he needs to be very careful.

On October 6, 1942, Ray is taken to a compound in Mersa, where he shares sleeping quarters with two British prisoners. Ray is not sure why he is moved around so much, or why he keeps getting tossed back and forth between the Italians and the Germans. But, wanting very much to stay alive, he complies with his captors.

The next day, 20 other prisoners join Ray and the British POWs, and the whole group is transported to Derna, on the Libyan coast. Among the other prisoners being transferred with Ray are two RAF officers: a flying officer by the name of McLarty, and a pilot by the name of Trevor-Harvie. Comparing notes, the three comrades discover that the pilot claiming to be from Southend-on-Sea had actually been a plant. That was how the guard had known to remove Larry's compass from the pack of cigarettes.

After leaving Derna, the prisoners spend the night at Lecee, and the next day they are put on a train for Bari, Italy. Once in Bari, Ray is quarantined for three weeks before being permitted into the POW compound. Much to his annoyance, he is never given a reason for this quarantine.

When Ray is finally let into the compound, he is greeted by horrific conditions. Medical supplies, or supplies of any kind, are almost non-existent, and the prisoners are suffering terribly. There are no parcels from the Red Cross, and many of the men are dying of starvation. Most of the prisoners are forced to catch and eat rats if they want to survive.

Christmas comes and goes, and the future seems bleak. Men are dying, and everyone is struggling to survive a day at a time. In February of 1943, things start to marginally improve. Ray is finally given some new clothes: a shirt and shorts. Red Cross parcels begin to arrive, and they are filled with food, tea, coffee, cigarettes, and other items of comfort. Almost overnight, the morale at the camp greatly improves.

On March 3, 1943, Ray is moved to the Sulmona POW camp where conditions are much better. He soon joins the escape committee. Ray copies maps and fashions clothing from blankets for the prisoners who plan to escape. He even takes part in digging a tunnel. During Ray's time in Sulmona, two officers manage to escape, but are later captured and returned.

On July 15, 1943, Ray is one of 160 POWs to be moved to a camp in Rimini, on the east coast of Italy. RAF officer McLarty is also among the men going to Rimini, and Ray and McLarty decide to stick together. While they are at the new camp, elaborate plans for an escape are put into action. On September 10, there is a prisoner revolt and a senior British officer takes over the camp. However, when news arrives that German troops will be arriving soon to regain control of the camp, the prisoners gather what they need and make for the hills. The chase is on. The Germans use dogs to comb the area surrounding the camp, and within two days, many of the escaped POWs have been recaptured. Ray and McLarty are not among them.

The two comrades have food and water, and they decide to lay low in the woods for a few days, until the search for the POWs dies down. But their plan fails. Unfortunately, both men are recaptured as soon as they leave the woods. Ray and McLarty, along with three other prisoners are forced by their German captors to begin the march back to the camp. It is a warm day, and in the heat of the afternoon the whole party takes a break. Ray and McLarty ask for permission to sit a fair distance away in the shade of a nearby rock. They are granted permission, and the two men go about making their second escape.

McLarty props a hat up on the rock so that the Germans will think they are still there. Then, wasting no time, Ray and McLarty roll down a steep hill and hide in the trees. When the guards realize what has happened, they begin an ardent and fruitless search for the prisoners, and unknowingly walk right past the pair's hiding spot in the underbrush.

This time, Ray and McLarty are more careful when leaving their hiding place. As they begin to make their way south towards Allied lines, they come across four Arab escapees and a Palestinian. Following the advice of these strangers, the two men head for a cave located near a mountain village. For a while, they live in this cave, and local villagers bring them clothes, cigarettes, food, and water.

Soon, there are over 30 escapees living near the village. On October 6, 1943, the Germans surround and raid the village. Ray and four other POWs evade capture, and a shepherd guides them up a mountain track. As they are travelling, they meet another group of escapees at Campogivde who are waiting to be guided through the lines. Ray and McLarty wait with the group for a few days, but on October 17, upon hearing rumours that the Germans are advancing, they make a dash for the nearby woods. Both men escape just before the Germans surround Campogivde and gun the whole area down. The Germans then start to comb the woods, shooting almost everyone they find.

The remaining fugitives split up into groups of four to make better time and to evade capture by the Germans. Six days later, Ray and McLarty arrive at Cupello, more than 200 kilometres south of Rimini as the crow flies. On October 25, they are guided safely through the lines to Lucera. On November 13, 1943, Ray is returned to London, ready to continue with his duties.

By the end of World War II, Flying Officer Raymond

Capture and Escape

Frederick Sherk was referred to as "Houdis," a reference to Houdini, which means that he had succeeded in escaping the enemy after crash landing on two separate occasions.

Chapter 11
A Heroine for the Allied Forces

S ergeant Joseph Arthur Angers is an air gunner with the Moose Squadron (No. 419) flying out of Mildenhall airbase, England. On June 17, 1942, he and his fellow crewmembers are returning from a bombing raid on Essen, Germany, when their Halifax is badly hit over Duisburg. As the bomber begins to burn and spiral, the crew is forced to jump.

Wounded from the crippling of the Halifax, Joseph fights to stay conscious as he pulls his ripcord at 15,000 feet. He slips in and out of consciousness during his descent, somehow managing to avoid being hit by the night fighters, heavy flak, flying shrapnel, and numerous explosions that seem to be all around him. Only partly aware of what is happening,

Joseph is jarred back to reality when his parachute catches in a tree. Through his pain he hears the sound of distant gunfire and knows that if he stays suspended in the tree he will be an easy target.

Summoning up a burst of energy, Joseph kicks away from the tree trunk and falls to the ground. It's an awkward landing, and pain shoots from his ankle all the way up his leg. Knowing that he must move fast in order to avoid being picked up by enemy patrols, Joseph ignores the pain and gathers up his chute. He grabs his escape kit and buries everything he doesn't need beneath a pile of underbrush. When he realizes that his ankle won't support his weight, he is forced to crawl away from the drop site.

Over the next few days, Joseph manages to make his way into occupied Holland by travelling only at night and staying away from the main roads. Exhausted and in desperate need of medical attention, he finds a Dutch peasant who is able to help him. The peasant manages to obtain medical aid for Joseph's injuries, and after a time of healing, takes him across the border to Turnhout, in Belgium, where he makes contact with the underground. The Resistance then smuggle him into France.

When Joseph arrives in France, the freedom fighters introduce him to his guide for the next leg of the journey, a woman known as the "Soul of the Belgian Underground." She is young, pretty, and brunette, and he is told that her name is Dedee. Weighing about 100 pounds, and standing just over 5 feet tall, the 22-year-old Dedee does not seem like a likely leader to Joseph. He is immediately concerned that his fate, and the fate of those who are escaping with him, should rest on the shoulders of this diminutive woman.

Two weeks later, Joseph is one of a group to leave Paris with Dedee. Following Dedee's usual daring routine, the small group travels coach class with German army officers. To divert attention away from her suspicious looking party, Dedee flirts with the officers and exchanges pleasantries on the train.

Once the group reaches St. Jean de Luz in southwest France, Dedee takes them to her "apartment." The party spends a few days in the flat, which is one floor above the home of the regional Gestapo agent. After gaining their forged passports and papers, they move on to Urrugne, to cross the Pyrenees into Spain.

Leaving for the Pyrenees at about midnight on a moonless night, Joseph's party meets another escape group at a rendezvous point. The navigator from Joseph's aircrew is in the other escape party. He and Joseph are both thrilled that the other is alive, and that they will be together for their trek over the mountains. Neither man, however, has had any word regarding the rest of their aircrew.

Carrying only emergency packs consisting of medical supplies, food, water, and their forged papers, the party sets out through the foothills of the Pyrenees. Unfortunately, smuggling has reached such proportions that the Germans have patrols everywhere in the mountains, and the officers are ordered to shoot first and ask questions later.

After hours of travelling by foot on uneven terrain, the tired and nervous party reaches their first peak. All of a sudden, two German soldiers ambush the group, firing rapidly in the air and yelling at the tops of their lungs to give the impression they're greater in number. As they run from the soldiers, Dedee, Joseph, and the navigator try to stay together through the thick underbrush, but become separated. The two Germans are in hot pursuit, and the navigator is caught. Joseph hesitates. He wants to help his friend, but quickly realizes there is nothing he can do. With a sick feeling in his stomach, he makes his way back to the rendezvous point with Dedee. It is a narrow escape, but Dedee, taking the situation in stride, is not willing to abort the route just yet.

What's left of the sombre party drifts back to the rendezvous point about 24 hours later. The group decides to wait a couple of days for things to die down before trying the escape route for a second time. Dedee feels that the Germans will probably relax a little, thinking that the escapees will be reluctant to try the route again now that they know the area is well guarded.

Travelling light once again, the party leaves a few nights later. This time, they manage to avoid the German patrols. The climb through the Pyrenees is long, and the men tire easily. Dedee, however, seems to have boundless energy, and she keeps the group moving at a steady pace.

After reaching the Spanish side of the Pyrenees, the group arrives at the Bidassoa River. The river is 46 metres wide and swollen from the frigid mountain streams that are feeding it. Its currents are treacherously swift. Before crossing the river, Dedee instructs the group to strip down, and to bundle their clothes and shoes together. Then, wading into the freezing water, joints aching with the cold, the group follows Dedee across in twos, holding their belongings above their heads.

Joseph's ankle, though healed, is still quite weak, and all the hiking over the rough terrain has taken its toll. Mid-river, his ankle collapses when he steps into a pothole on the river bed. Suddenly Joseph disappears, completely submerging. The icy water makes his head feel like it'll explode, and he shoots downstream with the current, gasping for breath and fighting to regain a foothold.

Another man dives after him, and the two struggle against the swift current for a moment, then find their footing and help each other to shore. Dedee now has a big problem on her hands: two wet and naked men, and no means to make a fire to get them warm. Joseph is shivering uncontrollably, and even though the water was freezing cold, his ankle is swollen and bruised.

Everyone is utterly exhausted, but they all pitch in to help, and the dry clothing is sorted and distributed to accommodate the two who lost their belongings in the river. Dedee permits a couple hours of rest before the group continues on.

Realizing that the break is for the men and not for her, Joseph is amazed at Dedee's resilience. He can't get over the fact that this small woman is putting her own life at risk to help a group of strangers, and that soon she will be returning to live with the very danger that the group is fleeing.

As they rest, Dedee tells Joseph about a man the Belgian Resistance refers to as "The Professor." At the beginning of the war, this man had been instrumental in fighting the enemy from within enemy territory. A university professor, he had risked his life for the cause until the Gestapo had finally tracked him down and executed him.

When Dedee finishes her story, the group sets out again, and soon they are out of the mountains completely. Their next contact point is San Sebastian, approximately 8 kilometres away. The group rests again while Dedee leaves to obtain an automobile for the remainder of their journey. Once the vehicle is secured, Dedee's job as guide is done. The group is safe. Saying a quick goodbye to her grateful charges, she returns alone on her 40th trip over the Pyrenees, through occupied land to Belgium, and back to her work in the Resistance.

When Dedee departs, Joseph feels a great personal loss and wonders if she will survive the war. As he watches her tiny figure retreat towards the mountains, he knows that he, like so many other RCAF airmen, owes her his life.

On January 22, 1943, Joseph Angers is reported safe to the Allied forces.

Two and a half years later, at the end of the war, Joseph contacts Major Count Temmerman, chief of the Belgian Underground, to find out more about his rescuers — specifically Dedee. He learns that her full name is Mademoiselle De Jongh, and is told a little about her work with the resistance. He also learns from the major that "The Professor" was Dedee's father.

After talking with Major Count Temmerman, Joseph receives Dedee's address. He writes to her, thanking her for her selflessness, for saving his life and the lives of the many others she led to safety. The pretty young woman had come into Joseph's life as a stranger, but she had left him as an angel of mercy.

"No award would have been too great for the magnificent young woman... For years, she fought against tremendous odds and expected nothing but bullets... She not only acted as guide for allied airmen from Paris across the Pyrenees to San Sebastian, but she … [also] organized false certificates of residence, false identification cards with photos and false passports. When a special seal was needed as a stamp of approval for a phoney document, she found a way to secure one."
Montreal Star, February 1946
(The words of Sergeant Joseph Angers, RCAF, in reaction to the news that Mlle De Jongh had been awarded the George Medal.)

Chapter 12
The Crew That Refused to Die

I t is November 1, 1944, and the Allied aircrews are preparing for a massive raid on Oberhausen, a heavily defended target in Germany. The very mention of Oberhausen makes even the most confident flyer sober with apprehension. Everyone's anxiety escalates upon learning that low cloud cover is obscuring the bombsite, making the operation extra tricky.

The aircrews are instructed that the bomber stream will be over the target between 17,000 and 21,000 feet. The planes will need to dive through the cloud cover in order to make visual contact with the marker flares and drop their load. Enemy fighter activity is expected to be intense, and ground defence is anticipated to include heavy anti-aircraft artillery as well as searchlights.

Among the many crews preparing for the mission to Oberhausen are a nearly all-Canadian group from No. 219 Squadron. The Canadian members of the crew include: Flying Officer Ronald L. Cox, pilot; Flying Officer Lyle W. Sitlington, wireless operator; Flying Officer Samuel Blair, navigator; and Flight Sergeant Raymond Austin Toane, rear gunner. Their kite for the operation is a Lancaster X KB-767, coded VR-U.

The flight to Oberhausen is long and cold. Ray, at the rear guns, feels the chill worse than the others. Stuck alone over the tail of the kite, his operation seems to be a solo act; often, his survival rests on one to one combat with the enemy fighters. As the Lancaster continues on its course, Ray checks his guns, then takes an outer glove off one hand and puts the hand under his arm to warm it. When that hand is warm enough, he does the same with the other.

"Damn cold up here," he mutters to no one in particular.

"We're nearing the target, it'll get hot soon enough," Pilot Ron Cox answers. There is nervous laughter from the rest of the crew.

Judging by the navigator's estimates, Ron starts the dive for the target drop. Thick cloud surrounds the kite, and for a few moments, they are flying blind. As there is no radio contact permitted, the crew can only hope another bomber doesn't fly into them. When the Lancaster levels out slightly, the target flares come into sight. There is smoke and flak everywhere; the sky is buzzing with activity, kites are being shot down all around them, and the Allied Spitfires are engaging enemy fighters.

Ron banks slightly to adjust his position and dives for the final approach. "Bombs gone," the bomb aimer notifies the crew. Ron levels the kite for a second or two so that the photos can be taken, then banks and pulls up, heading for home.

Soon after leaving the target area, the Lancaster is hit by a hail of bullets from an enemy Fw 190. Ray doesn't even see the fighter coming, but his guns jump to life, sending a string of deadly pearls in the direction of the attack. Breathing heavily, he quickly realizes the rear turret is hit. Panic swells up inside him. He wipes the sweat from his eyes, then looks at his fingers and sees that the warm, wet substance he is wiping isn't sweat at all; it's blood. Suddenly the pain hits him — his leg is burning, his face is stinging, his arms are stabbing. He swallows and tries to clear his mind.

"I'm hit," he yells into the intercom. By the response over the intercom he realizes his section isn't the only one hit. Keeping his eyes on the bubble for the return of the Fw 190, Ray wraps a belt around his leg to help slow the loss of blood from a gaping wound. Right now he needs to stay awake. With the loss of the kite's inner engines, the hydraulics will go, if they haven't all ready. He's surprised the crew still has the intercom. Knowing that any second, the enemy fighter will come back for the kill, he gets ready to shoot down the enemy.

While Ray is preparing for a showdown from his isolated station over the tail, the rest of the crew is also struggling.

Though the kite and a number of the crewmembers are badly wounded, no bail out order is given.

"Damage?" Ron demands.

"Fuselage and tail hit," a bodiless voice responds.

The navigator, Sam, is severely injured. Shrapnel has embedded itself in his back, and most of his equipment has been shot out. Suddenly, flames spring up out of nowhere. Without a thought to his pain, Sam grabs a nearby extinguisher and douses the fire. Although his back is throbbing, he knows he is needed to plot the next course, and he returns to his post. Wiping his own blood off the console, Sam starts calculating their next flight path.

As the men struggle to regain control, the kite dives and goes into another death spiral. Ron yells into the intercom for the engineer, and for a few seconds it looks as though they are done for.

But they aren't through yet. Ron manages to pull up and out of the spiral, levelling the heavy on three engines at about 1500 feet. As he continues to fight for control, the Lancaster jumps in the air as German anti-aircraft artillery finds its mark. More shrapnel shoots through the kite.

"I'm hit!" a chorus of voices call out, just before the intercom stops transmitting.

"Fire in the starboard wing!" Sam yells loudly to anyone who can hear him above the drone of the two remaining engines and the rattle and bang of the kite. He beats at the fire with his flight jacket, his boots, and his hands. The wound on his back is still causing him excruciating pain, and he is now bleeding from severe face lacerations. As he fights the fire, his jacket ignites and his hands are horribly burned. Once he has managed to put out the flames, he passes out from shock and pain.

The rest of the aircrew continue to struggle in their deteriorating kite. The Lancaster's starboard wing is hit, the inner engines are on fire, both tires are blown out, and all hydraulic systems are rendered unserviceable. After being revived by his other crewmembers Sam bravely returns to his post, plotting a course of return to the nearest airfield for the crippled bomber.

Lyle, the wireless operator, has serious wounds on his face and arm, but he is relieved to see that the kite's radio is still functional. In the rear turret, Ray is bandaging his leg to stop the bleeding. He also is also wounded in the face, and both arms are bleeding, but he remains at his post and continues to man the guns.

Again, the Lancaster lurches forward and dives into a spiral. Ron wrestles with the stick and controls. Seconds tick as the ground rises to meet the dying heavy. Then suddenly, the nose pulls up and they level once more. Ron barely has time to breath a sigh of relief when a hail of bullets fly past the cockpit — the Fw 190 has not finished with them yet.

Ray in the turret has no hydraulics to operate the swivels but fires anyway, as does the mid-upper gunner. The Fw 190 flies right into the hail of bullets. Hit but still flying, it heads for home. But while the crew is happy to see the enemy retreat, the fighter's second volley of bullets has set a fire in the bomber's rear compartment. As Lyle beats out the fire, Ron is able to level out and decides to head for Belgium. Sam, one step ahead, passes the course specs up to the pilot, and then painfully returns to what remains of his post.

When they are almost to Belgium, the kite's inner port engine re-fires, and Ron decides to try for the English coast. Sam, almost blinded by the blood from the wounds on his face, plots the course for the nearest British airbase. All the men remain in their positions.

As the battered Lancaster closes in on Manston airfield, Lyle reports their location and situation over the wireless. The crew is directed to a "safe" crash landing site, where attendants are standing by. The dying Lancaster approaches the site with two full engines and one feathering, no landing gear, and a severely wounded crew.

Ron pulls up the nose, keeps as level as possible, and slides the kite in with minimum fuss. There is a pause as the dying Lancaster settles on the tarmac, and then rescue crews rush in with fire trucks to extinguish the one engine still in flames. The wounded crewmembers struggle to abandon the aircraft, and are quickly attended to by ground and medical personnel. The men are in shock, not only from their wounds, but also from the fact that they actually made it home.

The aircrew that refused to die are taken away from the landing site on stretchers. After their wounds are treated at the nearby medical hut, the men are transported to the hospital. In time, all four Canadian heroes recover and are awarded medals for their bravery.

Bibliography

Aircrew Memories: A Collection of War Memories, the collected WWII and later memories of the members of the Aircrew Association, Vancouver Island Branch, Victoria, BC

Bolitho, Hector. *Command Performance.* Howell, Soskin, Publishers, 1946

Dumore, Spencer. *Wings for Victory.* McClelland & Stewart Inc., 1994

English, Allan, D. *The Cream of the Crop.* McGill-Queen's University Press, 1996

Lotz, Jim. *A Century of Service.* The Nova Scotia International Tattoo Society, 2000

McCaffery, Dan. *Canada's Warplanes.* James Lorimer & Company Ltd., Publishers, 2000

Mosley, Leonard. *The Battle of Britain.* Time-Life Books Inc., 1981

Bibliography

Russell, E.C. *Customs and Traditions of the Canadian Armed Forces.* Deneau Publishers & Company Ltd., 1981

Acknowledgments

During the many hours I have spent researching this book and others like it, I have come to realize that not only did the fallen war heroes give up their lives for their country, so did the survivors. Many of these survivors lost their childhood and innocence while overseas, and they will live with the horrors they have seen until they join those who fell before.

I have been humbled while writing this book, for while conducting interviews and research, I have walked with kings of honour and bravery, and I find myself very proud to be a Canadian.

I would especially like to thank Kenneth Owen Moore for the insightful interview, and for providing much of the background material in the form of books and photos. Also, the family of the late Lawrence George Cramer for history and service records, and photographs.

Acknowledgments are also due to the British Columbia Aviation Museum for the use of their resource library, and for the time spent answering questions and making suggestions on what stories to look for. Also, thank you for the loan of the World War II flyers uniform featured in the author's photograph, and for supplying some of the photographs reproduced in this book.

Acknowledgments

Finally, thanks to Ms. Sherry Johansen for her help with the grunt work, and for asking the best question of all: "What does this mean?"

Photograph: Blanshard Photography

About the Author

A mother of three, Cynthia J. Faryon is an internationally published author and freelance writer residing in Victoria, BC. Canadian born, she focuses her writing on Canadian content, covering topics such as travel, family issues, biography, and history.

Cynthia is currently working on her second book for the Amazing Stories series about a war bride who settled in Saskatchewan.

BY THE SAME AUTHOR

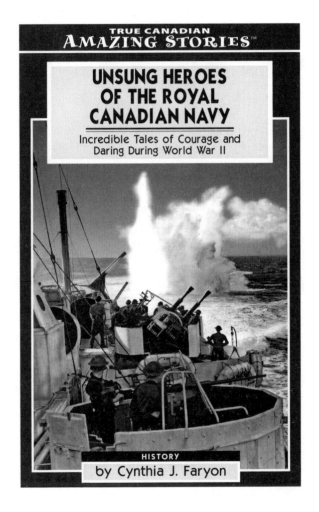

TRUE CANADIAN
AMAZING STORIES™

UNSUNG HEROES OF THE ROYAL CANADIAN NAVY

Incredible Tales of Courage and
Daring During World War II

HISTORY
by Cynthia J. Faryon

ISBN 1-55153-765-6

AMAZING STORIES™

A WAR BRIDE'S STORY

Risking it all for Love After World War II

ROMANCE/HISTORY
by Cynthia J. Faryon

ISBN 1-55153-959-4

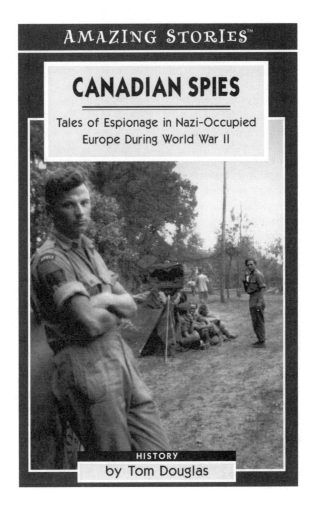

AMAZING STORIES™

CANADIAN SPIES

Tales of Espionage in Nazi-Occupied
Europe During World War II

HISTORY
by Tom Douglas

ISBN 1-55153-966-7

OTHER AMAZING STORIES

These titles are available wherever you buy books. If you have trouble finding the book you want, call the Altitude order desk at **1-800-957-6888**, e-mail your request to: **orderdesk@altitudepublishing.com** or visit our Web site at **www.amazingstories.ca**

New **AMAZING STORIES** titles are published every month.

Comments on other *Amazing Stories* from readers & reviewers

"Tightly written volumes filled with lots of wit and humour about famous and infamous Canadians."
Eric Shackleton, *The Globe and Mail*

"The heightened sense of drama and intrigue, combined with a good dose of human interest is what sets Amazing Stories *apart."*
Pamela Klaffke, *Calgary Herald*

"This is popular history as it should be... For this price, buy two and give one to a friend."
Terry Cook, a reader from Ottawa, on **Rebel Women**

"Glasner creates the moment of the explosion itself in graphic detail...she builds detail upon gruesome detail to create a convincingly authentic picture."
Peggy McKinnon, *The Sunday Herald*, on **The Halifax Explosion**

"It was wonderful...I found I could not put it down. I was sorry when it was completed."
Dorothy F. from Manitoba on **Marie-Anne Lagimodière**

"Stories are rich in description, and bristle with a clever, stylish realness."
Mark Weber, *Central Alberta Advisor*, on **Ghost Town Stories II**

"A compelling read. Bertin...has selected only the most intriguing tales, which she narrates with a wealth of detail."
Joyce Glasner, *New Brunswick Reader*, on **Strange Events**

"The resulting book is one readers will want to share with all the women in their lives."
Lynn Martel, *Rocky Mountain Outlook*, on **Women Explorers**

UNSUNG HEROES OF THE ROYAL CANADIAN NAVY

UNSUNG HEROES OF THE ROYAL CANADIAN NAVY

Incredible Tales of Courage and
Daring During World War II

HISTORY

by Cynthia J. Faryon

PUBLISHED BY ALTITUDE PUBLISHING CANADA LTD.
1500 Railway Avenue, Canmore, Alberta T1W 1P6
www.altitudepublishing.com
1-800-957-6888

Extreme care has been taken to ensure that all information presented in
this book is accurate and up to date. Neither the author nor the
publisher can be held responsible for any errors.

Publisher	Stephen Hutchings
Associate Publisher	Kara Turner
Series Editor	Jill Foran
Editor	Dianne Smyth
Digital Photo Colouring	Bryan Pezzi

We acknowledge the financial support of the Government
of Canada through the Book Publishing Industry Development
Program (BPIDP) for our publishing activities.

Altitude GreenTree Program
Altitude Publishing will plant twice as many trees as were used
in the manufacturing of this product.

National Library of Canada Cataloguing in Publication Data

Faryon, Cynthia J., 1956-
Unsung heroes of the Royal Canadian Navy / Cynthia Faryon.

(Amazing stories)
ISBN 1-55153-765-6

1. Canada. Royal Canadian Navy--History--World War, 1939-1945.
2. Canada. Royal Canadian Navy--Biography. 3. Sailors--Canada--Biography.
4. Heroes--Canada--Biography. I. Title. II. Series: Amazing stories
(Canmore, Alta.)

D779.C2F37 2005   940.54′5971   C2004-906265-4

Printed and bound in Canada by Friesens
2 4 6 8 9 7 5 3

To all the children and grandchildren
of veterans. This is part of your history.

And to Roger, who has stuck by me and supported
me in the writing and research of this book. Without
his belief in me, it would never have been completed.

Contents

Prologue

The great ship stands quietly in the morning sun, anxious to find the waves beneath her hull and thirsty for the company of the saltys who will man her. This great Tribal Class Destroyer was built for war. Adopting the tenacity and stubborn pride of the mateys who took two long years to give her life, she stands proudly in front of the men who will take her into battle.

The commissioning ceremony is a brief and simple affair, filled with naval tradition and quiet dignity. At the spoken command the new crew stands at ease in the shadow of the destroyer waiting patiently alongside the dock. All eyes are reverent during the prayer of dedication. The crew stands, heads bowed, arms crossed at the wrists, respectfully holding their caps. And, with a few words from the new captain, they remember their fallen comrades and swear to do this great ship justice in the world's fight for freedom. Downwind, the staccato sounds of shipbuilding remind them that their fight is far from over. For this crew and their ship, it is only the beginning. Not only will this destroyer be their weapon and their protector, it will be their home and their friend.

Clustered on the top of old barrels, piles of lumber, and the other vantage points along the dockside, the mateys (the men and women who built her) watch in solemn stillness as the finality of their labours settles on them. They are not officially part of this ceremony, but with pride and sadness they watch from a distance. Quietly, they say their goodbyes as the Canadian naval crew (the saltys), who had arrived just before the ceremony, lay claim to the mateys' creation.

This morning is the end of more than two years of emotional labour for the mateys. From thoughts to blueprints, from steel to ship, her building had been a grim yet proud chapter in their lives. Throughout the long months in which she had grown from an idea to a lethal weapon of war, they had been touched by the death and destruction that threatened the night skies. The mateys had seen the newsreels of the bombings in Europe, had witnessed the destruction, and had welcomed home their dead to their final resting places. They worked diligently day after day, knowing that many more Canadian boys would sacrifice their lives before this fight was finished. If they could have fought they would have, but we can't all go to war. Some are needed here at home. So, fuelled by familial stories of loss, the mateys' own incensed spirits entered the steel they forged as they built their ship, fighting back the only way they knew how.

From where they are gathered they can't hear the words with which the captain charges the crew. But when the hat is thrown into the air and the crew cheers, the mateys cheer, too, with shouts of "Godspeed!" "Make 'em pay!" "Bring her home safely!"

Then reluctantly, and more than a little sadly, the mateys leave their newborn in the hands of the Royal Canadian Navy (RCN). This new "lady" they have created from steel and iron is theirs no longer. She now belongs to the strong young hands of the navy crew who will take her from berth into the vast ocean beyond. They know that as long as there are memories of this great ship and stories shared of her exploits, she, like the lads on board, will never be forgotten. And all the battles, the deaths, the victories, will be remembered with awe and thankfulness for all who served and lived and fought to make this country free.

Chapter 1

The First Canadian Naval Shot of World War II

O n September 1, 1939, Adolf Hitler's army and air force cross into Poland. On September 3, Britain declares war on Germany. In a matter of days, most of the world has chosen sides.

After the initial German aggression, there is a pause before the fighting starts. Germany sits quietly waiting and Britain feeds her troops into mainland Europe. The trap is laid and Germany closes in on the Allies. All hell breaks loose with a fury of German fighting machines that leave the British troops breathless and collectively fighting for their lives. As they retreat to the coastline, with their backs against the English Channel, the massacre begins ... then suddenly slows. Like a panther waiting to pounce, the German army keeps the British on the beaches, letting the troops know, with an occasional strafing and a few shells flying overhead, that they can finish the men off at any time.

On a stretch of coast from Dunkirk to the southern port of St. Jean de Luz, two Polish divisions, along with a few French troops, are fighting desperately against the Germans. The situation is frantic and the Allies are being slaughtered like cattle, their young blood soaking the surf-smoothed stones along the beach. What the Brits swore would never happen is happening and thousands of troops are trapped without cover. Mercifully, the air support drops smoke, and the sea mist creeps over the beaches with eerie fingers of cold and damp, providing additional cover. The troops shiver and wait for the final blast that surely must be coming. The Germans, poised for the butchery of those still alive, are left waiting for the final order to finish the job they started.

A desperate cry for help goes out from Britain to Canada for ships to rescue the troops from the beaches of Dunkirk. The invasion of Great Britain is now a definite threat and the war looks all but lost.

And so the miracle that is known as Dunkirk is born. With a mission of mercy in everyone's heart, civilians — in whatever boats they have — brave the Atlantic from the English coast to the beaches of Dunkirk.

With an audacity, courage, and eagerness that humbles the rest of the world, civilians and military alike come to the aid of the troops. Once the boats make it across the Channel, bits and pieces of human tragedy gratefully hoist themselves on board and sail home in anything that will float. They leave behind their artillery, vehicles, ammunition, and many of their fallen. Even a rowboat, one cruelly buffeted by the Atlantic and crudely captained by a young teenager, is considered safer than the beaches and is viewed by the soldiers as godsent.

One of these brave rescuers is Robert "Bob" Timbrell of West Vancouver, British Columbia. British born, he joined the RCN at the outbreak of trouble. Appointed captain of the yacht HMS *Lanthony*, Timbrell makes six successful crossings before disaster hits. Then a German bomb hits the forecastle of the yacht, killing five of his crew members and cutting the fuel line. Limping to shore, the crew and army troops create a jetty out of trucks until the tide lifts the ship back into the water. The fuel line is repaired and Captain Timbrell arms the yacht with spare guns from some of the military vehicles left behind. His foresight serves him well. The boat is attacked by two E-Boats (German Ebling Ships) and he is able to fight them off. In all, Captain Timbrell is responsible for rescuing over 600 troops.

The HMCS *Restigouche* (fondly referred to as "Rustyguts" by her crew), the HMCS *Skeena*, and the HMCS *St. Laurent* ("Sally") are recalled from leave and ordered to ship out to England. A disgruntled lot of sailors begin to straggle back to their ships as dusk settles over the Halifax harbour. And the familiar pipe is heard: "Cable party muster on the forecastle!

... Special sea-duty men close up! ... Hands to stations for leaving harbour!"

The entire group of seamen groan, crawling back to their ships in whatever condition the orders find them, thinking it's simply more convoy duty. The ships make ready and slip their berths, setting a quick course for Plymouth.

Lieutenant Commander Nelson Lay in HMCS *Restigouche* is the senior commander of the group and leads the way across the Atlantic. Lieutenant Commander Henry "Harry" George De Wolf follows in the HMCS *St. Laurent*, and Lieutenant Commander Jimmy Hibbard brings up the rear in the HMCS *Skeena*. Commander Wallace Creery is captain of the HMCS *Fraser*, already in service overseas. They are all Canadian seamen and Canadian ships.

Nelson Lay, wanting to impress the British with Canadian seamanship, orders drills for the ships during the crossing. Lay slows the vessels from 16 knots, increases speed, pulls ahead, and then orders a reverse course. These exercises are conducted after dark, with all the ships blacked out and running on visuals only, because none of the ships have radar. The progress across the Atlantic is slow and the men complain to each other about how long the crossing is taking. After all, they now have a mission. Their troops are trapped and dying on a foreign beach and all of them want to come to the rescue, like the cavalry in an American western.

Harry De Wolf is also impatient. "You know," he grumbles to the bridge crew, "Lay and I will be known in the RN

(Royal Navy) as 'those two Canadians, De Wolf and De Lay.'"
But upon their arrival in Plymouth the first lord of the admiralty seems not to notice their "de lay," and he sends them a message of welcome: "The presence of the units of the Royal Canadian Navy in our midst inspires us to a still harder effort. Confident both of your skill and of your valour we wish you good luck in the fierce and exacting toil which lies before you."

However, it turns out the Canadians have missed the main evacuation and are ordered for clean-up along the continental coast.

The *Restigouche* patrols off the coastal town of Le Havre, and then heads for St. Valery to pick up the 51st Highlanders. There are pockets of Allied troops still left onshore, destroying all oil and machinery before retreating off the beaches. The flames mount so high in the sky that they can be seen at sea, and a dark grey pall hangs heavily along the coastline, filling the sinuses with an acrid smoke.

Arriving at St. Valery at about 5:30 a.m., Rustyguts finds another destroyer, a liner, half-a-dozen transports, several railway ferries, and many small boats evacuating the French and British wounded. Confusion reigns, and the Highlanders are nowhere to be found. Lieutenant Commander Lay takes command of the situation and tells his first lieutenant, Debby Piers, to send someone ashore to contact General Fortune of the Highlanders. The ships are sitting ducks this close to shore batteries, and no one knows exactly where and when the Germans will wake up and attack. Piers decides to volunteer himself. He came to fight in the war, and he feels that a little adventure ashore would suit him.

St. Valery, off the coast of France, is a village with a population of about 1000. It has a stone pier where the river joins the sea, and sheer cliffs separate the shore from the village. The Canadian ships keep a vigilant eye on those cliffs while they await word on the Highlanders, as there is no way of knowing what's advancing on the other side. A small cutter is launched for Piers and he climbs aboard, not knowing what he will find onshore. He's given a time limit, with orders to signal back as soon as he has word.

The small boat bounces through the surf toward the chaos onshore, and Piers is sure the whine of the engine will bring the Germans running. Heading full-speed at the beach, he hits a rock and bends the propeller, but everything else stays intact. Dragging the boat up onshore, he ties it off on an encroaching branch while glancing nervously around him. The beach is littered with shrapnel, torn uniforms, blast holes from shelling, and dried blood. A body rocks back and forth in the surf, entrails fanning out behind it like the tentacles of a jellyfish. Seagulls are wheeling overhead, and here and there a few of the birds fight over remains that Piers really doesn't want to identify. He steps over a lone boot and tries not to think of what might have happened to the man who was wearing it. Medics are still clearing the dead and the dying, so Piers leaves them to their macabre tasks and hikes up a trail to the cliff top.

A Canadian destoyer

Following the sound of machine-gun fire, Piers finds General Fortune of the 51st Highlanders aways inland. He tries to explain to the general that the ships have been ordered to take his men off the coast. The general has been out of touch with his headquarters for several days. And since the French commander in the area hasn't yet ordered his troops to evacuate, the general decides not to go either. He doesn't like the navy coming to "rescue" him, nor does he like the idea that his men will leave before the French troops. General Fortune decides that if he continues to hold the perimeter of the Dunkirk evacuation, more soldiers will get safely off to fight another day. Neither he nor Lay have been told that the main evacuation is finished, or that the remaining troops are surrounded by the German panzer divisions led by General Rommel.

In the distance the pounding boom of the enemy guns hits the eardrums with a dull thud. Piers can feel his blood pressure rise as he looks nervously around him, expecting the Germans to appear at any moment. "But we've got five, six, seven ships here, sir," he argues with the general. "We can take off thousands, and Captain Lay has received orders ..." But nothing Piers says persuades the general to abandon the fight. Piers is told to get back to his ship.

The machine-gun fire increases and shells start whizzing overhead. On the other side of the hill the sound of German tanks fills the air and men are running for cover. The French troops on the beaches decide not to wait for the order to evacuate, and gratefully accept transport on the waiting Canadian ships. Piers narrowly escapes the area as all hell breaks loose. Behind him, the 51st are captured and spend the next four years in German Prisoner of War (POW) camps.

Once back in his cutter, Piers discovers to his dismay that the boat will only make half-a-knot due to the damaged propeller. He signals the *Restigouche*, which is lying about four kilometres offshore and waiting anxiously for his news. By this time, the ship has been joined by the *St. Laurent*, which is filled with French troops. Lay gives orders to proceed closer inshore and to go and get Piers, rather than wait for him to reach them. The German guns are getting closer and the top of the cliffs are filled with tank movement.

The *Restigouche* reaches Piers's little boat, hooks it up to pulleys, and starts hoisting it up the side of the destroyer. Suddenly, panzer tanks open fire. Shells whiz overhead, pinging on the metal hull, splashing in the waves, exploding loudly. The crew scrambles, some to man the guns and give the Germans what for, and others to load the ammunition. Meanwhile, others struggle to hoist the cutter safely on deck. Smoke from the guns mixes with the burning of vehicles, and the noise drives the men's adrenaline higher. Whistle ... whoosh ... splat ... Kaboom! And a splatter of sea water hits the deck. Whistle ... whoosh ... splat ... Kaboom! And everyone ducks. Well, almost everyone. Lay is sitting calmly while his men are scrambling, and De Wolf, on the *St. Laurent*, wants in on the action.

Under a full head of steam, the *St. Laurent* comes to the rescue. De Wolf, often referred to as "hard-over Harry," isn't known to smile a great deal. But when he opens up with his 4.7-inch guns aimed at the cliffs above St. Valery, he has a huge grin on his face. His is the first Canadian ship to fire on the enemy in World War II. The crew cheers. They had come to fight the Germans, and finally the action has begun. With every boom of the gun the ship lurches and shudders. Pungent smoke fills the air and the men continue to cheer. "Hard-over-Harry" is still smiling broadly.

The *Restigouche*, after regrouping, joins in the foray. Both Canadian destroyers bang away at the tanks on top of the cliffs. The orders are shouted above the din, ammunition flies, hoisted from below decks and into the hands of the gun crew. Load! Load! LOAD! ... Wham! The *Restigouche* shudders and below decks the crew hears the strain on the hull and feels the recoil. Then the German guns answer back. Boom! ... Kathunk! Shells fly over the ships about a metre above the bridge. Whoooosh! They splash into the water, sending up an impressive spout. With the sound of each shell bursting, everyone on deck flings his body flat and holds his breath — even though once the shell explodes the danger is past. Commander Lay watches the action, still sitting calmly on his chair on the bridge.

The German guns straddle Rustyguts, trying to get a fix on their target. Boom! Whoosh! Too far on the port side. Boom! Whoosh! Too much to starboard. They're short again and again, trying to pinpoint the target. Commander Lay orders the guns to continue firing at the tanks while the ship zigzags, making things more difficult for the Germans. Shell splinters cut through the rigging and ping! ping! ping! off the upper and lower decks, leaving a ringing in the ears. Bullets ricochet, and the harsh smell from the guns fills everyone's nostrils. Those below decks hear the booms, feel the ship react, and keep the ammo coming. Dishes smash in the wild manoeuvres. Sailors grab whatever is screwed down in order to stay on their feet. The tension on board is mounting. This is no escort duty. This is war.

As soon as Piers is back on deck, he makes his way to

the bridge to report to the captain. By this time Rustyguts is doing 32 knots and zigzagging to avoid the shelling. The officer of the watch, the yeoman of signals, and the rest of the crew on the bridge are ducking down behind the canvas wind dodgers, supposedly to avoid the shells. The captain watches them and chuckles, as the canvas couldn't possibly offer protection against a 3-inch shell. With a slight smile still on his face, he looks at Piers amidst the smoke and noise. "Well, Number One?" Lay asks him. A shell explodes off the port side and Piers ducks. The captain barely flinches. Piers makes his report, ducking when shrapnel whizzes overhead or the guns boom. Yet there is Captain Lay, with his steel helmet on, sitting calmly in his chair as if nothing is happening.

After the report, since there are no more troops to evacuate, Lay orders the *St. Laurent* up the coast to continue to engage shore batteries while Rustyguts makes for Plymouth at 32 knots.

When the *Restigouche* nears the English harbour, a fighter plane dives at the ship from out of the sun. Lay sits straight up in his chair and yells, "Open fire!" He shows more excitement and emotion at this moment than during the whole battle off the coast. But the crew is taken by surprise and none of the 4.7-inch guns can be loaded and fired. After the aircraft has flown past, a few pitiful rounds from a Lewis gun splatter the sky aimlessly. The fighter circles and flashes a message to the vessel by Aldus light, "Damn poor shooting. But at least you're awake." The plane is British, piloted by a

Canadian fly boy with time on his hands who thought the navy boys looked bored. "I hope he has plenty to do in the battle later," is Lay's curt response.

Lay sets course to join the HMS *Calcutta* and the HMCS *Fraser*. They have just gone up the Gironde River, near Bordeaux, France, to blow up everything the advancing Germans might make use of. The HMCS *Restigouche* is to rendezvous with them, and escort them back to Plymouth.

But this never comes to pass.

Chapter 2
HMCS *Fraser* —
Collision at Sea

I t's the evening of June 25, 1940. The Canadian ships HMCS *Restigouche* and HMCS *Fraser*, as well as the British ship HMS *Calcutta*, are on a return trip from the coast of France. The ships are without radar, the night is dark, and the convoy is blacked out. In the quiet of the night, the whoosh and slap of the ocean on the hull of the destroyers is strangely peaceful. Too peaceful, think some of the crew. Dunkirk is fresh on their minds and every one of them is thinking about what the Nazis will do next.

The *Fraser* drops back to take a visual bearing of those behind, and the crew is suddenly ordered to change stations at top speed. The ship is preparing to make its way from the Gironde River estuary and across the Channel to England.

The Royal Navy's *Calcutta* is a 4290-tonne light cruiser, built at the end of World War I. On this occasion, Vice Admiral A.T.B. Curteis, flag officer commanding, Second Cruiser Squadron, is on board and in command of this small group. With tensions running high on the ships, most of the crews are starved for sleep.

The admiral orders a reduced speed of 20 knots and alters course, putting the *Fraser* on the *Calcutta's* starboard bow and the *Restigouche* on the cruiser's port quarter. Then he orders the destroyers to form a single line, reducing the speed of the formation to 14 knots. The *Calcutta* is to take the lead, with the *Fraser* next, and the *Restigouche* in the rear. At least, that is the plan. Lieutenant Commander Lay, captain of the *Restigouche*, temporarily increases speed to close up the formation behind the cruiser and then alters to starboard, being careful to leave the *Fraser* room to pull into the middle. Like synchronized swimmers, the *Restigouche* speeds forward while the *Fraser* swings inward to turn down *Calcutta's* starboard side — or so the *Calcutta* expects. But the *Fraser* is zigzagging without any intention of falling in line — the ship never received the order.

The commanding officer of the *Fraser*, Wallace Creery, tells the officer of the watch, Lieutenant Harold Groos, to carry on with the manoeuvres as scheduled. Groos gives the order "Port 10!" Creery tells Groos to increase speed and "swing a hard over!"

The *Calcutta* sees the move and misinterprets the

intention, expecting the *Fraser* to pass in front of the *Calcutta*. However, the *Fraser* is turning inward, to pass down the *Calcutta's* port side and make a complete turn in order to finish off the zigzag. Curteis, concerned about how close the *Fraser* will pass on the Calcutta's port side, orders "Starboard wheel!" and gives one short blast, cutting off the *Fraser's* complete turn. When the *Calcutta* sees the *Fraser* turn sharply to port, the commander realizes the ships are on a collision course and orders the engines to full reverse.

Seeing the *Calcutta's* change in direction and speed, Commander Creery realizes the *Fraser* can't turn sharply enough to avoid a collision. Creery takes over the wheel, ordering "Port 20!" and then "Hard-a-port!" The *Fraser* groans, dishes go flying, rivets pop, and those shipmates who are asleep in bunks roll onto the floor.

Creery realizes too late that he can't get the ship clear by a port turn. He then orders "Hard to starboard!" trying to pass across the bow of the larger ship, gunning the engines to outrun it and lessen the impact. The *Calcutta's* bow surges forward. Those on the bridge watch in mortal fascination as the bow of the *Calcutta* slices into their ship. The *Fraser* rips in two behind the "B" gun. The metal peels back from the hull and sparks fly in the night sky, filling the darkness with the shrill screech of ripping metal, mixing with the screams of the injured. The forward part of the ship breaks off, bobbing a few metres away like an apple in a tub of water. The wheelhouse and bridge structure are scooped onto the *Calcutta's* forecastle by the ship's forward thrust, ending up in one piece on the cruiser's bow. Creery leads the few bridge personnel to safety by jumping to the forecastle deck of the *Calcutta*. Able Seaman Todeus of the *Fraser* is yelling for help, as his feet have been badly crushed in the collision. Creery returns to the wrecked wheelhouse and rescues Todeus and Russ Milray, who was also badly crushed when the *Calcutta* was hit. Russ doesn't look good, and is taken to the sick bay for immediate medical attention.

The *Calcutta* lowers a small boat for the *Fraser's* survivors and surges on, signalling to Lieutenant Commander Lay in the *Restigouche* to pick up any remaining crew. Those left stranded watch the cruiser disappear into the darkness.

Tom Kellington is a stoker on watch in the engine room of the *Fraser* at the time of the ramming. The engines are still going astern, there is a hesitation, and then the lights go out. He doesn't feel much of a shock, no bumps or grinding noise can be heard above the throbbing of the engines. The lights simply die. Then the engines die. And then, complete silence.

Chief Engine Room Artificer Kent sends Kellington up the hatch to see what has happened. Kellington sees what he thinks is a rammed submarine tilted upwards, not realizing it's the *Fraser's* forward end. The forward boiler room is flooding, and when the tank suctions give way, everything dies.

Not sensing the seriousness of the situation, Kellington picks up some of his jerseys, which have fallen from the drying line around the air pump. When he gets back to the engine room it's empty. He drops the jerseys and gets out fast. Kellington jumps over the side of the wounded ship and is hauled into the *Fraser*'s whaler. "Give me an oar!" he roars, and sets to work, ready to row to England if necessary.

Commander Lay, in the *Restigouche*, has not been told that the *Fraser* has been rammed. He is only told to pick up survivors. Seeing the damage, Lay isn't sure if the ship was torpedoed or if it hit a submerged rock. He is amazed to find that the after-part of the Canadian ship is floating perfectly well. But there is no bow and no bridge, only the ship's smokestacks and stern.

It is now after 10 p.m. The easiest way to rescue the survivors still on board is to pull alongside the wreck at the back end of the ship and hold her fast. Scramble nets are tossed over the side for the survivors to climb to safety. "Heave up, lads," the men are encouraged. "Pass up the injured first, men."

Meanwhile, the severed bow drifts away in the darkness, upside down, trapping some of the crew below the waterline. Muffled banging fills the night air, and those already rescued watch anxiously to see what will happen to their trapped crew mates. Lay lowers his whaler, giving command of the rescue vessel to Canadian Lieutenant David Walter. Also ordered aboard are Lieutenant Harold Groos and Leading Signalman P.E. Palmer who has a hand-held night light for flashing communications. Groos motors slowly in the dark swells and drifts of the icy waters, pulling exhausted men from the chilly depths. The whaler fills up, and he orders the engines killed to better hear the men still in the water. When the whaler pulls back to the *Restigouche*, the *Fraser*'s propellers on the floating wreck begin turning. The *Fraser* rolls down on the whaler, throwing everyone into the water. One of the rescuers is tossed into the water and sinks. No one can reach him in time. Everyone else manages to reach the nets and safely climb on board. Those who are left on the *Fraser* start passing medical supplies and bottles of liquor up to their doctor, Blair McLean, who is now aboard the *Restigouche* and caring for the injured. Most of the men have fuel oil in their eyes and wounds. It floats on the water, and here and there small pools have ignited, giving off an eerie light over the swells.

The *Fraser*'s bow then capsizes, throwing more men into the icy seas. Carley floats (life rafts with slatted bottoms) are tossed out to them. The desperate calls from injured shipmates lost in the waves will haunt the survivors for the rest of their lives. The seamen feverishly work to save all who remain alive.

Finally, all who can be saved are safely aboard *Restigouche*. There is suddenly a loud sucking noise. The other half of the *Fraser*, floating high in the water and wallowing keel up, loses both forward guns as they fall into the water. The bow briefly rights again. Those trapped below tumble out and rush to the side nearest the *Restigouche*. They stretch out their arms and call out, hoping for rescue. With a whoosh! the *Fraser* turns keel up again, flinging the men into the water. Boats, Carley floats, and life buoys are lowered.

Men are yelling. The waves relentlessly grab and pull the men down. More survivors are brought on board.

The *Restigouche* is filled with people. Along with 59 evacuees from St. Jean de Luz, there are 11 officers and 96 men from the fore part of the *Fraser*. The wounded lie everywhere, with burns, cuts, and fuel-filled eyes, as well as broken bones and serious injuries caused by crushing. Kellington works frantically with Dr. McLean. Kellington is rushing back and forth to the engine room to heat water under the air pump because there are no hot water taps. He then runs the water to the doctor, who uses it to wash the oil off the injured. Before scrubbing the wounds, the doctor gives each man a tot of rum to help with the pain.

In the early morning mist, the harbour of Plymouth, England, lies sleepy and quiet. The throbbing of engines is heard, and through the fog a ghostly apparition creeps slowly to port. The *Calcutta*'s bow nudges the docking bay, and, gruesomely positioned on her forecastle deck, is the bridge of the *Fraser*.

Russ Milray, one of the men who was badly crushed, spent nearly two years in hospital in Devonport recovering from his injuries. He had more breaks in his body than could be counted. Gangrene set in quickly, and it seemed at first that Russ was a hopeless case. His legs had to be amputated to cut out all the infection, but gangrene set in again in the stumps. He had surgery after surgery to cut away the dead and dying flesh, and to save as much as could be saved. Still he hung in there, with that quiet stubbornness Canadians are famous for. Years later, in 1947, one of his Navy buddies from the *Fraser* met Russ Milray and his wife at a theatre in Toronto. Russ was smiling, cracking jokes, and looking healthy.

As for the *Fraser*, although the ship was done for, the adventures of its survivors were far from over. A few months later ...

Chapter 3
"Déjà vu, Margaree"

hen HMCS *Fraser* is lost in June 1940, arrangements are immediately made by the Canadian government to purchase a replacement from the Royal Navy. The HMS *Diana* has served in the Mediterranean and the Home Fleets, and the higher-ups decide she is the perfect replacement for the *Fraser*. She is sent to Albert Docks in London to be refitted, and is then commissioned as HMCS *Margaree*.

During the ship's refit the Germans hit the harbour with a vengeance. Twelve ships are damaged during one night's raid. But the *Margaree* is not touched. During the next night of bombing, a couple of sticks of explosives straddle her, and one sinks under the ship without exploding. The next morning the dockyard mateys brave the threat and pull her along the jetty a few hundred metres to get clear of the explosives. As soon as she is at a safe distance the bombs explode, sending a plume of water high into the air. The *Margaree* remains intact.

Word that HMCS *Margaree* is a "lucky" ship spreads among her new crew. This is comforting news since the majority of the crew are survivors from the HMCS *Fraser*. Thirteen of the wounded have recovered sufficiently to be assigned to the *Margaree*. Yes, they are all happy to hear she is a lucky ship.

Two of those reassigned to the *Margaree* are Dr. McLean and Lieutenant Landymore. Landymore was married a couple of months after surviving the ramming of the *Fraser*, and two months later here he is, climbing the gangplank of the *Fraser*'s replacement. As he steps foot on deck, he pats his front shirt pocket, where he keeps a picture of his wife, and hopes that the rumours are true. Landymore is determined to return to port safely to rejoin his bride.

The *Margaree* and her crew sail to Londonderry on a shakedown and workup cruise. One of the two sub-lieutenants has to sleep in the forward cabin, directly under the bridge. It's a tiny space with low head clearance. The occupant is chosen by the flip of a coin, something that will be talked about for years to come. Sub-Lieutenant Bob Timbrell wins the toss and makes himself comfortable in the cabin near the wardroom. It's a bigger cabin with a higher ceiling.

After Londonderry, the HMCS *Margaree* is ordered on convoy duty. The convoy gathers and sails on October 20,

1940. The ships travel in four columns, with the merchant vessel *Port Fairy* leading the port column, followed by the SS *Jamaica Planter*. The other three ships are in single columns starboard at 400-metre intervals. The group is travelling quicker than normal, and in a straight line instead of the evasive zigzagging most escorts use to avoid being an easy target for German U-boats. The *Margaree*'s crew is uneasy during the entire voyage. Even though she is rumoured to be a lucky boat, too many things don't feel right. She is like a cat that has survived nine times, and they are all wondering what will happen the next time her life is threatened.

The second night out the weather worsens. Rain squalls splatter the bridge screens, lessening visibility. All voyages are conducted under blackout conditions, and even with a scant 400 metres between ships, the crews experience the feeling of isolation. The wind begins to kick up the swells, snatching the tops off the waves and tearing at the rigging on deck. The salt in the wind stings the faces of those on watch and blinds their eyes, making the upper deck almost impassable. The ships in each column climb the swells to the top of each crest, rain splatters the bridges and upper decks in torrential blasts, and the lookouts take their visual bearings. Then the ships plunge back down into the watery valley with sea water swooshing over the sides of the vessels, over the forward gun, then crashing against the superstructure, which jars the hull and strains the rivets.

Life below deck is a tangle of wet uniforms and fitful

sleeps. Everything is damp, clothes smell of wet wool, body odour, and fish. Most men sleep with their life belts and clothing on. Cooking is impossible with the rolling of the vessels, so meals consist of sandwiches eaten to the constant and violent bruising motion of the ocean. Drinking a cup of coffee or kye (very strong, thick hot chocolate) becomes a balancing act, with the drinker wearing more than he sw–allows. Even using the head (the toilet on a ship) is a life-endangering event. Sitting on the throne is more than risky as the boat jostles and pitches, but flushing is even worse. If one does this at the wrong time, one chances being douched to death as the sea overpowers the valves and plumbing, soaking the sitter with whatever is in the bowl and pipes, and, even worse, creating a vacuum that threatens the continuation of the family name.

The *Margaree* is approximately two to three kilometres ahead of the convoy. She drops back closer to the group because of poor visibility. The signalman lets the rest of the convoy know of the change in speed. But in these conditions it's anyone's guess whether or not someone has seen the flashes. At midnight the first lieutenant turns the watch over to the relief, and advises him that the ship is gradually allowing the convoy to catch up with her.

The gun's crew is told to leave only two men at the gun mountings so the others can find some relief from the squall. Water is constantly drenching everything in fits from the sea and from the downpour from the sky. The men are miserable.

Taking pity on them, the officers tell them they can spell each other off, two at a time, giving leave to the others to find whatever comfort is available.

Aboard the *Port Fairy*, the first indication of trouble is in the early morning of October 22 at about one o'clock, when her chief officer observes the *Margaree* off the starboard bow. She is crossing too close in front for the *Port Fairy*'s speed and the roughness of the sea. He stops his engines, and when he sees that the *Margaree* is surging to port on the cresting waves, he orders full reverse, putting his wheel hard-a-port and sounding three short blasts to warn the destroyer as well as the *Jamaica Planter* behind him. He can't move to starboard because of the other convoy ships, and the *Margaree* — oblivious to the danger closing in on her — is continuing on her original path.

The *Port Fairy*'s engines hesitate in the tossing seas. Full reverse isn't engaging due to the swells lifting and surging forward in the current. The *Margaree*'s lookouts, struggling to see in the rain and wind, don't realize the other vessel is so close. They alter to port to take a wave, and cut directly across the bow of the *Port Fairy*. The timing could not possibly be worse for the two ships. The *Port Fairy* surges ahead on the force of a swell, and the *Margaree* hesitates in an undertow. The bridge crew in the *Port Fairy* give a yell and hang on tight, blasting the ship's horn to warn the crews of both ships, yet helpless to stop the collision. The *Margaree*'s bridge crew look up in time to see the bow of the *Port Fairy* descending on them from above. The men yell and brace themselves. Only God knows if they will survive the crash.

The *Port Fairy*'s stem slices through the *Margaree*'s bridge area, breaking the ship in half. The screams of the bridge crew are snatched away by the relentless wind and waves. Those below, still sleeping in their hammocks, haven't a chance. They receive no warning. The sub-lieutenant who lost the coin toss for sleeping quarters is asleep in his bunk below the bridge when the *Port Fairy* slices through his cabin. He is never seen again. The howl of the Atlantic squall is punctuated by the throbbing of the turbines. It drowns out the scraping of metal on metal and the ripping of the hull. The men crushed or broken are instantly thrown overboard, or pinned where they stand watch. Those alive know that when the ship begins to sink, they will go with her. Their home, their ship, will forever be their coffin.

The whole bow section of the *Margaree* sinks immediately. The "B" gun crew, who were ordered off the watch, miraculously survive the crash. The captain of the gun, who ordered the others to get out of the weather a short time before the collision, is at his post and watches in fascinated horror as the bow of the *Port Fairy* drives over him and the guns.

First Lieutenant Pat Russell is the senior surviving officer in the stern section. Without a bow, it's obvious the forward bulkheads will soon buckle. He orders everyone left to abandon ship.

Bob Timbrell had come off watch an hour earlier and was, at the time of the collision, asleep in his cabin beneath the after torpedo tubes. The impact broke the fuel tanks and his cabin is now drenched in fuel. He is thrown out of his bunk, landing hard, and tossed like green salad in the oil-fuel.

As there is nothing he can do about getting the stinking stuff off him, he grabs his greatcoat to protect himself from the weather up top, and rushes to the ladder. The electrical switchboard operator (Able Bodied Seaman Holman) and the ship's doctor (Blair McLean) are already at the ladder struggling to open the hatch to the upper deck. There are no engine noises now — only the sea pounding at the broken hull, and the creaking and groaning of a ship in the throes of death.

"She's sinking," says the doctor in a daze, reliving the collision of the HMCS *Fraser.* The sea had claimed the *Fraser,* and it seems to those who had survived the first collision that fate has come to claim them. The HMCS *Margaree* is no longer a lucky ship.

Bob Timbrell helps the others with the hatch, but their combined pushing and banging won't budge it. They search for something to batter it with. There is nothing. The three men can hear the sea boiling around the vessel. What's left of the ship groans, as if in pain. Trying not to panic, they decide that one of them will have to be used as a battering ram. As the lightest and the longest, Bob is lifted up by the doctor and the electrician to be used as leverage against the unwilling hatch.

"*Déjà vu,* Margaree"

"Stiffen those legs Timbrell!" they order him. With stiffened legs, poor Bob is hammered against the hatch feet-first. After a couple of tries, the hatch bursts open and the two fall on the deck, dropping Bob back down the ladder. He lands hard, breaking three or four ribs. The ramming party scuttles out. The "ram" picks himself up and follows the other two through the hatch and onto the deck, which is slick with fuel and sea water. Fire has broken out, and Timbrell realizes with a sick feeling in his stomach that, doused in oil as he is, his potential for becoming a human torch is very real.

Another surviving officer is Landymore. He and Russell climb forward to see if any men are trapped. The ship is as silent as a tomb. There are no shouts, not even the sound of escaping steam. There is simply the slapping of the sea, the wallowing of the wreck, and the empty sound of missing men. Landymore swallows hard and pulls his wife's picture from out of his front pocket. Wiping the splatter of rain off it, he takes a deep breath and exhales slowly. He will survive. He has to.

Russell and Landymore continue to comb the wreckage until they find the ramming party on deck. In the dark they can all see the *Port Fairy* alongside, struggling to stay close to the *Margaree* in the tossing seas. The group stare in silence at the hole where the forward end of their beloved ship is supposed to be. The forward end of their ship, and their crew mates, are gone.

Stunned, and with a weird feeling hitting the pit of their

stomachs, they are frozen in indecision. The surreal circumstances of their situation have them momentarily at a loss. Here they are, standing on a deck without a bridge or a forecastle, just the funnels and after end. There are supposed to be crew members in the engine room, the boiler room. There are supposed to be depth-charge crews and those sleeping aft. But the small group is standing alone, gaping in horror.

Both ships stop and the eerie silencing of the naval engines is filled with the violence of the squall. Buffeted by the wind, the hull of the wreck grinds and screeches on that of the rescue ship in teeth-clenching steel on steel. To McLean and Landymore, it's an all too familiar scene. A few scant months ago, they had heard the same sounds on the *Fraser*. Is it too soon to hope they are survivors of this collision, too? "Déjà vu, *Margaree*," whispers Landymore.

McLean and Timbrell leave the group to look for any men killed, injured, or trapped below. But there are no injuries left on board this time. To McLean's astonishment, the members of the crew either died or escaped injury completely. All men left living have found their way on deck. There is no one left alive below.

The disbelief is short-lived. There is work to be done. There are 10 depth charges set to 50 feet on the wreck, and these have to be made safe before they explode and destroy what's left of the *Margaree*, including the men onboard and on the *Port Fairy*. A couple of these charges have broken free and are careening dangerously to and fro across the deck with every swell. Russell orders Timbrell and Holman to deal with them, and the men scramble to get them under control. The four men breathe a sigh of relief when the explosives are finally set on "safe."

The *Port Fairy,* lying alongside the damaged destroyer, is crashing up and down against the wreck with each swell. Ladders are thrown down the sides for the survivors, and 28 seamen leap off the lunging wreck, clinging desperately to the side of the freighter for a breath, and then scrambling up and over to safety. A wave hits. Two seamen half jump and are half thrown as they leap off the pitching broken vessel. They lose their grip on the oily ladders and fall into the churning water between the ships. The *Port Fairy* plunges to the bottom of the swell, the wreck rises to the crest, and the two hulls smash together with a sickening, grinding thud. There are muffled cries as the two seamen are crushed between the hulls, their broken bodies sinking beneath the sea. One of the men lost is Dr. Blair McLean. The last that Lieutenant Landymore sees of his fellow *Fraser*-survivor is the doctor's hand reaching out of the waves before slowly disappearing.

The ships drift apart and four men are left on board the *Margaree*: Russell, Landymore, Timbrell, and Holman. The *Port Fairy* backs clear to avoid damage as the squall is worsening and they've been without the engines for long enough. The remaining *Margaree* men are on their own. A small Carley float captures their attention and Timbrell and Holman climb on top of the torpedo tubes to wrestle it from where it's stored. Grabbing either side of the float, they haul it on deck.

It is by now about 2:30 a.m., cold and dark, the squall all but blown out. The *Port Fairy* is out of sight and the remaining men are alone with the hollow wreck. The convoy has also moved on, adding to their sense of abandonment. There is a fresh breeze blowing. They are 500 metres west of Ireland. It's a long way to swim or paddle but they have incentive — on the one hand, the ocean is cold and wet, on the other, the wreck is sinking.

Timbrell passes the raft's line to Landymore as they prepare to throw the Carley float overboard. He wraps the cord once around his wrist and grasps the end, planting his feet firmly on deck so the float won't drift away when it hits the water. Timbrell and Holman heave the heavy raft over the side, their adrenaline pumping and hearts pounding. The raft sails high into the air and a long way from the *Margaree*. Too late they realize the line is only four feet long and Landymore is a small thin man. The line snaps taught and Landymore gives a yell as he sails over the side with the raft. The other three watch in horror as he hits the water with a splat and disappears from sight. The water is covered with fuel and when Landymore resurfaces, still holding on to the rope, he's spluttering and choking from the salt water he's inhaled. He looks up at the three men on deck as they look down at him. Then he holds up the rope, still firmly grasped in his hand. His face is glowing with oil from the wreck, the water is frigid, and he's still choking, but he has a great big smile on his face. "Landymore, did I give you permission to leave the ship?" Russell asks.

The remaining three jump into the ocean and pull themselves into the raft. They manage to paddle to safety and the *Port Fairy* returns an hour later and picks them up.

One hundred and forty-one men died that October night of 1940. Eighty-six of the 141 who went down with the *Margaree* had survived the *Fraser's* collision, only to die on her replacement.

Chapter 4
May I Have
Your Autograph?

The first settlers in northern Saskatchewan looked at the vastness of the prairies and renamed the desolate landscape Prince Albert, since most of them couldn't pronounce the Native name *Waskesiu*. A hundred years later, the HMCS *Waskesiu* stands forlornly at the dock in Halifax, waiting to be boarded by her crew. And like the early Saskatchewan settlers, the *Waskesiu* will battle the elements, against all odds, to achieve her goal. There are great hopes resting on this Canadian-built frigate, and promises that this new breed of anti-submarine escort ship will be more effective against the enemy than the corvettes.

The HMCS *Waskesiu*, under Lieutenant Commander James Fraser, and the HMS *Nene*, under Commander J.D.

May I Have Your Autograph?

Birch, join the SC-153 (slow convoy) as they move toward the United Kingdom east of mid-ocean. The convoy includes tankers with much-needed fuel. It is literally surrounded by escorts: 5 destroyers, 4 frigates, 11 captain's class frigates, 4 corvettes, 2 anti-submarine trawlers, and 1 rescue tug. A convoy is like a small city at sea. There's the lead ship, which is the head of government, there is a town doctor, there are fuel ships and supply ships. The little frigates and corvettes are like policemen walking the beat. They keep the laggers moving and keep order in the ranks. Onshore, life holds many unexpected events, and similar events happen at sea. Someone gets sick and the doctor is needed. The challenge in the middle of the ocean is how to get the doctor to the patient. Sometimes it's by motor launch. Other times it's by ship transfer with a pulley system, the doctor sliding down the cable to the deck of the other vessel.

At all times, Plymouth Headquarters tracks the U-boat activity in the Atlantic, and signals each convoy with the day's enemy activities. On the other side, each U-boat reports their position to their own headquarters in Germany. Like a complicated ballet, the Allied ships adjust course to avoid the U-boats, and the U-boats adjust their course to intercept. If the Allies are lucky, the convoys outmanoeuvre and outrun the U-boats.

SC-153 crawls steadily eastward, and it doesn't take long for the commander of this convoy to see that they won't be able to escape the Germans. All they can do is remain alert

Canadian crew men aboard the HMCS *Waskesiu*

and hope that the weather is bad enough to keep the U-boats under the surface.

On February 23 the day breaks dark and gloomy. The German submarine *U-257* is heading home after missing a rendezvous with a German blockade-runner. She is unaware of the convoy in her path. At 11 p.m. the U-boat discovers the group of Allied ships, and sets her sites on the HMCS *Waskesiu*. Commander Heinz Rahe orders the U-boat to dive, choosing to avoid confrontation because the submarine is short of supplies.

May I Have Your Autograph?

Early the next morning, a few minutes after two o'clock, *Waskesiu* Petty Officer M.J.T. Fortune, who is the asdic's (sonar radar's) first operator, discovers the U-boat on his asdic. The asdic's range is two kilometres, weather permitting. The *Waskesiu* has a very narrow margin for striking the U-boat, as the German sub can dive, zigzag, kill all engines and sink, or change to full speed ahead to avoid confrontation.

Manitoban Walter A. Fogg, the ship's telegraphist, holds his breath. The crew are excited to be in on the action. The captain of the *Waskesiu* slows the speed. Ping ... all that can be heard is breathing ...

"Hush, everyone," someone whispers.

"Shhhhhh ..." is the answering chorus.

Ping ... Ping ... Beep!

"There she is."

Ping ... Beep! Ping ... Beep!

"She's moving left, captain."

Canadian Lieutenant Commander Fraser has been in command of the *Waskesiu* for only 19 days. He slows the speed and orders a hedgehog attack first (unlike depth charges, hedgehogs need to strike the target in order to detonate). "Load! Load! LOAD!" the command is shouted down the line. Whumph! ... and the small frigate recoils with the power of the release. "Full speed ahead!" the captain yells, and the small boat leaps on top of the waves to avoid being caught by the explosions.

The ocean erupts and the sub is jarred but unharmed.

Rahe, the German commander, orders the U-boat deeper. He closes his eyes for a millisecond, trying to guess the thoughts of the man in charge of the ship on the surface. Fraser does the same. And as each crawls into the mind of the enemy, the two crews wait for the next order.

A flare is launched to mark the spot for the next attack. Fraser orders a speed of 15 knots, hard-a-port, and then back. The *Waskesiu* jumps and groans with the release of another charge then races away from the site once more. Fraser then orders a full stop, and waits.

Rahe also waits. He decides to play a game of cat and mouse and orders a course for due south. Then he decides to surface as a tease to the Canadian boat.

Fraser, instinctively sensing the sub's movements, orders the *Waskesiu* to 10, then 15 knots, preparing for a full-pattern attack. Contact is lost again. Fraser decides on a bold attack course. He puts himself in the place of the German commander and orders the *Waskesiu* to surge ahead, dropping a pattern of charges well in advance of where he believes his target is heading.

The sub bumps into the explosions, and the force tosses the U-boat around like a plastic boat in a child's bath. A few rivets pop and small leaks trickle ominously down the corners, reminding the crew of how vulnerable they are to the sea around them. The German commander changes his orders to surface and curses softly, sending the sub deeper to avoid rather than play with the *Waskesiu*. These Canadians are proving to be more of a challenge than he had expected. It is time to lay low.

On the surface, Fraser continues to hunt around the area until he regains contact on the asdic. With heightened adrenaline, he orders another full 10 charge attack on the sub. Whumph! The boat tosses and then leaps with the recoil. Silence ...

The Canadians search the water for signs of wreckage, but there is nothing. All attention is focused on the asdic. It is very quiet, the crew is listening intently for the "ping" that says their prey is still there. Fraser orders a cup of kye to settle his nerves, and balances the cup on his knee as he contemplates the situation. He knows the sub is there, he simply has to find her. Using the flare still burning on the water's surface as a starting point, he orders a box search of the area, closely monitoring the asdic. At 3:27 a.m., the *Waskesiu* is again in pursuit, and attack after attack is launched. Plumes of frothy white ocean are sent up into the dark sky with each blast.

Commander Birch, in the *Nene*, rushes to join the battle. He orders Captain Fraser to stand down (to stand aside or give over) so the *Nene* can locate the U-boat. Fraser sighs, and the *Waskesiu* waits, slowly circling. The crew crowds to the sides of the deck, and can faintly see and smell oil floating on the waves.

"Too easy," Fraser thinks to himself. He wonders if this is a simple ruse. U-boats often discharge items mixed with fuel to throw off the hunter. The *Waskesiu* anxiously waits for the arrival of the *Nene*, afraid the prey will escape while they are stuck waiting.

At 4:10 a.m. the *Nene* makes contact. The *Waskesiu* is idling along at only five knots. The sub is moving slowly northeast, and is very deep. W.A. Fogg sends the signal to the *Nene*. And the *Nene* orders Fraser to follow the sub's movements closely but to wait until daylight before attacking.

A short time later, the *Nene* decides the blip on the asdic is a whale and not a U-boat. Birch orders the *Waskesiu* to abandon the hunt and rejoin the convoy. "You're chasing shadows, man," Birch signals them. But Fraser trusts his navigator, Lieutenant Williams, who is monitoring the asdic. Fraser asks Birch for permission to make one more attack. Reluctantly, Birch agrees.

Increasing the speed to 10 knots, Fraser orders a deep depth-charge pattern, then changes the order to semi-deep at the last second and increases speed. Whumph! The *Waskesiu* jumps as explosions rock the frigate. Spouts of water reach high into the air and the crew cheers.

Commander Rahe in the U-boat curses angrily. The damn Canadians are too close, damaging the main engines and causing leaks in the control and engine room. Rahe orders the boat to the surface and swings about to ram the frigate, but finds his engines sluggish and unresponsive.

The *Waskesiu* hears the sub blowing tanks as it hits the surface. Fraser orders the gun armament to prepare to fire and increases speed until the U-boat is spotted on the port bow. "Starshell!" orders Fraser, and the sky is lit up with flares suspended by parachutes, which drift slowly down to the waves. In the light the U-boat is plainly visible. She lists to one side and starts to sink.

The *Nene* receives the coded message "Hearse Is Parked" just before the *Waskesiu* closes in and opens fire. The two Bren guns on her bridge fire 170 rounds while, on the forecastle, bursts from a machine gun pierce the early morning light. Thomas Stephenson, on the No. 1 Oerlikon gun, focuses on the sub's conning tower to prevent any of the Germans from making it to the guns in one piece.

The submarine crosses the *Waskesiu*'s bow about 100 metres away, and passes slowly down her port side, which is now illuminated by searchlights on the frigate. The U-boat is so close that the Canadians are unable to come around fast enough to ram her. The U-boat wallows and Rahe knows it's the sub's death knell. He orders his men to abandon ship. Then Rahe throws his life jacket and dingy to the men in the water — quickly re-enters the sinking U-boat — and closes the hatch firmly behind him.

The U-boat groans and, with a sucking noise, upends and sinks vertically, stern first. The German survivors fight with the waves to escape from the undertow, which is about to pull them down with the sub. Struggling in the bitterly cold Atlantic, they yell out to the Canadians, "Hallo! Hallo! Kamerad!"

The *Nene* and the *Waskesiu* lower their whalers to rescue the submariners who are yelling, blowing whistles, and waving their arms. The *Waskesiu* manages to take aboard only four Germans, hauling them out of the water and over the ship's stern. Using searchlights, the *Nene* is able to rescue another 15 men.

The Germans are well-treated on their way back to England. The four on the *Waskesiu* are given clothing, food, and drink, and they are soon exchanging war stories with the crew. Walter Fogg is happy to accept the Germans' autographs on the back of his HMCS *Waskesiu* official commissioning notice.

Walter Fogg now lives in Selkirk, Manitoba, with his wife. Upon being interviewed, he stated that the Canadians were known for three things during World War II — their marksmanship, their ability to survive the elements, and the humanity they offered a surrendered or wounded enemy.

Chapter 5
Bones

The crew isn't aware of it, but the departure, course, and speed of the Canadian destroyer HMCS *Assiniboine*, as well as the convoy, is known to German Admiral Doenitz. When "Bones" (the popular nickname of the *Assiniboine*) joins SC–94 convoy as an escort ship in early August 1942, German submarines are already on a course to intercept.

Lieutenant Commander Lemkhe of the *U-210* is ordered to take position as close to the edge of the "black pit" of the Atlantic as possible. Lemkhe is the infamous captain who sank a passenger liner at the outbreak of war, breaking the rules laid out by the superpowers giving safe passage for travellers. After hiding out until the furor died down at home, he

A Canadian frigate

is again ready and able for action. Looking for another notch on his belt, he is anxious for the chance to attack.

The black pit is the area beyond the fuel capacity of the Allied aircraft. Without the benefit of air protection, ships in this area are vulnerable to attack. In view of this problem, the British had come up with the convoy system, using faster, smaller boats as escorts for the lumbering fuel tankers and supply ships. The destroyers, corvettes, and frigates are heavily armed and, while not able to protect all the ships in the group, they definitely are a force to contend with. The U-boat captains all keep a close eye on the escorts while they hunt the fat fuel tankers. The fewer merchant vessels there are that reach port, the more difficult it is for Britain to feed her civilians and her military, and to fuel her military vehicles.

It is late afternoon on August 2. The day is dull and thick patches of fog inch across the ocean. The misty sea air has soaked everything above and below ship on the *Assiniboine*, and in some areas the fog creeps through doorways like smoke. The crew is wearing the best it has for the weather, but even so, there isn't a dry man aboard.

The tension on the escort ships is high, as there is a known wolf pack of U-boats in the area. The ships are staying in close formation and the crews, expecting trouble, are standing by their action stations. The crew on the *Assiniboine* is restless. The fog mutes the sound of the waves slapping against the hull, yet amplifies the throbbing of the engines below deck. The men strain their eyes and ears for the first sign of trouble. They know they are surrounded by at least 30 convoy ships, but the fog has a way of creating a feeling of isolation.

At 6 p.m. on August 3, the lead ship, the *Trehata*, signals a course change, but not everyone receives the order. HMCS *Nasturtium*, HMCS *Orillia*, and six merchantman ships continue on the old course, unknowingly leaving the safety of the group. For two days ships are sent out to locate the missing ones. Finally, on August 5, a radiogram from the *Orillia* reports their position as 33 metres south of the main convoy. The *Assiniboine*, one of Canada's Tribal Destroyers, is sent to herd the lost sheep and bring them home.

Before anyone can breathe a sigh of relief, the peace is shattered by an explosion. The SS *Spar* is torpedoed by Lieutenant Gerd Kelbling's *U-593* and sinks in minutes. Six metres away, the *Assiniboine* crew hear and feel the torpedoes exploding the hull of the *Spar*. Escorts race to the location and find debris and pools of oil burning eerily on the surface of the waves. Kelbling fires again at another ship in the convoy. The *Nasturtium* spots the torpedo track and all the ships turn "hard-a-starboard," watching the missiles pass by harmlessly. In retaliation, the *Nasturtium* makes a blind attack with depth charges. Then she lowers her boats to pick up the survivors of the *Spar*. Thirty-six men and the ship's dog are pulled out of the frigid waters while the U–boat sinks deeper to avoid the explosives. At 7:20 p.m., a large splash near the wreckage is spotted, but all the *Assiniboine* can find is bubbles. She stays in the area for a while and then rejoins the convoy.

On the morning of August 6, Canadian Seaman Bill Leggett is at his station as rangefinder director of the *Assiniboine* when the *U-210* is spotted a few metres away on the convoy's starboard bow. A break in the fog has blown its cover — a good thing, since the ship's British-fitted 286M radar had failed to detect its presence. Often this type of radar set is referred to by the seamen as "the Jerry's most effective secret weapon."

The *Assiniboine's* captain, John Stubbs, reports the sighting to the *Primrose* and orders a course straight for the U-boat. The sub hesitates, and then takes off with the *Assiniboine* hot on its tail. The ship stays starboard of the U-boat. If the *U-210* dives she will be forced to turn to port and the destroyer will have her.

The *Assiniboine* takes aim at the sub's conning tower and fires three salvoes (a direct order to overshoot then undershoot to determine distance) as she closes in on the enemy. The Germans fly into action with a wild series of manoeuvres, each one countered by the *Assiniboine*. A deadly game of cat and mouse ensues, with both ships trying to ram the other. The sky is littered with tracer, the destroyer recoils with every gun blast, and dishes go flying in the mess. Anyone who needs to use the head does so at considerable risk of personal injury. Each side is sure of its Atlantic supremacy. The power struggle escalates.

The HMS *Dianthus* is ordered to assist and she explodes on the scene in full throttle. Captain Stubbs swings slightly starboard of his target, opening up the distance for his guns to find aim and to cut off the U-boat's escape route. Meanwhile, the *Dianthus* is closing the gap from behind. The quarters are so close that the *Assiniboine* is unable to fire her 4.7-inch guns, and the U-boat stays close to prevent the Canadians from firing those guns. The Canadians man the mounted Lewis machine gun as well as the one-man guns. The sub fights a stubborn battle, diving to port. She is leaking. Oil is streaking the water with pockets of flame floating freely on the swells like splatters of blood. Still, Lemkhe fights on, ordering the wounded sub to dive.

The *Assiniboine* and the *Dianthus* start a box search once the sub disappears under the waves. After a few moments the search is called off. No wreckage is found and the asdic is silent. Everyone knows the danger has not passed as there are more U-boats reported in the vicinity. However, they still have a convoy to protect and Stubbs alters to the northeast to rejoin it. The *Assiniboine* is now 21 metres ahead, with the *Dianthus* five metres off her port beam. The escorts begin a zigzag pattern to cover more ocean in front of the merchant ships once they are again in their convoy position.

Captain Lemkhe, after an hour's silence, surfaces his vessel and heads again for the tankers, which are now a few kilometres ahead. He's closely monitoring the destroyers moving restlessly back and forth in front, and eagerly sets his sights for the fat merchant ships inside the escorts' circle.

The *Assiniboine*'s yeoman of signals sights the surfaced U-boat at about a kilometre away, shifting in and out of patches of dense fog. Stubbs turns the destroyer toward the point where the U-boat is last seen and informs the *Dianthus* that the game is not yet over. The two search for over an hour, until the conning tower of the *U-210* is again sighted. Lemkhe is lying quietly on the surface, believing the sub is hidden by fog. Seeing the Canadians change course toward him, the German guns his engines and disappears into the fog. A deadly game of hide and seek begins. Whenever the destroyer's 4.7-inch guns are on target, the target disappears in the mist like the ghost ship *Flying Dutchman*. Lemkhe seems to be enjoying the game, laughing with his crew and crawling inside the head of his enemy.

The destroyer speeds up and goes forward, swings around, and comes on the *U-210* unexpectedly from the front. Captain Lemkhe is on the bridge. While surprised by the closeness of the destroyer, he chooses to stand his ground. He fancies he is squaring off face-to-face with Stubbs. If he dives, his sub could slip away, but Lemkhe is enjoying the game. He tells his crew that he can beat the enemy on the surface since it's only a Canadian bucket. How good can these Canadians be? He turns the sub down the port side to get inside the destroyer's turning circle and beneath the aim of her main guns. He plans to swing wide quickly and then ram the destroyer behind the "B" guns. Or at least prevent the *Assiniboine* from firing and ramming him instead.

Stubbs is so close to Lemkhe that he swears he can hear the submarine commander breathing. As the sub twists and turns, Stubbs orders the guns to continue firing, more to keep his men busy than with any hope of actually hitting the U-boat. The *U-210* is returning fire bullet for bullet. Shells are whizzing past the heads of the Canadians and, angered by the audacity of the Germans, the gun crews are hammering right back. The distinct smell of explosives and burning cordite is filling the air, the fog drifts around them in damp curls, and the battle takes a personal turn. Which captain will out-manoeuvre the other? Whose crew is more accurate? Which vessel has a sharper turn? Will the Germans' stubbornness win out? As the fog lifts, the two commanding officers watch each other at their respective posts. Almost eye-to-eye, only a few metres apart, they observe each other's movements and try to calculate the other's next move.

Stubbs watches Lemkhe give wheel orders, and imagines the smirk on the German's face. Stubbs sets his jaw. A gun crew appears on the deck of the U–boat and makes a run for the forward guns, but the *Assiniboine*'s multiple .5 inch machine guns mow them down, then destroy the forward guns. All that the German crew has left are the machine guns on the bridge. With grim determination they rake the destroyer from stem to stern with a string of burning-hot bullets, setting the ship's bridge on fire and igniting the fuel tank of the motor launch on the deck below. The *Assiniboine*'s bridge crew race to put out the flames outside the wheelhouse and on the bridge. Meanwhile, Stubbs calmly sits and contemplates the other captain through the smoke. He gives his orders quietly, without emotion, as he stares down Lemkhe from across the water.

Lieutenant Commander Lemkhe orders his sub closer to the destroyer's side to prevent the *Assiniboine* from ramming the sub. Standing on his small bridge and shouting orders down the voice pipe to his control-room crew, Lemkhe knows his vessel's slightest shift in course and speed. It's as if the sub is an extension of his own body. The *Assiniboine* fires a direct hit on the Germans. Jerry fires a direct hit back at the

Canadians. Spouts of water rise up from the waves where shells land short or long. Smoke from the fire and the guns drifts on the ocean breeze, filling both sides with determination. German sailors are swept off the U-boat's casing by the destroyer's fire when they try to man their guns. But at the same time, German shells are hailing the *Assiniboine*'s bridge and forward guns.

Kenneth Watson is running back and forth, dodging the enemy guns while he diligently supplies round after round of ammo to his gun crew. Suddenly, in a storm of bullets, Watson is hit. He lands hard. Bullets continue to whiz overhead and his blood mixes with the sea water on the deck. Still, he's determined not to let the enemy win. Ignoring the burning in his leg and arm and the blood running into his boot, he picks up his load of ammunition. He delivers the load and turns back to get more. A fresh hail of bullets ping repeatedly onto the metal sheeting behind him, and then thud into his warm body. This time when he hits the deck he doesn't get up again, and the *Assiniboine* loses her youngest crew member.

In that same hail of bullets, Petty Officer Claude Daly is shot in the face. The German bullet passes through his cheek and out of his mouth. Choking on his own blood, his face burning from the wound, he moves Watson's body to one side and continues to carry out his duty. Suddenly, Seaman Bill Leggett is sprayed with shrapnel. It splatters over his body and seriously injures one of his arms. He is taken below decks, where the doctor applies a tourniquet. Thirteen others are also wounded. Those unable to continue the fight are moved below decks so they can be treated safely. Others, still wounded, set their jaws with Canadian pride and fight on.

"A" gun's crew has now been reduced to three due to casualties. Able Seamen Stanley Clarke and Morris Young keep the gun firing despite the shelling and the bullets flying over and around them. Able Seaman Roger Whynot can see that the "Y" gun on the *Assiniboine* isn't firing. Although he has no gunnery experience, he and Able Seaman Michael Scullion, as well as one other crew member clean out the jam. Then they load the gun and fire continuously at the U-boat, providing coverage for the fire crews.

The U-boat's guns fire repeatedly and knock out the *Assiniboine*'s main aerial, making it impossible for the destroyer to contact the other ships. Leading Telegraphist Walter Sutherland successfully climbs to the top of the ship and rigs a temporary aerial while ducking German bullets.

The fire on the *Assiniboine*'s bridge is still raging. The German guns concentrate on that area, hoping to disable the destroyer by blowing out her command post. There is an explosion and flames leap skyward. A member of the *Assiniboine* bridge crew is badly hit. With bullets and shrapnel flying around them and flames licking at the wheelhouse, Sub-Lieutenant Douglas Martin hoists his injured crew mate on his back in a fireman's hold. He climbs through the bullets and flames to the chart house where Surgeon Lieutenant Arnold Johnson has set up the medical station.

Meanwhile, Acting Chief Petty Officer Max Bernays, manning the wheel through all the turns and twists, orders First Lieutenant Ralph Hennessy and a damage-control party to fight the fire. Bernays carries on alone at the wheel. Flames and smoke fill the wheelhouse, making it difficult to see or breathe. At times it appears the fire will rage out of control and consume Hennessy. However, taking his duty to his ship seriously, he chooses to remain alone at his post for the next 40 minutes, doing the work of three men, including dispatching the 133 telegraph orders necessary to effectively battle the U-boat.

The bridge ladders are in flames, so the firefighters climb down the lower mast to reach the upper deck. Gunner Norman Wilkinson is wounded and sent to find medical help below. Seeing the flames, he ignores his injury and joins in the firefighting. Once he and the others climb down, they find Chiefs Don Portree and Charles Burgess already with a firefighting team in action. Portree grabs the nozzle of the fire hose and yells for the water valve to be turned on. The pressure hits with such unexpected force that he is flipped over the rails. Portree holds onto the hose for dear life, water spurting into the air. Other members of the party grab the hose and haul him up the side and onto the deck once more, successfully turning the hose onto the flames.

There is another small explosion and Seaman Norman Leckie leaps through the flames into the sick bay to rescue the medical supplies. Seaman Ed Bonsor leaves his post to help move the wounded out of harm's way. With smoke curling around him he piles hammocks against the ship's side to protect his injured crewmates from stray shrapnel. Above him, Stubbs continues his battle with the U-boat. With the firing of the big guns, the *Assiniboine* leaps with the recoil. Yet the sub seems to go undamaged. For a few moments, it appears the Canadians might lose the battle. Flames are leaping higher around the wheelhouse, and still the destroyer can't get the distance needed to lock onto the target.

Able Seaman John White is the first to locate the sub on radar. Regardless of the activity and fire around him, White is completely focused on his job. He reports the sub's exact location to the captain. Thanks to this information, Stubbs's manouevering is successful. Two shells from the *Assiniboine* hit the U-boat's conning tower, killing every man on the bridge — including Lemkhe. Though wounded and badly shaken, the Germans' first watch officer assumes command. He keeps his guns firing at the destroyer, hoping the Canadians will be so busy dodging bullets that the U-boat will be able to slip silently beneath the waves. The German lieutenant gives the order to dive.

Stubbs, seeing that his adversary Lemkhe is finished, anticipates the dive. He swings the *Assiniboine* around to ram the wounded vessel. After a couple of tries, he rams the U-boat right behind the conning tower and water pours into the sub. The diesel engines are flooded with sea water. They stall. The *U-210* is dead in the water, bobbing wounded and broken on the waves. It is now at the mercy of the ocean and the Canadians. But the Germans don't give up. With handguns and rifles they pour onto the sub's deck and continue the fight with the destroyer. Seaman Earl Costello grabs a .5-inch machine gun and peppers the sub with bullets, preventing any of the Jerries from reaching their forward guns. Then the *Assiniboine* rams the enemy again. The Germans throw their guns overboard and the battle is over. As soon as the order is given to abandon ship, the Germans scuttle the *U-210*, putting an explosive charge in the periscope shaft before surrendering. With hands raised, the remaining Germans climb up on the sub's deck through the forward hatch. Within two minutes there is an explosion and the sub sinks.

The *Assiniboine* has suffered major damage. Twenty of the crew are injured but, miraculously, only one crew member is dead. Medical Officer Johnstone and Norman Leckie are still working at a frantic pace.

Chapter 6
The Sinking of *U-94*, Canadian Style

I t's a balmy August and the year is 1942. There is a lull in the fighting off Iceland. Most of the U-boats are down off the US eastern seaboard. The convoy system of Canada and Britain has proven extremely effective against the U-boats, so the Germans have begun to focus on single American ships, finding them easier targets.

On August 25, the HMCS *Oakville*, a Canadian Flower Class Corvette-K178, zigzags on the port quarter of Convoy TQW-15. She has been ordered on escort duty with two other Canadian corvettes, the HMCS *Snowberry* and the HMCS *Halifax*. The convoy is also escorted by the Dutch *Jan Van Brackel* and by three small patrol craft of the US Navy. The command ship of this escort group is the powerful USS *Lea*, a destroyer.

By August 27 the group is slightly south of Haiti. Germany knows exactly where they are. So does Oberleutnant Otto Ites, commander of *U-94*. Ites is 24 years old and has served four years in U-boats. He has already sunk over 100,000 tons of shipping in this war and is thirsty for more. Back in April, Adolf Hitler had awarded him the Knight's Cross of the Iron Cross. He is proud of his accomplishments and is a challenging adversary. Ites is admired by his crew as a fighter and is personally well-liked. They call him "Onkel Otto." The Allies have other names for him, and no captain in a merchant ship wants to know that the Onkel is tracking his ship across the ocean.

On August 28, 1942, with only the sub's conning tower visible, Ites is stalking the convoy, closing the gap at dead-slow speed off their port bow. Gebeschus, his executive officer, is on the bridge with him. Ites quietly assesses the three escort ships, which are pacing restlessly back and forth in front of those tantalizing tankers he has crept four kilometres to destroy. He can taste the victory and yearns to see smoke and flames billowing skyward. Ites decides that by sneaking around the edge of the leading corvette, the HMCS *Snowberry*, he will have a clear target. Another ship to add to his list of kills.

It's a clear night, with a tropical wind force of four — residue from an earlier squall. Whitecaps are still apparent, and while the storm has all but blown itself out, the sea is still very rough. Most of the crews on the Canadian ships are lightly clad due to the humidity and those sleeping below decks have stripped down to their shorts. The HMCS *Oakville*'s first lieutenant, K.B. Culley, keeps his eyes on the surface whitecaps in the heavy swell. There is no reason to expect trouble but he senses the nearby sub and keeps a diligent watch for a telltale periscope.

Ites in the *U-94* estimates the convoy's speed at about 10 knots and orders an intercept course, decreasing speed to three knots. He decides that the tankers would be easy targets for his torpedoes, if it wasn't for the weaving *Snowberry*. Ites watches the escorts' movements and realizes that the *Snowberry* and the *Oakville* are zigzagging in tandem. And the *Snowberry* is staying on one leg of the zigzag for at least three minutes. He calculates the *Snowberry*'s next turn and cuts as close to the corvette as possible. He plans on slipping into the gap between the two Canadian ships, swinging around once clear, then firing on the fully loaded tankers.

Ites decides to ignore the small US Navy patrol craft darting between the escort ships, since it is a small threat. So intent is he on the corvettes and the manoeuvres around his intended targets, Ites doesn't see the US Navy's Catalina circling in the air above. But the pilot sees the U-boat. Its conning tower is in the silver path of the moon's light, looking black and threatening against the ocean. The aircraft circles and dives in quickly. The pilot knows a U-boat only needs 30 seconds to dive, so surprise is his best bet.

The Sinking of U-94, Canadian Style

"Bombs away!" the order is yelled. Pulling up and away, the Catalina banks to watch the show. Ites curses when he hears the engines of the aircraft above and sees the bomb doors open in silent slow motion. As death drops from above, Onkel orders the *U-94* to dive, but it is too late. The bombs explode in a perfect straddle, three charges on both sides of the conning tower. The *U-94*'s stern is blown high into the air, destroying her aft diving planes, which keep the U-boat level while on top of the water. Like a stranded fish gasping for air, the U-boat flounders for a moment in the waves as the victorious aircraft drops marker flares. The *U-94*, despite her wounds, continues to dive.

Sub-Lieutenant Graham Scott is the officer of the watch on the *Oakville*'s bridge. He hears the explosions as columns of white froth erupt into the night sky. He yells down the pipe, "Action stations!" And Lieutenant Commander Clarence King immediately orders full speed ahead and alters course toward the flares. The little *Oakville* jumps on top of the waves and races after the enemy.

The urgent jangle of the action-station bells on the *Oakville* jerks the crew from sleep, but the pitching of the ship under full engines ahead makes it difficult for them to rush up to the deck to their battle stations. Those who try to get into battle dress quickly give up the struggle and land on deck in whatever attire they were wearing to bed. Swarming up the ladder, the bridge crew push and shove past each other. There's a battle, and all of them want in on the action.

First Lieutenant Lawrence bursts into the asdic shack in time to see Leading Seaman Hartman shoving the cruising watch operator out of the seat and taking his place at the headset. All that can be seen of the plumes of water from the aircraft's depth-bombs is a rainbow mist in the moonlight. The last of the black conning tower is disappearing below the surface. Hartman swings the transmitter to the bearing of the depth-bombs' splashes. Ping ... sounds the oscillator. The sonar searches outward, the sound waves are coming back fainter and fainter.

Hartman swings his set to the right. Ping ... again, then the echoes fade. He swings his set to the left, trying to get a steady bead on the German sub below them. The aircraft above is using Morse code flashes in the night sky with a signal light. The pilot is watching the shadow of the black death as it descends to the ocean depths, and is letting all the ships know where the threat is headed. A lone marking flare drifts down in the night sky, and more than 100 sets of eyes watch it intently. The crew holds their breath and waits minutes that seem years long. Below them hides a U-boat, stalking the convoy. With their noses to the air, faces to the wind, the Canadians are waiting too, waiting for the wolf to pounce and give away his location.

"Fire a five-charge pattern when we cross the spot where those depth-bombs landed." The captain's quiet orders on the *Oakville* break the silence. Lieutenant Commander Clarence King had won a Distinguished Service Cross in World War I for sinking one U-boat and getting two probable kills. He's anxious for his first kill in this war, and, as all the great Canadian captains do, he attempts to think like the commander on the sub. He glances nervously over the waves toward the rest of the convoy. In his mind he sees the distance and location of each ship, and pictures the U-boat under the water. Which tanker will it go for first?

King orders a drop of five depth charges set to 30 metres. Whompff! ... The ship jumps, recoiling from the release of the explosives. The engines are gunned and the *Oakville* leaps on top of the waves to put distance between her and the charges. King knows he's shooting in the dark, and he knows that the charges will probably only keep the sub down. But if the sub stays down then the tankers are safe for the time being, as the sub needs to surface to fire torpedoes. Of course, no one will be totally safe until that German U-boat is put to rest for good.

The *Oakville*'s asdic is silent. The crew tenses, hearts beating as one. With a rumble the bombs explode. Water erupts to masthead height as the *Oakville* bucks, lurches, and trembles. The crew jumps into action like a well-oiled machine. King feels the hull groan and twist and mentally he strokes his ship. "Easy, girl," he whispers in the dark.

Hartman is sweeping for contact on the asdic, trying to ignore the activity and focus on his task. He swings to the right — ping. Before the reverberations die out there is a low drumming note in Hartman's earphones — the throb of turbines. He stands up and intuitively swings the oscillator further to

73

the right. He breaks into a huge grin. The low drumming in his earphones changes to a clamour as the submarine blows her ballast tanks. The *U-94* is surfacing. "We've got her!" Hartman yells. "The bugger is surfacing! The chase is on!"

The captain smiles. "There's the bastard!" he shouts. The black snout of the U-boat rears out of the boiling water ahead with water cascading off her deck as she swings left. The conning tower slices through a swell, glimmering ethereally in the silver moonlight. The Canadians feel a collective shiver and then brace for the spring.

King swings the corvette around to ram the sub. Rivets pop and the hull strains in a curve so tight the crew thinks King must ride motorcycles on land. "Load and fire starshell!" the captain commands. Flares light up the night sky, prompting the escorts to madly gather together the convoy. They know the flare means a U-boat is in the vicinity and they group their herd and move them out of harm's way.

King orders his first lieutenant to prepare to ram the U-boat and to get ready to shore-up the bulkheads after the impact. The submarine manoeuvres to pass closely under the ship's bow, to prevent being rammed. King has other ideas. "Hard-a-port!" he yells, racing the Germans for the turning space. But the sub arrives there first, and with only 30 metres to manoeuvre in, the *Oakville* can't make the turn. King curses. The *U-94* crashes down the port side of the Canadian corvette, grinding and bouncing off the hull. Onkel shakes his head at the determination of the small craft.

The Canadian crew lets fly the bullets at the bow of the submarine. King alters to starboard to once again try to widen the gap for ramming, and to give the guns room to fire. The guns roar out again and again, spitting fire and explosives at the German threat. The crew cheers above the booming of the guns and the throbbing of the engines. A shell explodes on the conning tower of the sub and the Canadians' enthusiasm grows.

The red tracer increases from the *Oakville*, ricocheting at wild angles off the thick hull of the *U-94*. Machine guns add to the cacophony and small arms begin firing at the U-boat, preventing the Germans from manning any of their guns. The corvette's bow swings around again. Ites knows what's coming and orders a turn to counter the *Oakville*'s swing into a ramming position. Onkel can't believe the bulldog tenacity of this small ship, trying time after time to ram the German steel without fear for her own safety.

Increasing the sub's speed, Ites dodges the corvette's movements yet again. He passes to the starboard of the *Oakville* under a hail of bullets. With precision and speed, the German gunners pour out of the forward hatch and make for their weapons. They are picked off one by one. The Canadians focus their attention on the Germans' 88mm deck gun. The gun starts to wiggle, then it rocks, and smoke starts to curl around it. Finally it topples into the water with a splash, followed by the cheering of the *Oakville* crew. But Ites manoeuvres the *U-94* with skill, gaining speed away from the corvette.

King gives chase in a rivet-popping, hull-bending turn that sends everything that is not tied down careening below like unguided missiles. Dishes smash and men hang on for dear life. Gaining momentum, the *Oakville* rams the U-boat, striking her a glancing blow on the starboard side. The *U-94* passes six metres off and down the port side of the corvette.

Stationed behind the ship's smokestack, six stokers who have not had a part in this battle decide that watching is just not good enough. Dragging out a box of glass pop bottles, the men start yelling curses at the Germans, who are only feet away. They throw the empties at the U-boat. In shock, the Germans stare at these madmen and duck. They're too stunned to shoot at the bottle throwers but are forced to avoid the glass that is smashing onto the deck of their sub.

King orders an additional depth charge and this one explodes directly under the *U-94*. The sub bucks and tosses about like a bull at a rodeo. For a few seconds the ocean spray obscures her from view, splattering the *Oakville* with salty foam. The U-boat slows and wallows in the kicking surf. King orders the corvette to swing out, and the *Oakville* revs her engines and leaps forward, ramming the U-boat squarely behind the conning tower. The corvette's bow rears up with the impact and she cries out from the wound. The *U-94* rolls uselessly in the waves. Beneath the bottom of the ship, the *Oakville* feels three distinct shocks, and the vessel jars. A ripping of metal is heard throughout the ship as the sub gashes the *Oakville*'s hull. The No. 2 boiler room on the little corvette and the lower asdic compartment both flood. The crew struggles to get the flooding under control. The *U-94* wallows astern and stops, sloshing backwards and forwards. Both vessels are severely damaged. The guns continue to send a steady stream of fire, with bullets winging off the sub at wild angles. Tracer is glowing white-hot in an uninterrupted stream.

The battle isn't over yet. King intends to capture the U-boat and orders a landing party on board the floundering submarine. Obediently, the men slide down the ladder and scramble for their gear. Seaman Harold Lawrence, in his haste to join the battle, is clothed only in his life belt and underwear.

When the 12 crew members muster on the port side the gun is silent as they prepare to leap onto the deck of the crippled submarine. The party thinks that the *Oakville's* gun has been silenced for their leap, but in fact the gun has misfired and First Lieutenant Culley is trying to clear the jam. He discharges the shell, throws it over the side, reloads, and swings the muzzle over close to Lawrence's right ear — just as Lawrence and Powell are leaning over the rail preparing to leap. One startled look over their shoulders at the sound of the gun swivelling, and the boarding party scuttles for safety. "Fire!" Whompff! The ship jumps with recoil.

The blast blows Lawrence and Powell onto the deck below. Momentarily stunned, they get back up, and in spite of bleeding noses and bruises, they spring into the air and onto the heaving German submarine. The waistband on Lawrence's underwear snaps on impact. Stunned by the shell blast, he kicks his shorts off and stands naked and glowing white in the moonlight. Lawrence and Powell are the only two who make it onto the sub. Suddenly a wave surges over the casing, washing Lawrence over the side. Powell reaches out and grabs him by the life belt, dragging him back onto the deck of the sub.

The crew of the *Oakville*, highly excited by the frenzy of the battle, rain a hail of bullets on the sub from one end to the other. They don't realize they're shooting at their own crew members. Lawrence and Powell dive for cover. The bullets ricochet off the metal deck with a whizzing clunking sound while the pair, keeping as low as possible, make for the bridge. Powell wears a proud grin, Lawrence is wearing only a life belt.

Suddenly, a German steps out from behind the forward gun and pauses for a second at the sight of the two Canadians. Pumped with adrenaline, Lawrence hits him with his pistol barrel and knocks him into the waves. Rounding the conning tower, they're confronted by two more Germans emerging from the hatch below. The Canadians rush forward, surprising the enemy in more ways than one. One German takes a horrified look at Lawrence's lack of clothing and instantly jumps into the smashing sea. Powell rushes the other and kicks him over the side to join his shocked crew mate, who is treading water close to the doomed U-boat.

The Sinking of U-94, *Canadian Style*

Soon the two lone Canadians find themselves surrounded by 26 Germans, all pouring out from below. The
Canadians have the only pistols, but only one Canadian
has clothes on. At this point, even with the guns, Lawrence
begins to feel he's at a disadvantage. He debates whether or
not to borrow a German uniform, but he dismisses the idea
as unpatriotic.

Powell herds the submariners to the after gun-platform,
which is pocked by bullet holes. The forward end of the
bridge is crumpled from the ramming and the hatch is stuck
open at about 50 degrees. Lawrence slides over a body, wrig-
gles underneath the hatch, and drops down into the guts of
the U-boat to see if anything can be salvaged. It is a waste of
time, as the Germans have already scuttled the dying U-boat
and destroyed its important papers. Lawrence climbs back
out. The U-boat rolls, then rolls again, and the watertight
bulkhead gives way as Lawrence quickly orders everyone into
the water. The *U-94* sinks a short time later.

The USS *Lea* is combing the area looking for survivors and
is signalled by King to rescue the boarding party as well. King
is now temporarily stopped by the *Oakville*'s flooded engine
room, and is on minimal power. The *Lea* collects 21 Germans.

Lawrence is pulled from the water, still wearing only
his life belt. The American crew aren't sure if he is German or
Canadian. Quickly, Lawrence resorts to some salty Canadian
slang to convince his American rescuers that he is from the
Oakville and not part of the U-boat's crew.

79

"We figured you had to be Canadian," one seaman responds. "No self-respecting German would ever be caught out of uniform."

The *Oakville* sends out a dinghy to pick up Petty Officer Powell along with five German prisoners. Oberleutnant Otto Ites has three bullet wounds, but he is one of the rescued. Nineteen of the German crew are never found.

No injuries are reported from the flying bottles.

Lawrence is issued a new uniform.

Chapter 7
Tribal Kill

The naval grapevine talks about the Tribal Class Destroyers as being slow and under-gunned. The crews of the HMCS *Haida* and the HMCS *Athabaskan* don't agree. The Tribals, they argue, have more guns than River Class Destroyers, and at least seven times the firepower of an ordinary destroyer, if not more. They are often referred to as pocket cruisers, and by the end of World War II, the *Haida* is one of the most celebrated ships in Canadian history. Lieutenant Commander Henry "Harry" George De Wolf is the commander of the *Haida*, and John Stubbs (previously the captain of the *Assiniboine*) is now commanding the *Athabaskan*.

The ships' companies come from every province in Canada. As each new recruit arrives on board, a familiar cry is heard. "Anyone here from the west?" And in salty language someone answers, telling him what they think of the west. A similar query is raised about the east, and again a strong voice yells out what they can do with the east. A good-natured argument then breaks out, and the air buzzes with typical seamen's banter, as friends recognize friends and homesick Canadians compare hometowns and talk of loved ones.

The Tribals are more than just fighting ships to the homesick Canadians. These ships are the saltys' homes, and they're run like a village. All on board put the ship first, their mates second, and themselves last — in true Canadian naval tradition.

The mascot on the *Athabaskan* is a ginger cat who walked up the gangplank one sunny afternoon and has run the ship from that day forward — as only a cat can do. The ship's crew have named her "Ginger," of course. And, although they call her a she, Ginger is a he.

On the *Haida*, the mascot is a small scruffy terrier-like dog with a wet tongue and a wagging tail. The gun crew picked him out from a litter while on shore leave, once they got the okay from the officer of the day (ODO) for a "purebred Airedale pup." The pup is anything but a purebred. However the ODO, himself a dog-lover, tweaked the pup's ear and agreed to have him on board in spite of his dubious parentage. The pup quickly let the ship's two ducks and Angora rabbit know who's boss.

One afternoon, as the *Haida* was being refuelled at

sea, the hose from the tanker that was fuelling bunker "B" came loose. Oil fuel sprayed high in the air and covered the deck and the dog in a black sticky mess. The ship's doctor scrubbed up the wretched animal, and the dog was given the name "Bunker B."

Now, as the ship is standing by, Bunker B (still in late puppyhood) stands with his head cocked to one side, growling at his favourite toy, a leather glove. He is getting saltier every day; he stands completely still during inspection, and knows to bark aggressively at the officers. The gun crew are his gods and he follows them faithfully.

The HMCS *Haida* is part of the 10th Destroyer Flotilla, referred to as Force 26. The ships in this group are the cruiser *Black Prince* and the Canadian Tribal Destroyers *Haida*, *Huron*, and *Athabaskan*, as well as the British destroyer HMS *Ashanti*. Force 26 is one ship short, as the *Tartar* is under a refit. The remaining ships are at port waiting for orders.

Shortly after tea, the captain's sea boat comes alongside the *Haida*. Captain De Wolf climbs up the ladder and retires to his quarters. "Cooks to the galley" is piped earlier than usual, confirming a rumour of an upcoming mission. All hands eat an early supper at 5:30 p.m. The time for sleeping and relaxation is over now. Throughout the ship there is a quiet sense of preparation against the night that is approaching. This is the final harbour hour, and many spend it writing letters home.

"Special sea duty men" is piped at 6:45 p.m., and "Hands fall in" is piped 10 minutes later. The waiting is over.

Each division lines up on deck. The captain climbs up to the bridge, dressed in his sea gear. With a quiet command, the mooring to the buoy is slipped. As the ship swings, obedient to her engines and rudder, she turns down harbour. The sea boat, still alongside, is hooked onto a rope hanging down from hinged booms davits (hinged booms) and is swung up and hoisted on board. As her crew climbs out onto the main deck, the davits are swung inboard and snugged down.

It's always an interesting passage going out from Plymouth. The waterway is narrow, with the shores very close. Sea birds wheel above. Those on board watch the people walking along the shore, a few wave, and the seamen wave back.

The *Haida* passes the signal station, a low, flat-roofed structure perched on a hilltop. The hands come to attention as the pipe for "Still" sounds, and then the men on deck stand easy as the ship motors swiftly by. Bunker B stands still, too, and only his lip curls when the officer walks by. The officer frowns at the dog. The gun crew hide their smiles.

The wind is freshening now as they near the seagate (an anti-submarine net across the harbour suspended by cables). Boats patrol outside the gates and all vessels are checked before the nets are rolled back to allow access to the harbour. Over to port, behind the net, the waiting cruiser slips her moorings to escort them through.

Clear of the seagate, the crew look to catch their last glimpse of the harbour. Each man tries not to think of this being their last sight of "home," but the thought is never too far from their minds. The sunset lights the rooftops and windows with the last colours of the day. Soon England, blacked out for war, will be nothing more than a lump of darkness. Ahead of the ships are the blackened seas of the wind-whipped Channel and the enemy coastline.

The night's work begins and the crew are suddenly too busy to think of shore. Guns and ammunition are checked and re-checked. The Kaaa-thump! of the pom-pom is heard as it opens fire. Then the Oerlikon gunners, targeting the bursts of the pom-pom shells in the evening skies, open fire with tracer on the English side of the Channel. Soon they will be crossing too close to the enemy lines for such attention-drawing displays.

The deadlights on the ships are screwed down on portholes. Hatches are closed and thick canvas curtains are drawn into place across all openings to the deck as the ship travels in blackout conditions. Every man off duty heads below to sleep. When action stations are sounded at 10:30 p.m. they know there will be no rest for any of them until dawn.

Force 26 sails southward across the Channel toward the French coast. "Give me a hand chum," says a westerner to Able Seaman Norman Goodale as he attempts to get a lammy coat (a large overcoat) over his bulky life jacket. It's a tough task under the best of conditions, but the sea air is damp tonight and the lammy keeps sticking to the life jacket. Heavy underwear, thick socks, sweaters, life jackets, ear protectors, anti-flash hoods, steel helmets, lammy coats, and other paraphernalia are being shrugged and strapped on by all the crew. This is for warmth and not meant to be worn in case of a dumping in the ocean. However, warmth is necessary and in the case of an emergency most of this will be easily and quickly peeled away.

Bunker B dances around the men of the *Haida* while they get ready. Red tells him to stay in his bed and keep out of trouble. The men have already made him a hammock, and they promise to find him a life jacket and a helmet when they find the time. Bunker B doesn't understand the words, but he wiggles and wags and drools over the attention.

The buzzers sound their insistent clamour throughout the ship. "Show time," Able Seaman Norman Goodale announces to anyone within earshot. At first Bunker B refuses to be left behind as the hands climb out to the dark decks. Red grabs the dog and hands him over to a rating (a seaman) to confine in a safe place. "Keep him in the Transmitting Station, chum," he requests, "and keep him safe."

Along the decks men are moving swiftly. Magazine hatches are opened, fire-control squads close hatches to sections that will not be in use, and the ship is readied for action. Tensions increase, and men watch the waves nervously.

Up on the bridge the captain, the action officer of the watch, the signalmen, and the gunnery, torpedo, and observer officers are all alert and ready. The captain is the only man who seems calm, sipping a cup of the infamous kye. The different stations all over the ship report to the bridge crew that all is secure and ready. The captain gives the stand-by order and, as they close in on the enemy coastline, the small force of Allied ships is alert and on guard.

Visibility is good, about three-and-a-half kilometres. It's a dark, moonless night, which is ideal for keeping a low profile, but makes it difficult to keep track of the other ships in the group. The *Haida*, with the *Athabaskan* close astern, forms the starboard sub-division of Force 26. The *Black Prince* is on their port side, with the *Huron* and the *Ashanti* forming the port sub-division a bit farther afield.

At 1:00 a.m. a shore light is sighted along the coast of France. Ten minutes later a shore searchlight is spotted from the Ile de Batz lighthouse, raking the dark sky with its ominous beam. "Must be looking for planes," remarks the navigator to no one in particular. A while later, a flash of gunfire is seen, but so far there is no indication that the Canadian ships have been spotted. A few minutes later, another shore light and more flashes of gunfire. The senior officer in the cruiser orders a course change to put more ocean between the ships and the enemy coast.

Ping ... Ping ... Ping ... ships appear on radar and they are heading right for Force 26. "Increase speed to 30 knots for intercept!" the captain orders, and the *Haida* and the *Athabaskan* rev the turbines to close in on the enemy destroyers. The German destroyers head full-speed away and the chase eastward begins. Stokers and engine-room artificers are kept busy, and the throbbing increases as the

Unsung Heroes of the Royal Canadian Navy

ships cut through the waves. Excitement replaces anxiety. The order for action stations sounds, and gun crews wait impatiently for the order to open fire. The ammunition hoists below decks are loaded and ready, and with the engines providing a battle cry, the warriors are all in place.

The sharp crack of the *Black Prince* cruiser's gun spits flame and breaks the darkness first. Starshell burst above in an umbrella of white stars, illuminating the enemy at 4000 metres. The destroyers rush the enemy at full speed, and the hum of the turbines rises to a scull-cracking whine as the ships race through the seas. The *Haida* moves in fast with the *Athabaskan* close astern. Ginger the cat has found a nice perch on the bridge of the *Athabaskan* to watch the action, and the crew see it as a good omen.

The Canadian Tribals' job is to engage the enemy, and the *Haida*'s bridge crew searches the seas intently after the starshell bursts. The Germans have laid a smoke screen, cutting down visibility in the dark night. Cautiously, the destroyers close in. Whoompff! The enemy opens fire. Starshell of their own breaks the dark of the night, and shells whiz overhead, sploshing in the cresting seas on the far side of the two Canadian ships.

"Shoot to the left! To the left!" signals the *Haida* to the *Black Prince*, and the cruiser corrects the range and fires starshell again, high into the air. There's a tense moment and the starshell bursts again, flooding the horizon with an eerie light.

88

"There they are! There they are!" And dotted black against the horizon are three, possibly four, enemy destroyers travelling east under a smoke screen. The time is 2:26 a.m.

"Open fire!" says the captain. "Commence! Commence! Commence!" Well-oiled hoists slam into place, loaded with ammunition as the hatches below the guns are opened.

"Load! ... Load! ... LOAD!!" Whoomff! Fire leaps from the muzzle of the gun as the *Ashanti* jerks from the recoil. It's a hit on the left-hand German ship. Whoomff! Another hit. The *Black Prince* opens fire from "A" turret, while continuing to use "B" turret for starshell to keep the fleeing Germans within sight. The pungent smell of cordite mingles with the night air as the *Haida* opens fire with "A" and "B" guns. As the ship heels with the recoil, the crew are sure they can feel the hull bend from the power of their guns.

The track of the four shells from the *Haida's* two forward guns blazes a bright trail in the night sky. The bridge crew watch in fascination as the shells arch across the expanse of ocean toward the enemy ships. The *Black Prince* is now firing steadily, and so are the *Haida, Huron, Ashanti,* and *Athabaskan.* The enemy ships turn around and open fire on Force 26. The sounds of whizzing shells and spattering ocean fill the air, punctuated by the return fire from the Canadian ships as they close in on the enemy. The German destroyers swing away and open up their engines to find refuge behind their smoke screen.

"A hit! A hit!" the crews on the Allied ships yell as a glow of flame bursts on an enemy ship, visible even through the smoke. A second hit is spotted on another enemy ship. The Tribals race full-speed ahead, straight at the enemy. Suddenly, the sky turns black as the "B" gun turret on the *Black Prince* becomes silent. The Allied ships are too close. The cruiser swings seaward to clear herself. The Germans take advantage of the break and fire a number of torpedoes. The captain of the *Black Prince* orders hard-a-port, and a torpedo passes on her starboard side. More torpedoes are sighted and the *Black Prince* shoots north full-speed ahead to avoid being hit.

De Wolf, on the *Haida*, is now in command of the destroyers. Illumination is ordered from the *Athabaskan* for the *Haida*, and from the *Ashanti* for the *Huron*. All four ships continue shelling the Germans.

At 3:00 a.m., the enemy destroyers finally emerge from their smoke screen for a moment, and dive back into it again. The *Haida* signals to everyone to watch for torpedoes. Following the contour of the coastline as close as possible, the *Haida* and the *Athabaskan* find themselves close to the enemy's smoke screen. As the coastline veers south, they pull ahead of the *Huron* and the *Ashanti*. Shore batteries open up and the *Huron* and the *Ashanti* are soon engaged while all four Tribals continue firing on the enemy ships ahead. The two groups close in and the fight becomes personal, heightening to a ship-on-ship battle.

The Germans run, ducking right through a known minefield and the Tribals follow them with teeth-clenching determination. Up ahead are the islands of Sept Iles. Tense and alert, the *Haida*'s bridge crew watch for the Jerries' next move. The navigator is keeping a close eye on the charts for sunken rocks close to the shore. Shore batteries are hammering away, so the captains of the ships keep their vessels just out of reach. Navigators are worth their weight in gold during battles such as this. Without their keen eyes, concentration, and ability to ignore the booming guns and the battle all around them, ships could easily land helplessly on rocks.

Up ahead, the smoke screen looks as if it's thinner. As the crews of the Tribals watch, they catch a glimpse of something at the edge of the smoke screen that looks like a ship attempting to double-back. It's a fleeting glimpse, followed by a pause in shooting. The *Haida* takes a chance and darts closer, altering course for her "X" gun mounting to fire starshell. Whoompff! The ship jumps. Well-aimed, the first burst falls directly over and behind the target, casting a shadow of the ship on the cloud of smoke like shadow puppets on a sheet.

Streaking out, clear of the smoke screen, a German destroyer makes a run for it, trying to come around behind the Canadians and pin them between the guns of their other ships. A German Ebling (E-boat) turns broadside to the *Haida* and attacks, giving the other German ships a clear path. The *Haida* signals a 90 degree turn to starboard, ordering the other two Tribals to keep the Germans contained while the *Athabaskan* and the *Haida* turn to face the enemy. The *Haida*'s guns swing and aim steadily on the target up ahead.

The bridge crew of the *Athabaskan* watches intently as the drama of the moment unfolds before them in the eerie light of the starshell mixing with drifting smoke. One moment the enemy is in plain view, speeding along, then the *Haida's* guns crash with salvo after salvo, hiding the night sky and filling the sea breeze with the stench of explosives. There's smoke. There's confusion. There are flames shooting from the guns ...

The first series of shells is a direct hit, catching the E-boat amidships, about three metres below her main deck. The plates crumple like tinfoil. The explosives carve their path through the steel, exploding inside the guts of the ship. A shell crashes aft below deck level, another below the bridge, and finally one smashes into her behind the first.

Great geysers of steam rise from the enemy destroyer amidships. She slows and stops. Red tongues of fire leap into the sky from where the shells hit, quickly exploding into a blazing inferno on her main deck.

The *Athabaskan's* shells are also smashing through the bows and fires break out there as well. Across the flame-lit expanse of water between the Canadian ships and the burning German destroyer, only a few metres away, the Canadians can hear the roar and hiss of escaping steam. The Tribals circle, closing in for the kill.

Meanwhile, the *Huron's* and the *Ashanti's* prey has escaped, so they turn around to join the battle. A group of survivors attempt to escape the burning E-boat on a life raft, but with German guns still being fired at the Tribals, the *Haida* has no choice but to continue the battle. A salvo, intended to strike below the waterline, crashes into the enemy's crippled hull and sends the raft and the men hurtling skyward. It sobers the crew, and while they pause their barrage on the enemy, the German guns jump to life again. The bullets whiz overhead, causing the Canadians on deck to duck. Finally, the enemy guns fade out and only the roar and crackle of the flames can be heard from the E-boat. The silhouettes of Force 26 show like black shadows against the fire-lit horizon.

As the Tribals circle, high on the bridge of the mortally wounded German ship, a lone gunner lets off a few more rounds. Streaking across the narrow gap, the tracer sweeps along the *Haida*'s length. Shooting from a position amidships, with flames dancing around him and shells whizzing past, the lone German gunner makes a gallant last stand, forcing the men on the Tribals to take cover. His shells hit the *Huron*'s bridge and upper rigging, smashing the port navigation lights and the port side of the stoker's mess. Another shell shoots away the pom-pom feed rail, killing Leading Seaman Gosnell on the *Athabaskan* and injuring four others.

Shore batteries open up on the group once again, but the *Black Prince* returns their fire, forcing them to cease. The guns of the Tribals fire repeatedly at the wreck, with a stream of coloured tracer zipping along the enemy's decks, ricocheting over her bridge and after structure. The guns on the E-boat, later identified as T-29s, finally lie silent. The lone gunner lies silent as well.

The Tribals close in for the final sinking. Shell after shell rips into the dead ship, sending up showers of sparks against the black masses of oily smoke billowing in the night. The white clouds of the smoke screen are replaced with a black cloud of death, and here and there on the darkened swells of the ocean, are a few scattered pools of brightly burning fuel. The Tribals alter course again for another round. But then, as they watch, the Ebling rolls to port. Her bow dips, and the fires sizzle, smoke, and sputter as she slips swiftly under the sea. From the *Haida*'s foredeck comes the sound of hoarse cheering as the gun crews watch her go. It's 4:20 a.m. Norman Goodale and the rest of the crew are triumphant. And a little sad.

The Tribals catch up to the *Black Prince* at daybreak, and Force 26 sets a course for Plymouth at 25 knots. It has been a successful night's hunting and all the ships sail into the harbour with battle ensigns flying. Several men have suffered minor wounds. Red proudly exhibits a grazed arm and Joe, the lad who intends to marry Sally, has a dented helmet and a bump on the head to show for his night's work. Goodale has escaped injury. And Bunker B? He hid out in the mess during the shooting.

The remaining damaged enemy ships have probably escaped into a protected port along the coast of France. It's a battle for another night, but another night is closer than any of the Tribals suspect.

Tribal Kill

The outcome of the battle soon to come will stagger most who witness it, and will be recorded in many history books ...

Chapter 8
White and Scarlet, "We fight as one"

As they sail up the harbour the Tribals are scrutinized with interest. The news of their successful battle reaches Plymouth before the ships arrive in port. Once they do arrive, ship after ship salutes them. The crews are happy. The sinking of a German E-boat is a milestone, and the *Athabaskan* and the *Haida* are proud to have been part of it. Bunker B rides on deck with the rest of the *Haida* gun crew, and in celebration, he has a red bandana around his neck.

"Have you dead or injured on board?" the harbour officer calls out.

"We have both," is the answer, and the crew watches in silence as the wounded and dead are taken off the docks by the waiting ambulances.

Dockyard mateys swarm aboard like mother hens to patch the holes that the enemy fire has made in the hull. They tighten the fittings that have been loosened by the vibration of high speeds, as well as the recoil shuddering caused by the firing of the ship's own guns. The crew on the *Haida* mentions the way the ship's hull seemed to bend in the rolling seas. They are told it will be reported and investigated at a later date.

Steam radiators had shaken loose of their fittings and fallen off the walls. Chunks of asbestos had vibrated off overhead pipes. Dishes, which had broken loose from lashed cupboards, lay broken on the decks. Hastily abandoned sea gear litters the deck among the salted swirls of dried sea water. It's a mess to clean up, but it could have been worse. A great deal worse.

Approximately 2100 rounds of ammunition have been fired, and it all needs to be replaced and stored in the proper magazines. Stores are brought on board, damaged equipment replaced, and the fuel bunkers filled. Bunker B watches all this excitement with interest. He seems to think that all the activity is for him as he trots through the soapy water when the ratings wash the deck. Soon the *Athabaskan* and the *Haida* are set to go back to sea.

The night before shipping out, the *Athabaskan* and the *Haida* are in harbour together, both tied to a buoy on which someone has painted "The Canadians." It has been a day of rest, writing letters and playing cards with the crew from the other ship. Late in the afternoon a heavy consignment of mail, parcels, and cigarettes from Canada reaches the ships, and most of the men spend their down time reading the news from home. The cat makes herself at home on both ships. And Bunker finds the gun crew of the *Athabaskan* just as friendly as his own. Time passes quickly until seven o'clock brings the order to slip.

It has been a fine day, a day of sunshine, a day with good company. The crews would have preferred another night in to get caught up on their sleep, but war has its own timetable, so it's grumble and go. The Coastal Forces mine-laying craft will be operating inshore in French waters tonight, and the two Tribals are ordered to watch their backs.

The *Haida* slips the buoy first, turning around and heading for the gate to the Channel. The *Athabaskan* has a little trouble getting clear and scrapes Number 6 Buoy as she swings around. This causes a slight delay, so she increases her speed to catch up. At the seagate the *Haida* slows to pass through. The *Athabaskan* slows and falls in behind.

Down on the quarterdeck a group of officers on the *Haida* are talking. A lieutenant, looking back at the *Athabaskan*, says she'll be lucky, she'll get back all right. He has a premonition of trouble. He figures that the *Haida*, being the lead ship, will draw most of the attention. "There should be more than two of us," grumbles another.

The *Athabaskan* and the *Haida* sail across the Channel as sisters, with a spirit between them that ships of war rarely experience. As they slowly separate before opening up the engines, the *Athabaskan*'s cat makes a vain effort to jump aboard the *Haida*. Petty Officers Gerald MacAvoy and John Manson of the *Athabaskan* grab the cat to stop it from falling overboard. Someone says, "That's not a good sign."

"For some strange reason," notes *Haida* petty officer George Goodwill, watching the cat with interest, "it's been coming over to our ship lately, and every time we gently toss it back."

"Not a good sign at all," says Norman Goodale.

Once they are surging across the Channel, all thoughts of foreboding are pushed aside as the ships make ready for the night's operation. They all know D-Day is coming, and hunting U-boats now will make the waters safe for the big invasion. With the lessons of Dunkirk fresh in everyone's mind, the Canadians take their orders very seriously.

When the Tribals arrive on the scene, the mine layers are already underway, using the darkness as cover. The weather is ideal for the operation. There is a clear sky, a waning moon to provide good visibility, and a smooth sea with a gentle swell.

The *Athabaskan*, reflecting the moonlight, looks like a ship of silver as she cruises. She is plainly visible. Like the *Haida*, her crew are ready for action. This is not a new task for the crew; mine laying is a common occurrence. But tonight ... tonight it's different. Call it intuition or a sailor's fancy, but there is something in the air that has the crews of both ships on edge. All are trying not to think of the night of August 27, 1943, when the *Athabaskan* was attacked and hit by 18 enemy Dornier-217s. HMS *Egret*, a British sloop, was sunk that night, and a glide bomb had hit the *Athabaskan*. She managed to sail into port under her own power but with a serious list to starboard. That night wasn't without casualties. And in this war, there are no guarantees.

On the bridge of the *Athabaskan*, Lieutenant Commander Stubbs is discussing battle plans with his first lieutenant, Robin Hayward. "I hope they come out," he says, referring to the German ships that escaped the previous night, "because we're ready and willing. I hate it when they disappear like that."

In the engine room below, Lieutenant Theodore Izard is thinking about his wife, Pam, now safely settled with his parents in Victoria, British Columbia. The two had met and married in Plymouth six months earlier. Now she's on the other side of the world waiting to start their new life together. "It shouldn't be long before *Athabaskan* goes to Canada," he says hopefully. "Admiral Nelles said it would be soon, and then we'll have a real honeymoon. Boy! What a day that'll be." He touches the picture of his bride and puts it lovingly in his breast pocket.

At 2:00 a.m. on April 29, the Tribals are in position and start patrolling. Radar is unreliable for some unknown reason, and all watches visually rake the waves for any sight or sound of enemy ships. German ships have been reported to be travelling westward at 20 knots between St. Malo and

Roche Douvres. The Canadians are ready for them, both crews anxious for a rematch.

Up on *Haida*'s bridge, De Wolf stands alone with binoculars in his hands. Some distance away, on his right, with head and shoulders silhouetted in the moonlight, is the officer of the watch. The two are silent as their eyes study the coastline. De Wolf looks nervously over at the sister ship, the *Athabaskan*. She is gleaming silver in the moonlight, and the captain knows that if she stands out to him, then she is in full sight of anyone onshore.

At 3:00 a.m. an officer from the bridge on the *Haida* comes aft and stops to have a cup of kye with the surgeon lieutenant in sick bay. "Quiet night so far," he informs the doctor. "We're about 20 metres off Ile de Bas. Should be heading home soon. I'll be glad when we do. I've had a hunch of trouble coming all night. Still, it's not likely anything will happen now," he adds and laughs nervously.

A second signal from Plymouth Headquarters at 3:07 a.m. orders the Tribals to intercept the enemy ships. The crews' senses heighten. New energy is put forth with the news. It's now obvious that they are heading in to finish the battle that was started a few nights ago. All hands are alert and at action stations. Hearts are pumping, and the ship and men become of one mind.

Bunker B, much to his disgust, has been banished to one of the seaman's quarters. They still haven't outfitted him with a life jacket as yet, and Norman Goodale hopes he will be okay.

The enemy ships are now in sight, and at 4:12 a.m., the *Haida* opens fire with starshell lighting up the sky. Two minutes later the *T-24* and *T-27* are sighted racing westward and the chase is on. "There they are!" someone yells. "Load! Load! LOAD!"

The Canadians open up with all guns in a wild chase after the enemy. The Jerries lay a smoke screen and regroup in its shelter while continuing to shoot torpedoes at the Allied ships. All the Allied torpedoes are pointed at the other German Ebling. The crews on the Tribals cheer, yelling that the German torpedo man must be on the side of the Allies.

The Germans hammer at the Canadians with their main guns. The *Athabaskan* seems to be the enemy's target. German starshell bursts over her and salvoes whiz through her rigging, splashing in the water around her. Lieutenant Commander Dunn Lantier, the radar officer, is informed by his radar operator that two objects starboard are heading in their direction and travelling fast. Thirty seconds later, explosions rock the Tribal, and John Laidler, the radar operator, is blown overboard by the force. When he rises to the surface of the water, he's coughing and choking on fuel. It's stinging his eyes and burning his throat. He tries to call out, but realizes that no one can hear him as the *Athabaskan* is 300 metres away and still moving. Even with fuel in his eyes, he can see that her "X" and "Y" guns are destroyed and that her gun crews are wiped out. Smoke is rising from her port side and something about the way she's riding the waves says she is in real trouble. Fortunately, Laidler finds a Kisbie buoy and clings to it. All he can do is wait in the frigid water and hope someone finds him as he watches his ship slow until she lies dead in the water with flames reaching into the night sky.

Meanwhile, unaware of her sister ship's plight, the *Haida* continues the chase, hammering on the fleeing enemy with her guns. From the bridge, Commander De Wolf is planning his next move when he gets word from Lieutenant Commander Stubbs, "We seem to be badly damaged aft."

The message is punctuated by German guns closing in for the kill. The *Haida* crew watch in horror until the torpedo control officer asks the captain, "Why don't we make smoke?"

As the *Haida* swings to starboard, a stoker crawls out on the afterdeck. Braving the blast from the "Y" guns he reaches up and opens the valve, turning on the chemical smoke producers. They work immediately. The *Haida* begins belching white clouds of chemical smoke, then circles the *Athabaskan*, desperately trying to provide cover for the Tribal. The *Haida* steers valiantly between her wounded sister and the enemy while attacking the Germans with enthusiasm. Her crew fires round after round until *T-24*, badly hit, limps to the east. The *T-27* breaks away to the south, with *Haida* on her trail.

During this time, the *Athabaskan* drifts at the mercy of the currents as her men work fiendishly to save her. The fire at the stern ignites the ammunition. Exploding shells and shrapnel fly in all directions. Smoke and flames reach hungrily into the sky, a beacon for the enemy. The *Haida*'s smoke screen helps some, but it fails to hide her sister ship completely. The shore batteries open up, and the *Athabaskan* becomes the target of a turkey shoot.

Even in the thick of the ammunition flying overhead, the well-trained men remain calm. With Canadian determination, every man is working to save the ship.

Lieutenant Commander Lantier then fires the last round of starshell from "B" gun. It's the last round ever fired from the broken ship.

There is feverish activity on the crippled ship's decks. Up forward, the bosun's party works frantically to rig the towing hawser. The 70-ton portable pump is pulled into position amidships. The feedline is hoisted overboard and several men make their way aft to fight the raging flames. The wounded are helped below for medical attention. On the bridge, Lieutenant Commander Stubbs is calmly giving orders. The *Athabaskan* is settling deeper into the water and her time is running out. Stubb sighs, then gives the order: "Prepare to abandon ship! All hands stand by their Abandon Ship Stations!"

The men proceed silently to their stations, scarcely able to believe the order they have just heard. A signalman's life jacket strap is loose and an officer bends over the man to snug it up for him. The captain remains on the bridge and watches them go. One of the men has the ship's cat. At the last second he jumps into the waves and is seen swimming toward the French coastline.

Suddenly, a torpedo rips into the hull of the floundering Canadian ship. First Lieutenant Lawrence, on his way to the bridge, is killed instantly. A horrific roar erupts as ammunition, fuel, and tanks explode, creating a huge blowtorch aimed skyward. It is nothing short of a holocaust. The deck tilts and then collapses as internal explosions blow it outwards with heat that melts the metal.

When it's over only one man on deck is still alive. A 19-year-old stoker, Ernest Takalo, is lying on the deck facing the bridge section. The flash burn lights up the entire deck. It is so bright, in fact, that Takalo can see the individual hair strokes from the paint job on the steel plating of the forecastle. Lieutenant William Clark, climbing down from the bridge to the signal deck, is hit with a ball of flame that scoops him overboard. Observers on the *Haida*, which is still pursuing the enemy, see a bright flash. They hear an incredible explosion, and with one voice they gasp at the funnel of flames and smoke. "My God," they cry, "It's the *Athabaskan!*"

The *Haida* shudders in the shock wave, and an escaped Bunker B, terrified by the noise and fear around him, leaps off the deck and into the waves, never to be seen again.

From No. 1 boiler back, the *Athabaskan* is a blazing inferno. What went up with the force of the explosion is now raining burning blobs of fuel on the survivors of the crippled ship. Men run, blindly screaming and beating at the flames landing on them from above. In desperation, many leap headfirst into the sea. The smell of burning of flesh is mixed with the stench of burning oil. And the sound of the crackling flames licking at the vessel is amplified by the sizzle of burning bodies meeting the cold ocean waves.

The ship lurches violently and most of those who are still on board tumble helplessly over the side. "Abandon ship! All hands abandon ship!" the captain yells hoarsely. The gunner's mate hears the order while he is leaning against a railing. He tries to vault over it into the water below, but his arm is broken in two places and won't support his weight. With blood streaming from a gash on his head he looks dumbly at the rail, trying to understand why he can't leap overboard. The ship heels over and he sits down heavily. Feeling queasy and slightly detached from the reality of the situation, he lies down and gravity slides him under the rail and into the sea.

Nineteen-year-old Seaman James Aikins is in the carpenter's shop when he hears the order. He can't escape, as the deck door is jammed tight. Running through the mess to the passageway, he reaches out to open the No. 2 boiler room door and it explodes in his hand. He is thrown backwards and drenched by a scalding spray of water, sustaining burns to most of his body. He slides down the guardrail and drops his scalded body into the frigid waters below. Fighting for consciousness, he manages to grab onto some debris. He clings to it for dear life.

"Abandon ship! Abandon ship!" That heart-stopping cry in the night — the blast of explosions, the sizzle of flesh,

White and Scarlet, "We fight as one"

and the smell of death — signals the end of the mighty and proud *Athabaskan.*

But what of her men?

Chapter 9
Abandoned Ship, Abandoned Survivors

S toker Robert Gracie and his shipmates waste no time in obeying the order to abandon ship. The HMCS *Athabaskan* is sinking. The shock is traumatic as the group hits the water, but the bold survivors swim valiantly away from the doomed ship. Stoker Gracie is swimming frantically. He can hear the main mast creaking and ripping, and he knows it's falling. Looking up, he sees it looming above him and with renewed strength he strikes out at the water. There's a mighty splash and a whoosh of water overtakes him, but the mast itself falls clear.

Almost completely engulfed in flames, the *Athabaskan* lists horribly and sinks deeper into the water. Chief Petty Officer William Mitchell is still aboard, pinned to the main deck by a heavy beam. Both legs are crushed, the pain is almost more than he can bear. He calls out but in the noise and confusion no one seems to notice him. Suddenly, Able Seaman Donald Newman and Leading Signalman Allen Thrasher appear out of the smoke like angels. They work feverishly, using a steel bar for leverage, and soon Mitchell is free and sliding over the side and into the water. Newman yells down at him apologetically as Mitchell hits the water. "That's all we can do for you," he says, then disappears back into the smoke. Using only his arms, with his legs drifting uselessly behind him, Mitchell pulls himself through the freezing ocean waves to a safe distance. Without a doubt, he knows that if he makes it, he'll owe his life to those two mates.

A group of men are frantically trying to activate the *Athabaskan's* motor launch when the pulleys jam. Able Seaman Russell Phillips crawls underneath to yank the launch loose. Pulling with all his might, he doesn't realize that there is nothing supporting the heavy boat. Suddenly it comes crashing down on him, breaking his arm and dislocating his shoulder. The others rally around and soon the boat is launched. Phillips is lowered gently over the side into the water.

In the forecastle of the *Athabaskan*, gobs of flaming fuel are raining down on Able Seamen Samuel Fillatre and Lester McKeeman, but they refuse to leave the area until they first get their gun captain, Leading Seaman "Buck" Parsons, safely over the side. Meanwhile, Able Seaman Laidler, continuing to hold tightly to his Kisbie buoy, watches the *Athabaskan* through her final ordeal. He hears the sounds of her destruction, as ruptured watertight bulkheads cave in under the deadly weight of water, and machinery tears away from normally secure bedplates. The *Athabaskan*, in her final death throes, cries like a child. And it feels to Laidler like he is watching a friend dying in agony. The ship had guarded and protected him from the very beginning. Now he is helpless to save her. Choked with emotion and grief, Laidler turns his face against the buoy and closes his eyes.

As the Tribal tilts slowly to a vertical position, gear and equipment begin to crash like stones and boulders cascading down the side of a mountain. Each and every item — pots, pans, and tools — clatters and bangs as it slides and tumbles. The great ship moans. And suddenly, above the cacophony, comes a loud and very distinctive crash. "There goes the piano!" shouts a voice in the darkness.

Now vertical, the ship seems to poise there a moment and then slips swiftly backwards, down into the encompassing waters with a sizzling hiss. The Tribal Class Destroyer disappears and darkness envelopes the sea and its survivors. Their ship, their home, their friend, is dead, sunk beneath the ocean she once ruled, to rest in its depths in a cold and watery grave. Only those trapped in her final moments keep her company.

While the *Athabaskan* endures her agony, the *Haida* loses no time in hunting down the enemy ships, which had fled in different directions. Harassed by the Canadian Tribal's fire, the *T-24* speeds eastward while the *T-27* makes off to the south. The *Haida* fires a direct hit and continues to fire unmercifully on the *T-27*. If her gunners had been fast before, they are fighting desperately now. "For the *Athabaskan!*" they yell as they load and fire.

"Another hit!" Flames leap high on the first German destroyer and it smoulders in the smoke. The second enemy ship slows and falls behind the first. Suddenly, in the heat of battle, the *Haida* is illuminated by a strange bright light, which is followed by a rumbling noise astern. Her frantic men above deck pause momentarily to look. It's too bright for starshell and their gaze is greeted by a deadly rising column of white smoke. Higher and higher it bursts from the sea, flames, smoke, and debris shooting into the air. "My God!" the crew of the *Haida* gasps. "There goes the *Athabaskan!*"

Able Seaman David Gold is stunned by the horrific sight, and he gazes in shock and disbelief, wondering at the holocaust that has destroyed his ship's sister. "We're next for sure," he groans to his shipmates. They turn and fight in earnest now, desperate to get the upper hand of the battle so they can begin to search for survivors.

The *Haida* is closing the gap between her and the German ship. The *T-27* is beginning to show the effects of the devastating shelling. Flames are leaping from her hull as the fleeing enemy comes dangerously close to the French coastline. Suddenly, without warning, she swings around toward the *Haida* in a bold attempt to escape the trap. But then *T-27* slows and stops completely, leaning to port at an even sharper angle than before. The grim rocky shores of Finistrere have caught her. She's run aground.

Realizing that further action is pointless and that the other German ship has escaped, Commander De Wolf orders a ceasefire and heads back to where the *Athabaskan* was last seen.

Disregarding the threat of enemy ships, De Wolf orders his illumination officer to fire one starshell for a better look at the situation. It reveals nothing. The *Athabaskan* is nowhere to be seen. As the flare dies out, scores of life jacket lights dot the waves. The mighty *Athabaskan* is nowhere to be seen. All that is left is a spattering of survivors fighting to stay alive, broken and freezing in the unforgiving Atlantic.

The crew of the *Haida*, stricken with grief, rushes to save the survivors.

The *Haida* eases gently into the mass of struggling seamen and stops. "We'll stop for 15 minutes, under orders from Plymouth," states the commander. Headquarters has ordered the *Haida* to leave by daybreak.

The sight imbeds itself on the rescuers. Men — friends — grouped in the waves below are yelling, blowing whistles, and shouting for the *Haida* to help them. For those on the ship's sides, it's possible to climb aboard using the scramble nets, but for those in front or in the rear, it's a different story. A light wind is causing the *Haida* to drift away faster than the men can swim to her, and rescue seems cruelly out of reach. The seriously wounded are helpless, at the mercy of others. Even the uninjured are having trouble making it to safety. The friendly ship's propellers are put in motion to manoeuvre closer and correct the drift, but they're shut down quickly and survivors are being sucked in by the mighty slicing of the screws.

Those not ordered to man the guns or keep watch above are forming lines to pull the men from the water. The deck is now smeared with oil, and everyone who has contact with the survivors is soon covered in it as well. The fumes are unbelievable, and injuries, burns, and cuts are instantly covered in the stinking, stinging, and sometimes smouldering fuel.

Leading Cook Bernard Laurin had thrown himself off the deck of the *Athabaskan* right before she sank. He had come up choking and gagging from the oil and salt water he had swallowed. Laurin swims as far from the wreck as possible. He rubs his eyes, trying to free them of fuel. He thinks briefly of his family and wonders how they will feel to hear that he went down with his ship. Then, with renewed vigour, he strikes out for a float. With burned and swollen fingers he grasps onto the side. If anyone survives, it will be him. He is determined not put his wife and family through the heartache if he can help it.

A few moments later, Lieutenant Commander Stubbs swims up to him. He says that he has been blown off the bridge. Laurin notices the captain's face and hands are burned, but otherwise Stubbs appears to be in reasonable condition. Then, out of the darkness, the *Haida* comes into view. "Swim for it, son," the captain orders, and Laurin swims until he is scooped up into friendly arms and ushered below deck to warm blankets and tots of rum.

Lieutenant William Clark and Sub-Lieutenant Robert Annett strike out from their Carley float when the *Haida* appears. Soon the exhausted men realize they can't make it to the ship. Grasping a cork net, Clark looks around for his companion and sees only water. Annett is nowhere to be seen. Clark realizes he is now among 14 other men. By dawn only four are left. In the pale light, Clark sees a nearby Carley float, swims over to it, and paddles back to pull the remaining three survivors off the cork net and into the raft, away from hypothermia and death.

Petty Officer George Casswell drifts away from the main group after a few hours in the water. Alone and giving up hope, he is unaware of the *Haida* and the rescue going on a short distance away. As his body temperature lowers, he experiences a feeling of warmth and well-being. Beyond exhausted, he starts thinking how nice it would be simply to let go and drift off to sleep. Thinking of his family gathering together for his memorial, he shocks himself awake. To fight off death, he starts reciting the Lord's Prayer over and over again.

Suddenly the *Haida*'s cutter appears and the half-frozen sailor is hauled aboard. "Canadian or German?" Casswell demands. "Cause if you're damn Nazis, then toss me back in the water."

"I assure you, we're Canadians. The *Haida* is right over there waiting for us to bring you in." Casswell smiles, then promptly collapses.

The men on the *Haida* who are ordered to stand by their battle positions, such as Petty Officer Fred Polischuk, watch the rescue going on below them with feelings of helplessness. Their friends and fellow Canadians need them. Yet, with daybreak kissing the night sky, they have to stay where they are in case of trouble. With every tick of the clock, the danger to all of them grows. Every last life raft, life jacket, and life boat, have been tossed overboard for the survivors. If attacked, the crew of the *Haida* will have to pray. Every single man left on board is well aware that there will be no surviving a sinking ship without that emergency equipment.

Hearing the men's desperate pleas, the rescuers increase their efforts. The minutes are ticking by, but there are so many men in the water. It's obvious to everyone that not all of them will be pulled aboard in time. The minutes slip by far too quickly and they work diligently against the threat of daylight. A rescue line of strong young hands and arms reaches out to grasp the oil-soaked survivors.

Lieutenant Commander Stubbs moves in amongst his men in the water. All he can do is offer them words of encouragement and inspire them to keep struggling against death. Swimming close to the nets on the lee side of the *Haida*, he looks up at the sky. Dawn is breaking. The ship is now vulnerable to shore batteries and German destroyers. He is filled with panic. "Get out of here, *Haida*! E-boats!" Again, he yells desperately to the *Haida*. "Do you hear me? Get the hell out of here!"

It is the last command he will ever give. John Hamilton Stubbs, the commander of the fated *Assiniboine*, and the last commander of the mighty *Athabaskan*, swims off into the awakening dawn and is never seen alive again.

Rough and ready sailors, with salty language and sea-hardened hands, gently cut clothing off the wounded, and tenderly wash fuel out of eyes and injuries. They spoon-feed hot liquids into the chilled, and rub down cold bodies, bringing back heat and feeling, and then cover them with blankets. More than one wipes away tears as friends who succumbed to the elements are brought on board, lifeless and still.

The 15 minutes comes and goes. De Wolf paces on the bridge, watching the horizon with nervous and anxious eyes. There isn't going to be enough time. With more sailors brought on board, and less emergency equipment available, one torpedo could bring catastrophe to all those they have rescued. Not to mention jeopardizing the life of his ship and his men. Bobbing lights, spread far and wide, show too many men still in the water. Men who might never make it. Shouting down encouragement, he glances for enemy ships, urging on the rescuers, yelling for the men to move faster ... swim harder ... haul up the injured quicker.

The first streaks of dawn are finally breaking through. Sunrise is moments away, and with every ticking minute, the *Haida* and the rescue operation become sitting ducks. Still, the captain orders five more minutes — five more precious minutes.

"I'll warn you every minute," he adds to the order. His compassion has won the moment, but common sense dictates that time has come to an end. The crew gets a short reprieve to collect as many survivors as possible. Then Plymouth and fate will have to decide what the next move will be.

Able Seaman Digby Deal is hauled aboard, oily and cold, but uninjured. He helps get Lieutenant Jack Scott safely on deck. But when the men start cutting away Scott's clothing, Digby bolts for the ocean. "Are you kidding?" yells the seaman as Digby scrambles down the net.

"My friend Moar is still out there and I can't leave him behind. I promised him." He jumps back into the waves and swims to a Carley float. Able Seaman Raymond Moar has a broken back. Without assistance he will never make it.

At the same time De Wolf calls out the minutes.

"Just one more moment," thinks Commander De Wolf to himself. But the *Haida*'s asdic operator notifies him of the possibility of approaching enemy craft. Commander De Wolf has no choice. "Slow ahead," he orders, staring straight ahead.

Men still in the water panic as the *Haida* starts up the engines. They are begging, pleading, yelling curses. Fighting for their lives, they swim to reach the nets and ropes still hanging off the side of the destroyer. Commander De Wolf has already disregarded three orders to leave the area. He now has absolutely no choice. He prays silently for those he leaves behind, knowing their cries from the still-darkened sea will haunt his nights forever.

The *Haida* trembles and vibrates as the turbines throb. Petty Officer H.P. Murray and Telegraphist S.A. Turner are still on one of the scramble nets trying to rescue the survivors as the ship starts to move. They look at the hands reaching out to them and grab for just one more. The ocean current around their legs gets stronger and, handing off the last of the survivors, they both struggle to unhook themselves from the nets. The waves are now waist high, and the force is making it impossible to climb up. Hands from above reach down, gripping ... pulling ... tugging ... but it's no use. The *Haida* picks up speed and suddenly the rope breaks. The wake surges over the two men and washes them straight into the turning screws.

The handful of men on deck look after them in stunned silence. It is too much to comprehend that these two lads, who have played such a courageous part in saving so many of the survivors from the *Athabaskan*, should meet this terrible fate after such heroism.

Able Seaman George Howard is swimming close to the *Haida* when she begins to move. The wake of the destroyer threatens to drown him. As the *Haida* pulls away, 22-year-old Able Seaman Ted Hewitt is frantically trying to shed his heavier clothing. He struggles for every breath, taking in gulps of sea water mixed with fuel. He gasps and chokes, arms caught in the sleeves of his greatcoat, the frigid Atlantic tugging him down to where his beloved ship lies. Despair engulfs him and looking around he sees over 100 pairs of eyes all watching the departing ship with the same hopelessness that he is feeling.

Hewitt is sure that if the *Haida* leaves without him, his life is over. With all his might he swims for a loose line and hangs on, yelling with all his strength. Someone on deck notices his body being slammed against the wake and calls his crew mates to help haul the man up the side. The Atlantic has other ideas. Time after time the waves seem to reach out and grab the man, threatening to snatch him back to the waters below. Still, he hangs on. Finally, they have him aboard. He is the last survivor of the *Athabaskan* to be rescued by the *Haida*.

Meanwhile, right after the cutter has been dropped by the departing ship for the survivors to climb into, Acting Leading Seaman William McClure, Able Seaman Jack Hannan, and Stoker William Cummings decide to jump in and help with the rescue efforts. McClure assumes command of the cutter and orders a slow ahead to look for survivors. Petty Officer Casswell is the first to be picked up, followed by Able Seamen Jean Audet, Stanley Buck, and Charles Burgess, as well as Signalmen Thomas Eady and Guy Norris.

Shortly after, the cutter's engine sputters, backfires, and dies. Alone in enemy waters without a ship in sight, the men hit, kick, curse, and play with the motor to get it to start again. But the motor stubbornly refuses to fire. As the cutter drifts, more survivors are found and pulled aboard. Murray and Turner, who were washed off the net when the *Haida* pulled away, had managed to avoid the churning screws and had drifted out on the swells. They are only in the water five minutes when the cutter finds them.

By now, the *Haida* has set course for Plymouth, leaving the grave of her sister ship far behind. Below decks, in the dim light of the battle lamps, is an unforgettable sight. Survivors are everywhere in the confined quarters. In the after flats the air reeks with the stench of fuel oil. No heat can be turned on and no smoking is permitted below decks for fear of fire.

The *Haida* had rescued 42 of the *Athabaskan*'s crew-members. So, for the doctor and his assistants, the work is only beginning. Morphine is administered to the men with the worst injuries, and cleaning the fuel-fed wounds is a challenge. The badly injured and those who were crushed by the ship in its last minutes of life can only be made comfortable until they reach harbour. One man, badly injured, is taken to the captain's cabin for a blood transfusion because he is not going to survive to see a hospital without one. All on board know that over 200 of their friends and shipmates are still lying in or below the waves.

Able Seaman Wilfred Henrickson still clings to the side of a Carley float, but wonders why he is bothering. His head is drooping into the sea and he's swallowing oil and water. Exhausted, he is ready to die. There is no room on the float and no rescue in sight. On the float, Able Seaman William Bint sees the hopelessness in the young man's face and convinces him to trade places for a bit.

The Carley floats and cork net floats gradually become less and less crowded as men give up, or give out. These men slide silently beneath the waves. Floating corpses bump lightly against the living, adding a touch of the macabre to the scene. The living are floating face up. The dead face down. Those who are dead are reverently pushed aside to make room for the living. Mourning will come later — if there is a later.

Far away from the main groups, two lonely figures bob on the swells. Thirty-four-year-old Able Seaman Lester McKeeman (an old man in the eyes of his shipmates, who call him "Pappy") is supporting a young injured sailor on his back, trying to keep the boy's spirits up by talking to him. They babble about home, families, friends, shipmates, and a host of other things. Occasionally there is silence as the teenaged *Athabaskan* crew member lapses into unconsciousness. His laboured breathing is now the only sign of life in him. McKeeman is trying to hang on for the kid's sake. If he were alone, he thinks, he would no longer be alive. The waves lapping and pulling at him are slowly winning. Right now, death is almost welcome. He is so very tired.

When daylight breaks and the first rays of sunlight creep across the water, McKeeman's young friend has grown still. Sobbing for himself as much as for the lad, McKeeman unhooks the death-stiffened fingers from around his neck and lets the lifeless form drift silently away. "Christ Jesus Almighty — forgive me!" sobs the seaman. It's one of the most agonizing things he has ever had to do. And, with the dying of the young one, he feels a part of himself die too.

Finally, German ships are seen approaching. Their rescuers have come in the form of their enemies. For all those survivors left behind by the Allied forces, the POW camps await them. One of the ships that comes to their rescue is the *T-24*.

Far out in the Channel, the *Haida*'s cutter is slowly making its way home. The men are wet and cold. But with hard tack, water, and malted milk tablets, they are better off than those left at the site of the sinking. Suddenly, on the horizon looms a German mine sweeper that changes course and heads directly for the small boat. Darting into a mine field, the men pray the Germans will give up. For a moment it looks as though the vessel is planning to fire on them. It hesitates, then swings around. leaving the survivors to their fate. Every man on that little boat knows their situation is desperate and that the odds are against them.

The *Haida*'s cutter is finally sighted by a squadron of RAF planes and the exhausted survivors are picked up by an Air/ Sea Rescue launch and taken to Penzance. By midnight they are resting, warm, and comfortable. But a disquieting thought stays with them all, "What about the rest of the gang?"

That question, for some, comes many years after the war. Commander Stubbs's body washed ashore with 59 others near Plouescat, Brittany, and they were all buried nearby. Under the cover of night, 1000 people from all over the French island gathered together to mark the seamen's graves with a cascade of beautiful flowers — a gesture of their respect for *les libérateurs canadiens.*

Epilogue

Able-Bodied Seaman Norman Goodale, who served on the *Haida* in 1944, has since relived those two nights, over and over again. To this day, he can still hear the cries of the men in the water, calling out from the waves. Goodale married and came back to Canada after the war, and 20 years later he settled in a subdivision in a small town in Quebec. Soon after moving in, he found out that a few doors down lived Dan Wiggins, a gunners mate and survivor from the *Athabaskan*. Subsequently, the two families spent many hours together, and the two men spoke frequently of that fateful night the *Athabaskan* was lost.

Around this same time, Norm and his wife, Joan, decided they needed some work done on their house. They called a man one street over who was a carpenter. A German by the name of Willy Zerter came over and saw the picture of Norm in his World War II navy uniform. It didn't take the three men long to discover that Willy had been a gunner on the *T-27*, the German destroyer that had been beached at Mencham off Kerlouan by the *Haida* during the night the *Athabaskan* went down.

"My Commander, Kapitanleutnant Gotzmann commented on how quickly and accurately the British shot that night," Willy told his new Canadian friends. "We beached on purpose to avoid the firing. We had no idea the ships were Canadian, only that they were bull dogs."

"We were the Royal Canadian Navy," Norm said quietly, "a force to be proud of, a force to be reckoned with."

Further Reading

Burrow, Len. *Unlucky Lady.* Canada's Wings, Inc., 1982.

Douglas, W.A.B. and Brereton Greenhous. *Out of the Shadows.* Dundurn Press, 1996.

Ireland, Bernard. *Naval History of WWII.* HarperCollins Publishers, 1998.

Lamb, James B. *The Corvette Navy.* Toronto: The Macmillan Company of Canada, 1988.

Lawrence, Hal. *A Bloody War.* Toronto: The Macmillan Company of Canada Limited, 1979.

Lord, Walter. *The Miracle of Dunkirk.* Penguin Books, 1982.

Nelson, CPO Mark. *The History of the Naval Reserve in Winnipeg 1923–2003: Winnipeg's Navy.*

Richards, Lieut. Commander (Mad) S.T.R. *Operation Sick Bay.* Cantaur Publishing, 1994.

Acknowledgments

I would like to thank W.A. Fogg for the photos in this book and his interview regarding his time spent on the HMCS *Minas* and *Waskesiu*. I would also like to thank Norm Goodale, John Jeffrey Coates from the HMCS *Haida*, John Lipton, and a number of Navy veterans who wish to be nameless. They shared their stories and their history with me, an experience I will always treasure.

Photo Credits

About the Author

Cynthia J. Faryon lives in Richer, Manitoba with her husband, youngest daughter, and their two dogs.

Amazing Author Question and Answer

What was your inspiration for writing about the heroes of the Royal Canadian Navy?

My father was in the Air Force during WWII. I grew up hearing him yelling in the night from nightmares on occasion, especially after watching a war movie. We weren't permitted to chew gum, crunch potato chips, or set off fireworks because his nerves were so bad. We all knew it was because of shell shock during the war, but my father would never talk about his experiences. After he passed away in 1988, I started digging into his past and discovered his amazing story. I only wished I could have learned about it from him while he was alive, and by writing these books, I'm hoping to help others discover their own family heroes while they are still alive.

What surprised you most while you were conducting your research?

How interesting Canadian history is when you personalize it. WWII was always nothing more than boring statistics to me as a child growing up. Putting faces to the men who fought the famous battles and discovering the human side of the war makes it so real.

What do you most admire about the people in this Amazing Story?

They are simply ordinary people who rose to greatness under duress. To go into a veteran's home and see him as a nice, elderly gentleman, a grandfatherly type, then to hear his story of battle and survival is incredible. People have so many sides to them I find it fascinating.

Did you run into any difficulties while researching this book?

Finding veterans still alive and willing to talk about their experiences was a challenge. The Internet became my best tool. I sent out emails to various organizations and posted messages on many, many sites. It gave me access to veterans all over. Through emails and phone calls I was able to reach many men in this book. Every time I found one of them and spoke to them on the phone I felt humbled, excited, and honoured. I felt I already knew them.

What part of the writing process did you enjoy most?

Weaving the human story from the facts, dates, and technical history. Putting the real person with his feelings, fears, and deeds into the story so the reader will feel like he or she has gotten to know him personally.

Why did you become a writer? Who inspired you?

My mother and my father's rich past. My mother was an orphan and separated from her sister for 65 years. The two were reunited by accident, and after meeting my aunt for the first time and hearing her life story, I knew I had to write a book about it. So I wrote Sisters Torn, and when that was finished I felt something was missing from my life. So I started to freelance, and then started writing for Amazing Stories.

What is your next project?

Another Amazing Story, titled *Unsung Heroes of the Canadian Army*. And after that I have some ideas for fiction.

Who are your Canadian heroes?

The real Canadian heroes are those who touch us emotionally with their lives and their integrity. Among the Canadians who have influenced me the most are Terry Fox, Rick Hanson, and my father, Lawrence Cramer.

Which other Amazing Stories titles would you recommend?

All of them. This is a great series and should be in every household and every school. We have a rich history and Canadians need to become more aware of our amazing country and those who have made it what it is.

AMAZING STORIES

by the same author

AMAZING STORIES™

UNSUNG HEROES
OF THE ROYAL
CANADIAN AIR FORCE

Incredible Tales of Courage and
Daring During World War II

HISTORY
by Cynthia J. Faryon

UNSUNG HEROES OF THE ROYAL CANADIAN AIR FORCE

Incredible Tales of Courage and Daring During World War II

"That he was a hero is merely incidental to the fact that he died in pain — that he was robbed of life — and that he is lost to his generation. There is glory in living for an ideal as well as in dying for it." Hector Bolitho, 1946

More than 250,000 courageous men and women were enlisted in the Royal Canadian Air Force during World War II. These Canadians fought valiantly in every major air operation from the Battle of Britain to the bombing of Germany. Thousands lost their lives. Those who survived to tell their stories were forever changed. Here are some of their incredible stories.

True stories. Truly Canadian.

ISBN 1-55153-977-2

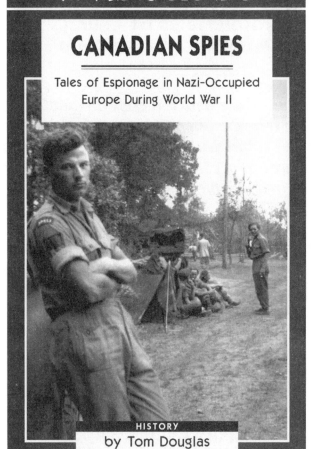

CANADIAN SPIES
Tales of Espionage in Nazi-Occupied Europe During World War II

"Dumais sprang to his feet and began running away from the direction of the train. This time, he was spotted and bullets screamed by his head. When he reached a dense clump of bushes, he dived into them and held his breath."

During World War II, some of the most treacherous jobs were those performed by men and women located deep within enemy territory. Always in danger of being exposed and subjected to torture, imprisonment, and even death, their stories are chilling accounts of bravery and luck — and, in some cases, what happens when the luck runs out.

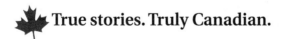 True stories. Truly Canadian.

ISBN 1-55153-966-7

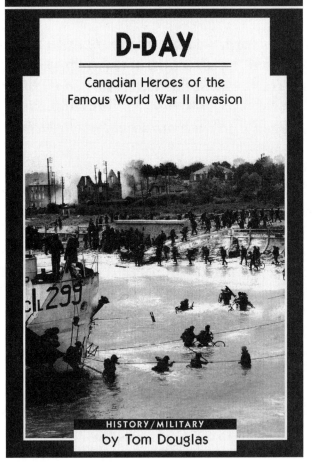

AMAZING STORIES™

D-DAY

Canadian Heroes of the
Famous World War II Invasion

HISTORY/MILITARY
by Tom Douglas

D-DAY
Canadian Heroes of the
Famous World War II Invasion

"As the Canadian armour neared the highway, Meyer yelled 'Attack!' and all hell broke loose."

On June 6, 1944, a daring and ambitious invasion of Europe changed the course of World War II, eventually leading to the surrender of Nazi Germany. During the night, through storms and high seas, the Allied forces swept towards the beaches of Normandy in France. This is the story of the bravery, the heroism, and the sheer dumb luck of the more than 14,000 Canadians who played a crucial role in that incredible event.

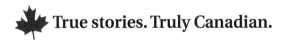 True stories. Truly Canadian.

ISBN 1-55153-795-8

AMAZING STORIES™

GREAT MILITARY LEADERS

Charismatic Canadian Commanders

MILITARY/HISTORY
by Norman Leach

GREAT MILITARY LEADERS
Charismatic Canadian Commanders

"I never saw his equal for true grit...He lay all day with his body torn and bleeding, and it was only at night when the stretcher bearers could approach the trench to get out the wounded that he was carried away, and then he went last."

The history of Canada is filled with charismatic and talented military leaders. Each of the men featured in this collection was wildly successful in business and used his private wealth to provide Canada with a military unit at its times of greatest need. Today these respected units continue to serve Canada and Canadians.

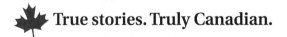 True stories. Truly Canadian.

ISBN 1-55153-773-7

KLONDIKE JOE BOYLE
Heroic Adventures From
Gold Fields to Battlefields

"...man with the heart of a Viking
and the simple faith of a child."
Joe Boyle epitaph

An adventurer and a natural leader, Joe White-
side Boyle blazed the White Pass to the Yukon
and was among the few who scratched a fortune
from the Klondike. During World War I, he was
a spymaster working behind Russian lines. He
cheated death many times to become the "Sav-
iour of Rumania," and in the process fell in love
with a queen.

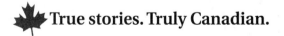True stories. Truly Canadian.

ISBN 1-55153-969-1

OTHER AMAZING STORIES

These titles are available wherever you buy books. If you have trouble finding the book you want, call the Altitude order desk at **1-800-957-6888**, e-mail your request to: **orderdesk@altitudepublishing.com** or visit our Web site **at www.amazingstories.ca**

New **AMAZING STORIES** titles are published every month.